THE TURNING POINT

ALSO BY GREGG BRADEN

Books

Deep Truth
The Divine Matrix
Fractal Time
The God Code
*The Isaiah Effect**
Secrets of the Lost Mode of Prayer
The Spontaneous Healing of Belief
*Walking Between the Worlds**

Audio Programs

An Ancient Magical Prayer (with Deepak Chopra)
Awakening the Power of a Modern God
Deep Truth
The Divine Matrix
The Divine Name (with Jonathan Goldman)
Fractal Time
*The Gregg Braden Audio Collection**
Speaking the Lost Language of God
The Spontaneous Healing of Belief
Unleashing the Power of the God Code

DVD

The Science of Miracles

*All of the above are available from Hay House except items marked with an asterisk.

Please visit:
Hay House USA: www.hayhouse.com®
Hay House Australia: www.hayhouse.com.au
Hay House UK: www.hayhouse.co.uk
Hay House South Africa: www.hayhouse.co.za
Hay House India: www.hayhouse.co.in

THE TURNING POINT

Creating Resilience in a Time of *EXTREMES*

GREGG BRADEN

HAY HOUSE, INC.
Carlsbad, California • New York City
London • Sydney • Johannesburg
Vancouver • Hong Kong • New Delhi

Published and distributed in the United States by: Hay House, Inc.: www.hayhouse.com® • ***Published and distributed in Australia by:*** Hay House Australia Pty. Ltd.: www.hayhouse.com.au • ***Published and distributed in the United Kingdom by:*** Hay House UK, Ltd.: www.hayhouse.co.uk • ***Published and distributed in the Republic of South Africa by:*** Hay House SA (Pty), Ltd.: www.hayhouse.co.za • ***Distributed in Canada by:*** Raincoast: www.raincoast.com • ***Published in India by:*** Hay House Publishers India: www.hayhouse.co.in

Cover design: Amy Rose Grigoriou • *Interior design:* Nick C. Welch

Grateful acknowledgment is made to the Institute of HeartMath for permission to reproduce the steps for "Attitude Breathing" Copyright © 2013 Institute of HeartMath; and for permission to reprint the illustration in Figure 4.1. Additional grateful acknowledgment is made for illustrations licensed through Dreamstime stock images, member of P.A.C.A. and C.E.P.I.C.

Library of Congress Cataloging-in-Publication Data

Braden, Gregg.
The turning point : creating resilience in a time of extremes / Gregg Braden. -- 1st edition.
pages cm
ISBN 978-1-4019-2923-7 (hardback)
1. Resilience (Personality trait) 2. Change (Psychology) I. Title.
BF698.35.R47B73 2014
155.2'5--dc23
2013030339

Hardcover ISBN: 978-1-4019-2923-7

17 16 15 14 4 3 2 1
1st edition, January 2014

Printed in the United States of America

"We are drowning in information,
while starving for wisdom. The world henceforth
will be run by synthesizers, people able to put
together the right information at the right time,
think critically about it, and make
important choices wisely."

— E. O. Wilson (1929–),
EVOLUTIONARY BIOLOGIST

CONTENTS

INTRODUCTION

The Power of Resilience in a Time of Extremes

If you've ever been on a journey of any kind, then you know the routine. To prepare for the trip, you first get an idea of where you're going. You check the weather conditions, study maps, and then pack what's needed to keep your routines alive while you're traveling.

The key here is that when you know where you're going, you know what to take with you. And when you find yourself going somewhere you've never been, you prepare for the unknown. It's this simple idea that's at the heart of this book.

Our Journey

We're all on a journey, and it's a big one. Our journey is leading us to a place no one has ever been. There are no travel guides or Internet trip advisors to tell us precisely what our destination looks like or exactly what we'll need when we get there. Rather than planning a temporary excursion to an exotic place that we can return from after a few days, we hold one-way tickets. This is a different kind of journey altogether. We're not just going to another location somewhere on Earth. We're going to another world hidden within our everyday lives—and it's the choices we're making today that are taking us there.

Together we're barreling down the fast lane of a superhighway that's crossing the boundaries of traditional beliefs, religions, and habits of the past. In doing so, we're also blowing right past the limits of what we thought was possible. These very experiences are our passports leading us to the new world that's emerging before our eyes.

Our Destination

I can't say for sure what our destination will look like. After the dust settles and we learn to adapt to our changing climate rather than trying to control it, after new and sustainable economies replace those that are fractured and failing today, after we embrace the technology that provides every bit of the energy we need without the devastating side effects of fossil fuels, I can only imagine what our lives and the world will be like. And when I do, I see a better place for us all.

I see a world where we've raised the standard of living for everyone, rather than lowering it for many in order to support only a few. I see a world where war is obsolete and using the threat of war to solve our problems no longer makes any sense. I see a world where our love of cooperation is greater than the fear that drives violent competition. And I see the shift in thinking that makes each of these things possible. To get to that shift, however, we must begin by recognizing the realities that we face and the promise that they hold. A good place to begin is by acknowledging the fact that we're living in a time of extremes.

A Time of Extremes

We're living in a time when we can expect *big* things to happen—*big* shifts in the world and *big* changes in our lives. And just to be clear, the extremes I'm talking about don't necessarily have to be considered bad things. It's just that they're *big* things, and they're happening in our lives as well as our world. While the reasons for the extremes will be explored in the upcoming chapters, the key here is that we're living a rare era of transition.

We're living the emergence of a new "normal," and the success of our transition hinges upon: (1) our willingness to acknowledge the shift, and (2) how we learn to adapt to it. Our globalized culture of jobs, money, markets, and resources means that it's now impossible to separate the extremes in the world from what they mean in our everyday lives.

The crisis of climate change is a perfect example of this connection; the record-setting droughts caused by shifts in global weather patterns translate directly into the higher prices we pay for food at our local markets. The extreme debt and failing economies on the other side of the planet translate directly into higher costs at the gas pump and higher ticket prices for the buses, trains, and taxis that take us to work each day. Because of these and other extremes, business loans have become scarce, and the interest we're being paid on our savings and retirement accounts is at a record low. The global slowdown of industry translates directly into the loss of jobs and benefits in our local communities.

These are the kinds of extremes in the world that are creating big changes in our lives. Among the many uncertainties they bring, though, there's one thing that we can be sure of: our lives are changing in ways that we're not prepared for, at a speed that we've never known.

The Key

I'm an optimist by nature. I see real reasons for optimism in our lives. At the same time I'm also a realist. I am under no illusions when it comes to the huge amount of work that it's taking to give birth to the new world that lies before us. Our ability to successfully meet the challenges that are converging in our lives begins by our acknowledging what may be the most obvious yet difficult question we could ask of ourselves: *How can we deal with the issues if we're not honest about the issues?*

Our willingness to acknowledge the magnitude of this simple question is the key to developing more resilience in our time of extremes.

Everyone Is on the Journey

A big difference between trips that we may have taken in the past and the big journey that we're on now is that today we don't get to pick our traveling companions. The reason is simple: Everyone on Earth is on our journey. No one can be left behind. Our world today is so deeply interconnected on so many levels that it's impossible for the transformation that's emerging in one part not to show up in other places as well. I've seen this firsthand in my travels to some of the most remote and isolated places remaining in the world—like Tibet, for example.

In 2005, following a number of previous pilgrimages to the monasteries of the Tibetan Plateau, I saw for the first time the eerie glow of cell phones illuminating the dark recesses of centuries-old buildings as the pockets under the robes of monks and nuns lit up. For the people living in these secluded monasteries, their former world of isolation is now on a path of connectivity. The change that this path carries is a promise that their traditions will never be same.

A Crisis in Thinking

We don't need to go to Tibet, however, to see the evidence of how dramatically the world is shifting. Change is reflected everywhere, both in the ways in which the world works, as well as in the ways things *no longer* work. The era of an oil-based economy, for example, is giving way to a new economy based upon forms of energy that are cleaner and more sustainable. The centralized production of our food from corporate farms half a world away is giving way to the healthy and sustainable production from small farms that invigorate local economies. The practice of creating wealth from industries that destroy our planet is giving way to socially responsible models of investing.

And as the world of the past slips away and the new one emerges, the clash of new against old highlights another, even greater crisis, one that we all face, yet which we'll probably never read about or hear discussed in the popular media. It's a silent crisis that's like the proverbial elephant in the room—something that everyone sees yet no one acknowledges.

Arguably the greatest crisis that we face in our time of extremes is a crisis in thinking. And our thinking is the very key to the way we deal with the needs of the emerging world. You and I are being tasked with something that's never been done. We're being challenged to radically shift the way in which we think of ourselves and our relationship to the world, and to do so faster than any generation in history has ever done before.

Our willingness to think differently about ourselves and the world will be the key to the success of our journey. And while it's definitely a big journey that we're on, it's also a short trip, because the world we're traveling to is already here. It's with us right now.

We Have the Solutions

Fortunately for us, the technology to solve the biggest challenges we face has already been discovered. The biggest problems we could ever imagine are already solved. The advanced principles are already understood. They all exist in this moment, right here, right now, and are at our fingertips. All that stands between us and the new world—where energy comes from clean, abundant sources and is accessible to every member of our global family; where clean, healthy food is plentiful and accessible to every mouth on the planet; where every human is able to obtain the basic necessities to live a comfortable, meaningful life—is the *thinking* that makes room in our lives for what already exists in the world.

Are we willing to embrace the thinking that makes such possibilities a priority? Will we allow the science that reveals the deepest truths about our relationship to ourselves, one another, and the earth to become the passport for our journey?

This book was created to help answer just such questions.

The Big Picture

As you read the pages that follow, I invite you to keep five facts in mind:

Fact 1: Now is different. From the breakdown of national economies and the end of so-called cheap oil, to the realities of climate change and the failure of the belief that war can settle our differences, a convergence of extreme conditions unlike anything known in the history of the world is upon us. It's *because* now is different that the thinking of the past no longer works to solve our problems.

Fact 2: The *turning point* of thriving transformation can replace the *tipping point* of extremes. Nature provides a time when every crisis can be turned into transformation, when simply surviving the extremes in the world can be turned into a thriving way of life. That time is a *turning point.* A turning point emerges when a new force—a fact, a discovery, an experience—changes the way we address our course of events. *What matters is that turning points of life may be spontaneous, or they may be created.*

Fact 3: Life gets better, and resilience is the key. It's important to remember that the only things breaking down in our lives right now are ways of living and thinking that are no longer sustainable. Personal resilience makes room for big shifts in our lives, and is our greatest ally in our time of extremes.

Fact 4: We already have new solutions. We already have the solutions necessary to create turning points of transformation in our lives. We don't need to reinvent the wheel. Rather, we need to build the "road" of thinking that gives the "wheel" of solutions something to travel upon.

Fact 5: The biggest crisis is the most difficult to accept. The single factor that lies between crisis and transformation is one that has eluded scientists, politicians, and religious leaders alike. It's a *crisis in thinking.* We must embrace the thinking that allows us to accept the existing solutions into our lives.

It's these five facts that cut to the very heart of what we're up against and hold the keys to the next step of transformation for ourselves and our world. Our ability to thrive in the midst of such monumental change—*our resilience*—is the first step to ensure the success of our journey.

In This Book

Throughout the chapters that follow, I invite you to share a truthful and factual journey of very real possibilities. This is not a honey-sweet depiction of life seen through rose-colored glasses. Instead, this is an honest assessment of the realities that have arrived at our doorstep and meaningful strategies that can guide each of us in the choices that will transform everything.

In the following pages, we'll answer the big questions on everyone's mind: *What's causing the extremes in our world? What do global extremes mean in our personal lives? How do we make everyday life better for ourselves and our families?*

As you read, you'll discover:

- Strategies we can implement in our lives right now to create turning points of transformation
- The keys to resilience during times of change for our families and societies
- The path to successfully adapting the way in which we think of jobs and careers, and our money and finances, in a transformed world
- The facts that have led to our time of extremes
- Why it's possible to elevate each of us to a higher standard of clean, healthy, and sustainable living

It's important that you know from the very beginning what you can expect from this book, why it was written, what it is, and what it is not.

- *The Turning Point is not a science book.* Although I will share the leading-edge science that invites us to rethink our relationship to the world and the way we've been conditioned to solve our problems, this work has not been written to conform to the format or standards of a classroom science textbook or a technical journal.
- *This is not a peer-reviewed research paper.* Each chapter *has not* gone through the lengthy review process of a certified board or a selected panel of experts conditioned to see our world through the eyes of a single field of study, such as physics, mathematics, or psychology.
- *This book is well researched and well documented.* It has been written in a reader-friendly way that incorporates case studies, historical records, and personal experiences that support an empowering way of seeing ourselves in the world.
- *This book is an example of what happens when we cross the traditional boundaries between science and spirituality.* By marrying the discoveries of 20th-century biology, the earth sciences, and social change, we gain a powerful framework within which to place the dramatic shifts of our age and a context that helps us deal with those changes.

When the Facts Are Clear, the Choices Become Obvious

In the past, we've all been led to think of ourselves, our nations, our religions, and our lives in ways that have that helped us make sense of our world—through stories based on what our families and communities accepted as true at some given point in time. If we're honest with ourselves and acknowledge the fact that the world is changing, then it makes sense that our stories must change as well. I invite you to consider the facts in this book and then explore what they mean to you. Talk them over with the people in your life. In doing so, you'll discover for yourself if, and how, your story changes.

The Turning Point is written with one purpose in mind: to empower us in the choices that lead to thriving lives in a new, transformed, and sustainable world. I believe it's possible to move onto this path, while preserving the traditions from our cultures and heritage that make our time in this world so rich. The key to our transformation is simply this: the better we know ourselves, the better equipped we will be to make our choices wisely.

— **Gregg Braden**

Santa Fe, New Mexico

AUTHOR'S NOTE

Turning Points vs. Choice Points

In my previous book *Fractal Time,* I included a discussion of choice points and the opportunities for change they bring into our lives. I'd like to take a moment to address the difference between the "choice points" in *Fractal Time* and the "turning points" we'll explore in the following pages.

In summary, a *choice point* is a precise window in time. It has a beginning and an end that can be known and mathematically calculated. A choice point is based upon significant events of the past that trigger repeating patterns of change throughout time. Using the simple mathematics of nature, we can discover when these cycles will repeat and when the patterns are most conducive to positive change.

By contrast, a *turning point* is not bound to a specific moment in time. While natural laws allow for turning points in our lives, when and how they show up is more of a holistic and intuitive experience. Turning points may be spontaneously created by the events of our everyday lives, or they may be created intentionally by us. The beauty of turning points is that we must cross them *before* we reach a tipping point of no return.

We can think of turning points as nature's answers to life's extremes and an opportunity to fulfill the promise identified in these words, attributed to the 6th-century B.C.E. Chinese philosopher Lao-tzu: "If you do not change direction, you may end up where you are heading."[1]

CHAPTER ONE

NOW IS DIFFERENT:

Our Time of Extremes

"Not till we are lost, in other words, not till we have lost the world, do we begin to find ourselves."

— HENRY DAVID THOREAU (1817–1862),
AMERICAN ESSAYIST AND PHILOSOPHER

The first rays of the morning sun were just breaking over the horizon as I stepped down from my truck onto the ground of the ice-covered parking lot. Although the glaze under my feet was unusual for the time of year, simply knowing that fact didn't make my walk to the cashier inside any less treacherous. The leather soles of my boots were worthless when it came to traction on the ice, and my walk became more of an awkward skate.

I was passing through a small town in southern Colorado on my way to a meeting in Taos, New Mexico, later in the day. Remembering the long stretch of wilderness I had to cross to get there from past trips, I'd stopped at the convenience store to fill my tank with gas and grab a hot tea. As I stepped through the door into the warm air inside, an older-looking man was sipping coffee from a thermos at a table near the window. He had just seen the whole display of me slipping and sliding from my truck to the door. As I passed his table, without even looking up at me he said, "Slick out there, ain't it?"

"So you saw my dance?" I asked jokingly.

"Yeah, I saw the whole show. Those boots of yours ain't no good in this kind of weather. You need to get some of these," he said, pointing to his thick rubber-soled work boots under the table.

"I've got some," I replied, "but they're back at home. I usually come through here later in the day when the sun's up and the ice is gone. I got a late start out of town last night, though, and didn't want to drive over the pass in the storm. So I spent the night at the Best Western." I pointed in the direction of the only hotel in town.

I thought that was the end of our exchange, so what I heard next took me completely by surprise.

"Yeah, I know what you mean," the man said. "It ain't s'posed to be so cold this time of year. But everything's changed. The native people told us this was comin' . . . all of it. They told us the rain would stop, the weather would change, and people would go crazy tryin' to figure it all out. Problem is, nobody believed 'em."

The man's words were completely unexpected and totally out of context for the morning—at least for me they were. For him, however, these were obviously things that were on his mind. For the first time, he peeked up at me from under the brim of his threadbare John Deere cap.

He looked directly into my eyes, and with a big breath said, "Now everything's haywire. It's all messed up, man. It stopped rainin' in the rainy season. My wheat stopped growin' when it's s'posed to. My cows can't find any grass to eat."

He continued, "It ain't good. But what are you gonna do? You gotta keep livin'. You gotta keep tryin' and just do the best you can. But I'll tell you one thing—this ain't business as usual, that's for sure." The old man stood up to leave, and took one more sip from his thermos. I'd barely spoken, yet I felt I'd just experienced an extraordinary conversation.

As he turned and walked toward the door, he finished, "You take care now, young man. There's a whole lotta nothin' between where you're at now and where you're goin'."

I watched as he walked to his old International Harvester pickup. I knew they'd stopped making those trucks over 30 years earlier. I followed him out the door, stood, and watched until the rumble of his truck faded into the sounds of the morning. I thought about what he'd said and wondered if it was true.

It's a fact that the world has changed in big ways, but it's hard to put a finger on precisely when the change began. There was one thing the old man said that I couldn't deny: We're living a time that is extraordinary by any measure. Our world today is truly no longer business as usual!

Now Is Different

It's true. Now *is* different. The world that we grew up with is gone, and it's not coming back. It disappeared before our eyes. While we were shopping for the weekly groceries, putting meals on the table for our families, and caring for our aging parents, the familiar world we've known and trusted disappeared. The problem is that no one told us this was happening. No one told us that our lives were being changed forever.

There was no announcement in the headlines of *The Wall Street Journal* or *USA Today.* There was no media special on the cable channels, no investigative report on the nightly news, and no exposé on a glossy magazine cover to catch our attention at an airport newsstand. Because the world we knew no longer exists, and its disappearance has never been widely acknowledged in mainstream thinking, we've never had the opportunity to acknowledge the greatest shift in our lives, impacting the greatest number of people in the history of the world! We've never had the chance to say good-bye to the things that are gone and mourn their passing.

We saw evidence of our world vanishing as the mom-and-pop shops that used to line the streets of our small communities gave way the big-box stores that drove them out of business. The family-owned farms that we used to rely upon for our eggs and milk every week have become a rare sight even in the rural areas of America. The neighborhood shops that we counted on to fix everything from the holes in our shoes and our tires, to the lawnmowers that trimmed the grass we used to grow in front of the homes that we used to own are becoming memories of another time. An entire way of life has vanished, and it happened so fast that many people still don't know it's gone and never coming back. They don't realize that we're in a vulnerable world of transition, and for now, a time of extremes.

This is where the problem begins. Because they don't know the shift has happened, they're still waiting for the world of the past to return. They're waiting for life to get back to "normal." Consciously for some, unconsciously for others, they're clinging to an idea of the world that used to be, to the way things used to work, and to where they fit into that world. Many people have put their lives on hold until that familiar world returns. They've put off making big decisions, like when to get married, when to have children, and when to look for a new job in a new industry to replace the one that no longer exists. They've put these things off because they're waiting for the world to settle down and get back to normal. While they're waiting, they're missing the best part of life: life itself!

An entire way of life has vanished, and we've never had an opportunity to mourn its passing so that we can let it go.

Waiting for "Normal" to Return

I remember a conversation I had a few years ago that beautifully illustrates what I mean by waiting for life to "get back to normal." I was talking to a gas-station attendant in a small mountain town about the weak economy and how people in the area were coping.

"How are things in this part of the world?" I asked. "Has business been good here?"

With a shrug, the woman behind the counter stopped counting the change in the cash register and looked at me. "Do you really want to know?" she asked.

"Absolutely," I said with a smile as I handed her my credit card. "I wouldn't ask if I didn't."

"Nothing's been the same here since the mine closed," she began. "People were making good money. They had good jobs, good benefits, and job security. At least, they *thought* they had job security. Then everything changed. Everything just went to hell. It's always been a mixed bag around here with the mine. When it's open, things are great. When it closes, it's pure hell and people go through hell. A few years ago the price of the ore dropped so low that the mine had to close, and just like that there were hundreds of people with no jobs."

"That's got to be tough," I replied. "How much of the town works in the mine?"

"When it's open, it's the biggest employer in the county," she explained. "In the good times, they ran 24/7, using around 600 people to cover three shifts up there."

"Wow, that's quite an operation! How many people live in the town itself?" I asked.

"Our population is about 1,850 people," she replied. "About a third of the town has worked in that mine. When it's good, it's really good. And when it's bad, well . . ."

"So what's everyone doing now?" I asked. "How are they making a living?"

"Oh, they're around," she said. "They're doing whatever they can to get by. Some of the guys are mechanics working on cars by the gas station down the road. Some are cutting winter firewood for locals or baling hay. They're doing just about whatever they can to get by until the mine reopens."

"How do you know the mine will reopen?" I asked. "How long's it been since it closed down?"

"It closed five years and two months ago," she said. "There's a skeleton crew working there now to keep things moving. We keep hearing rumors that it's starting up again, but nobody knows for sure. All we can do is hope."

"I'll hope with you, and keep you in my prayers," I told her as I signed my receipt.

Another customer was coming in as I turned and walked back outside to the beauty of the mountains that towered over the town. I was amazed by what I had heard. Driving back to the main road, I couldn't help thinking of the parallels between what the woman behind the counter had just shared about her small community and what's happening on a bigger scale in the world at large. Perhaps more important, I'd experienced firsthand the way in which people often deal with the kind of change that tears at the fabric of their security and their lives.

In the case of the mine, it was closed because the world changed. The ore that the livelihoods of those townspeople once depended upon is now being mined in China for a cheaper price. That change is one facet of an even larger shift in the balance of global resources. For the mining community, it's a shift in favor of another economy located in another country.

The point here is that people who are reluctant to release the security of doing what's familiar to them are missing the opportunity to create even greater security in the new world that's emerging.

We sometimes justify our reluctance to let go of the past through a belief that the changes we see are temporary. In the same way that music-industry executives believed the revolution of rock 'n' roll was a temporary craze when it first appeared in the 1950s, or the way some technology "experts" believed computers would be a passing fad when they burst onto the scene in the 1960s, when we see so much change on such a large scale happening so quickly, it's a sure sign that we've outgrown the world of the past. And that's why it's impossible to return. Our reluctance to accept that the changes exist may even compromise our ability to adapt—we can only cope with changes that we acknowledge.

How can we thrive in the new world if we're focused on waiting for the old world to return?

A Radical Shift

There are layers of change in the emerging world that surrounds us. We no longer live in the isolated countries that formed the foundation of our policies and thinking during the 20th century. We no longer live in nations with isolated economies, isolated technologies, isolated energy grids, and isolated defense and communications systems. These facts have led to the certainty of where we find ourselves right now, in this very moment: we're living with a new set of rules for our lives, our careers, and the big picture of the world.

The way we think about money and financial security now isn't the same way our parents or their parents thought about money and financial security. The way we thought of careers in the past, in terms of company loyalty and local jobs, is giving way to a less loyal and more global view. The role that religion and spirituality has played in our lives is taking on new meaning as we try to apply 2,500-year-old ideas to 21st-century crises. Our ideas of medicine, disease, and healing are converging into a new, holistic model of wellness for us and our families. The very principles that have helped us feel secure in our communities and homes are changing. Facts like these lead us to one of the most crucial, yet least understood realizations of our era: *we're living a time of many extremes, and they're all happening at once!*

The best minds of our time are in agreement that you and I are living a radical shift in the world and our lives that's unlike any other in recorded history. So precisely what are we facing today that no generation before us has had to face? While answering this question could fill the pages of an entire book—and other authors have done a beautiful job of doing just that—to do so is not the reason I'm making this point. Rather, it's to provide the background for why we now need to think differently.

With these ideas in mind, the following is a summary of the climate, population, energy, and economic conditions that make "now" so different from times past.

Climate Extremes

It's not just our imagination. It's not just the emphatic warnings of overzealous environmentalists that tell us we're in a time of climate extremes. It's not just the elders of the world's indigenous communities sharing the wisdom and warnings of their ancestors regarding our era. It's the data itself that tells the story. And the data tells us that we're living a rare era of cyclic change that few humans in the past have ever experienced. Since the mid-1990s, our global family has met with the crises, and risen to face the aftermath, of a growing number of weather-related extremes—from record-setting floods, hurricanes, tornadoes, and temperatures, to killer superstorms—that have had consequences unparalleled in recorded history.

- **Fact:** We've crossed vital ecological thresholds that are necessary for Earth's survival (such as too-high levels of CO_2 and species extinction).[1]
- **Fact:** There has been a two-and-a-half-fold increase in the number of devastating floods worldwide that occurred between February and May 2010 as compared to the number of floods during the same season of the year in each of the years between 2002 and 2006.
- **Fact:** There has been an increase in the number of North Atlantic tropical storms that the National Weather Service documented between 1998 and 2007, a trend that continues to the present day.
- **Fact:** There has been a dramatic surge in the number of wildfires (associated with drought) since 1998 in North America and throughout much of Australia and Europe.

While it's certainly not unusual for weather-related disasters to occur, it *is* unusual for there to be so many of them occurring in so many places in the world at the same time. "Each year we have extreme weather," Omar Baddour, the chief of the data management applications division at the World Meteorological Organization in

Geneva, Switzerland, has explained, "but it's unusual to have so many extreme events around the world at once."[2] Even while Baddour was alerting us that global weather events for winter 2012 would go beyond business as usual, a bizarre series of storms were wreaking havoc across the globe. These included massive floods in the United Kingdom, extensive fires in Australia, and an epic storm of both rain and snow that threatened the lives of 160,000 Syrian refugees living in temporary camps set up in makeshift shelters in Lebanon. Before the winter months arrived, it was already clear that 2012 would be a year for the record books. By year's end, the extremes had left a legacy that included:

- The world's ninth-warmest recorded year since 1850
- Record low rainfall in the United States and the most severe and extensive drought in at least 25 years
- Record high temperatures in the United States, with 197 all-time highs tied or broken
- Superstorm Sandy, which brought a record 32.5-foot-high wave to New York Harbor

A study published in the journal *Climatic Change* tells us without reservation that extremes such as these are more than just local anomalies. They're happening on a worldwide basis, and the world simply isn't prepared for how quickly the climate is changing. "The last decade brought unprecedented heat waves," says the lead author for the report, Dim Coumou. "For instance in the U.S. in 2012, in Russia in 2010, in Australia in 2009, and in Europe in 2003."[3] Coumou summarizes the impact of such extremes in one sentence, stating, "Heat extremes are causing many deaths, major forest fires, and harvest losses—societies and ecosystems are not adapted to ever new record-breaking temperatures."[4]

While the decades-old controversy regarding the existence and causes of climate extremes appears to be far from resolved, the data of the earth itself reveals the facts. It's a fact that the history of the planet is one of dynamic change in climate and weather patterns. It's also a fact that patterns of the past suggest we should be experiencing a time of warming at present.

The ice-core data represented in the top graph in Figure 1.1 clearly shows Earth's cycles of warming and cooling over the last 420,000 years. The "0" on the right-hand side of the scale is the present day. It indicates that we're now at a place in the cycles where it's reasonable to expect a general warming of the planet. The question is, *How much should we expect?*

The bottom graph in Figure 1.1 gives us a clearer picture of what our warming has looked like for a smaller period of time. Here, the revised indicators for the last 2,000 years show that temperatures during the medieval warming period (MWP), between 820 C.E. and 1040 C.E., were nearly four times greater than what we're experiencing today. Another warming episode in the late 1200s involved temperatures twice as high as today.[5] While the variations are in fractions of a degree Celsius, I'm sharing them here to offer a rounded perspective on climate change and what it's meant in the past.

It's interesting to note that these temperature changes occurred without the factors that are commonly believed to be the cause of such extremes, such as industrial sources of CO_2. The question is, *Why?* If the CO_2 was not the trigger at that time, what was? And what does it mean for us today? These are questions we must honestly answer if we are to address the issues of climate change in a meaningful way.

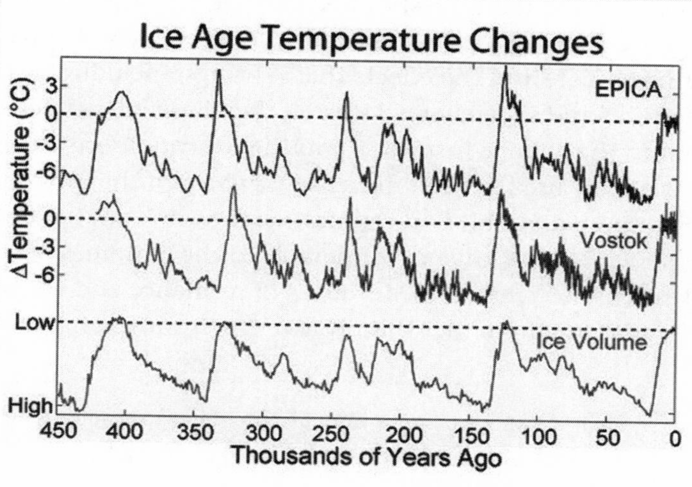

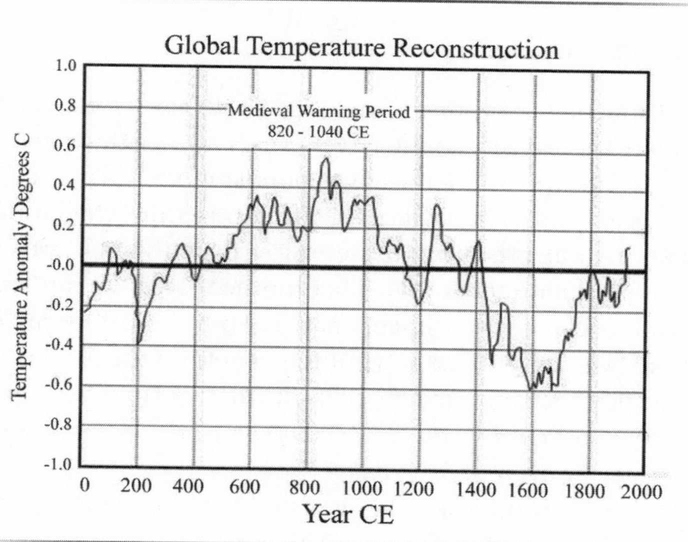

Figure 1.1. It is a fact that the world's climate is changing, and that warming is a part of this change. The top graph shows historic cycles of warming, as well as cooling, indicated by ice cores over the past 420,000 years. Source: Petit/NOAA/GNU free documentation license. The bottom graph shows temperature deviations for the last 2,000 years, both above and below levels considered normal. Here the data clearly shows the cyclic warming and cooling of the past, including the medieval warming period (MWP) with temperatures of 0.5°C above the norm, and the cooling that followed.
Source: Adapted from *Energy and Environment,* vol. 19, no. 1 (2008).

This is where the honesty of acknowledging the data comes in. If, as the data suggests, we're experiencing the new normal of a changing climate and the effects that it brings, including warmer temperatures and supercharged storms, then it makes perfect sense to adapt to the change instead of waiting for conditions to return to the way they used to be. It makes sense to adapt the way we live, grow our food, and build our homes—and to rethink the choices of the past that now leave us vulnerable to the extremes of today. It makes sense to reexamine our ideas of resilience and the role it plays in adapting to, rather than recovering from, change.

We're experiencing a time of climate extremes that is unlike anything in living memory.

Population Extremes

As I touched upon in my previous book, *Deep Truth,* from the end of the last ice age, about 12,000 years ago, until sometime in the mid-1600s, the size of the entire population of Earth is believed to have been pretty much stable. During that time, the number of people born was offsetting those losing their lives to everything from woolly mammoths and saber-toothed tigers to the brutally cold winters caused by climate change. So for 11,500 years or so, there had been fewer than 500 million people on the planet. To put this into perspective, it means that during this time *the number of people being sustained by the resources of our planet was less than half the number now living in India today.*

After 1650, conditions changed and the population began to grow. The illustration in Figure 1.2 gives us a sense of how quickly that growth happened.

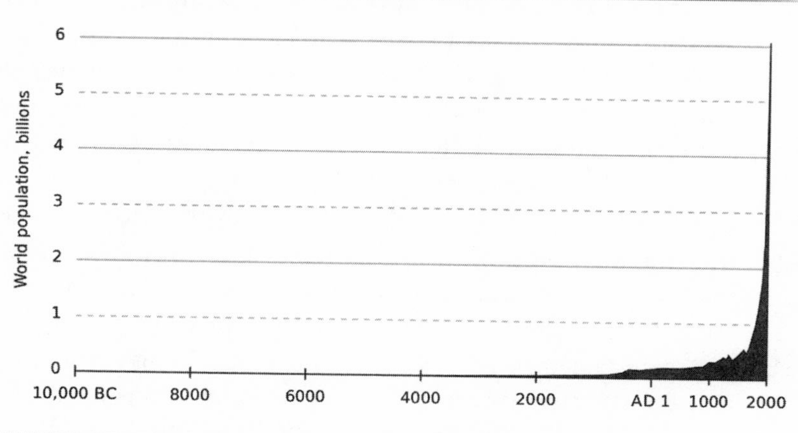

Figure 1.2. Estimate of Earth's total population from 10,000 B.C.E. to 2000 C.E. The steep increase approaching 2000 began to be evident in 1804 when the global population reached the 1 billion mark. The dramatic population growth since that milestone is unprecedented in the history of the world and a key factor in the increased demand for energy, food, and other resources needed to sustain our global family. Source: El T, public domain.

Between 1650 and 1804, the population doubled to 1 billion people. After the first doubling, it took only 123 years to double again to 2 billion. Since that time, the trend has continued, with each doubling taking less time. As the number of people in the world increased to 3 billion, 4 billion, 5 billion, and 6 billion, the number of years it took to add each additional billion people shrank from hundreds to 33, 14, 13, and 12, respectively. In 2012, our global family reached a new record of about 7 billion people. While the speed of population growth appears to have slowed since then, it continues.

As Joel E. Cohen, Ph.D., mathematical biologist and head of the Laboratory of Populations at The Rockefeller University, states in *Scientific American,* "The peak population growth rate ever reached, about 2.1 percent a year, occurred between 1965 and 1970. Human population never grew with such speed before the 20th century and is never again likely to grow with such speed."[6]

The good news in Cohen's assessment is that the population explosion appears to have topped off about 40 years ago. The flip side is that most of those born during that peak are still alive and need to find the resources in terms of food, water, homes, and jobs to sustain them through their life spans, now with an average expectancy of 67 years worldwide. This is where politics, technology, lifestyle, and age-old customs are converging to create the hotbed of social crises that we see today.

The U.S. Central Intelligence Agency (CIA), whose vast resources for data collection provide some of the most accurate and timely information possible, describes the need to record such statistics: "The [population] growth rate is a factor in determining how great a burden would be imposed on a country by the changing needs of its people for infrastructure (e.g., schools, hospitals, housing, roads), resources (e.g., food, water, electricity), and jobs. Rapid population growth can be seen as threatening by neighboring countries."[7]

While the rate of population growth in our world peaked between 1965 and 1970, we still need to find the resources to sustain those born during the peak through their expected life spans.

Energy Extremes

There's a direct link between the number of people in the world and the demand for energy. While we'll explore the relationship between population and energy in later chapters, the point here is that the world's growing population, and also the growing numbers of people aspiring to Western ideas of an energy-intensive lifestyle, has pushed the demand for energy up to record levels. For the last century or so, that demand has been met mostly through the use of fossil fuels.

During the 19th century, coal was so abundant in Europe and North America, and so inexpensive, that it quickly became the fuel of choice for the world. For more than 100 years, coal powered the steam engines for the factories, ships, and railroads of the Industrial

Revolution. In 1800, it's estimated that the world produced about 10 million tons of coal per year to satisfy its energy needs. By 1900, that number increased 110-fold to over *1 billion* tons. Today, coal remains the primary source of energy used to power the turbines that create electricity for the world. In 2010, 7.2 billion tons were produced worldwide.

At the current rate of use, the U.S. Energy Information Administration estimates that the world has about a century and a half of remaining "economically exploitable" coal reserves.[8] Coal, however, is not the energy used for things beyond the world's industrial power grids. When it comes to heating our homes, cooking on our kitchen stoves, and fueling our automobiles, we rely upon oil.

Following World War II, oil became safe, cheap, and popular. Oil has been the fuel of choice for domestic energy uses since that time. While the world's oil reserves looked nearly inexhaustible at the start of the oil era, crude oil is in fact a finite resource, and it's unreasonable to rely upon this shrinking resource for the growing energy needs of the world in the future. While this makes sense intuitively, it was a geologist in the 1950s who put this fact into perspective and gave us a timeline for the world's oil. That geologist was M. King Hubbert, Ph.D.

In what has become the key to determining how long we can expect the world's oil supplies to last, Hubbert placed the telltale factors for oil (estimated reserves, proven reserves, recoverable reserves, and so on) into a formula to describe how much exists and how long before it is exhausted.[9] The result was the statistical curve that now carries his name, *Hubbert's curve*—more commonly known as the *peak oil curve.* Figure 1.3 on the next page shows the theoretical peak oil curve and the actual curve from U.S. oil production. The real-world data correlates almost exactly with the predicted curve. Compelling results such as these are now applied to global estimates to give us a realistic idea of how long the world's reserves will last.

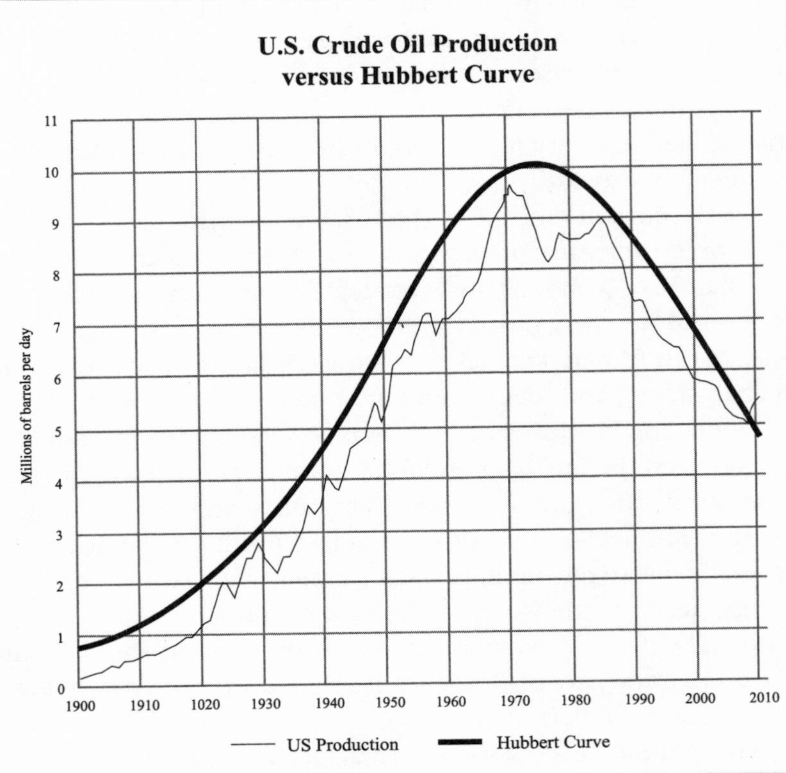

Figure 1.3. This illustration shows geologist Dr. M. King Hubbert's estimates for peak oil production in the United States, along with the curve showing the actual production. This comparison illustrates the accuracy of Hubbert's calculations and makes a compelling case for the accuracy of similar calculations on a global basis. Source: U.S. Energy Information Administration.

The result? *We've already passed the time of peak oil,* and it happened approximately 25 years ago—in the mid-1980s. We've now entered an era of relying upon oil that's harder to retrieve and more expensive to produce to meet the global demand for energy. The dilemma is that while we know that the "cheap" oil is gone and the world's reserves are shrinking, the demand for oil is actually still increasing every year. Figure 1.4 below shows how this demand first began to exceed production in the mid-1980s. While a growing environmental awareness, coupled with more efficient automobiles, has actually lessened the demand for oil in the developed Western nations, the world's overall demand continues to grow, largely due to emerging economies, such as those of India and China.

Until recently the amount of oil available has for the most part been able to keep pace with what is needed. It's clear, however, that this relationship cannot last under the present conditions.

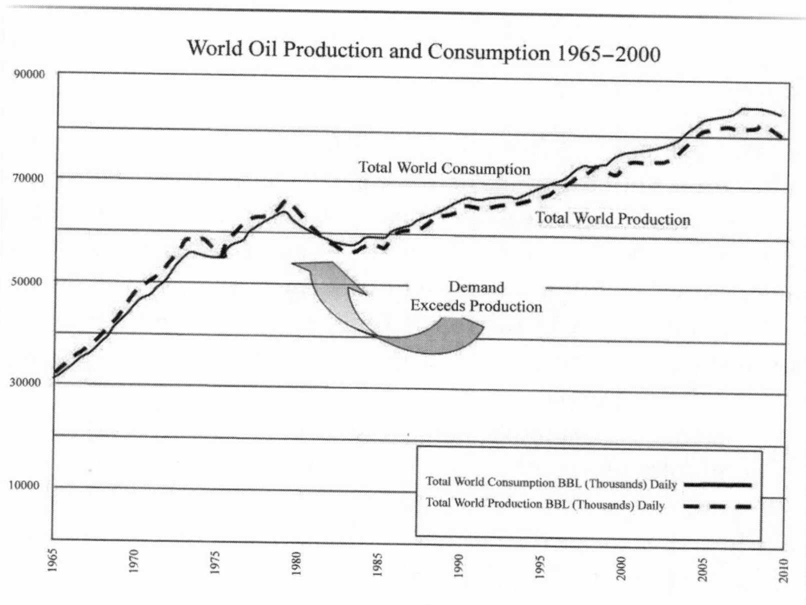

Figure 1.4. This illustration shows the global production of oil compared to the global demand. The data shows that two trends are clear: (1) the demand for oil became greater than the available oil in the mid-1980s, and (2) the gap between demand and production is growing. Source: BP Statistical Review of World Energy (June 2011).

Now that the availability of cheap oil is declining, scientists have to look deeper into the oceans under many miles of water and deeper in the earth under many miles of rock for the remaining deposits. Both of these factors make the drilling more difficult and increase the costs of retrieval, making crude oil less profitable to produce. The term that describes this relationship is *return on investment* (ROI). The decreasing ROI on oil production today is already a factor that's giving new meaning to the term *peak oil.*

While oil will continue to be an important way to meet the energy needs of the world for the foreseeable future, it's becoming less so because other, renewable forms of energy and advances in natural-gas technology are turning the energy equation of the world upside down.

Economic Extremes

When I look out from the stage into the audience during my seminars, it's not uncommon to see participants' eyes glaze over at the very mention of the word *economy.* Many people automatically link the word with money, a topic that seems boring and too technical. But when I share with them that the economy of the world is about much more than money, they become curious. "How can you have an economy without money?" they'll ask. The answer surprises some people.

Whether we're talking about the economy of a family or the economy of a planet, the truth is that it *may* include money, but it doesn't have to. Our global economy is part of the fabric of relationships that weave the families, communities, and nations of the world together. It's the means for us to share the things we have with other people who need them, and for them to do the same with us. Without an economy, we couldn't share the food, energy, medicine, and goods that are vital for our lives each day.

With this idea of an economy in mind, the audience suddenly moves from being only slightly curious to intensely interested. Suddenly the meaning of the topic becomes crystal clear: we're talking about their lives and the very essence of the changes that are affecting them each and every day.

While the topic of the world economy would be interesting to explore at any time, it's crucial to do so in our time of extremes for one very important reason: it's in trouble. Depending upon which expert you ask, some will say that the global economy is fractured and needs healing. Others will say that it's broken and *beyond* healing. Almost universally, however, all will agree that the global economy as we've known it is teetering on the brink of a collapse unlike any we've ever seen.

While the reasons contributing to such a precarious situation are many, and we could trace the roots of our vulnerability to a number of factors that began in the last century with the banking system itself, to do so is beyond the scope of what I can do justice to in a few pages. And while such information is interesting, it's really not the focus of the changes we can make in our lives today to be more resilient. So I'll limit this portion of the book to two key elements that are converging upon the economic landscape of the world. Both are contributing to our time of extremes and affecting *your* life right now.

These factors are:

1. The reserve currencies of the world
2. The unprecedented levels of debt

Each of these ideas alone is simple to understand. When we put them together, they tell a story. This story will become important in later chapters of this book, which relate to creating resilience in your life.

So, let's begin. . . .

Factor 1: The Money Everybody Uses

Following World War II, the United States had arguably the strongest economy in the world, based on the strongest and most stable currency: the U.S. dollar. Because of its strength and reliability, the dollar was adopted as the currency of choice to be used between countries for big purchases of things like oil, gold, and food. On July 22, 1944, it officially became the reserve currency of the world. The definition of a *reserve currency* is a "currency that is held in significant quantities by many governments and institutions as part of their foreign exchange reserves."[10]

Having a global reserve currency has its advantages and its disadvantages. For the country issuing the currency, it's a good thing, because it ensures there is always a demand for its money. It also gives that issuing nation an advantage when it comes to exchange rates and buying imported commodities. The downside is that the health of the reserve currency affects every economy that uses it.

Today, the world uses multiple reserve currencies. These different currencies are held in a "basket" of which the U.S. dollar and the European euro make up a combined 90 percent. As the primary reserve currencies, large amounts of these two currencies are held in the world's financial institutions and banks (see Figure 1.5). The additional 10 percent of the reserve basket is made up of other currencies such as the British pound sterling, the Japanese yen, and the Swiss franc.

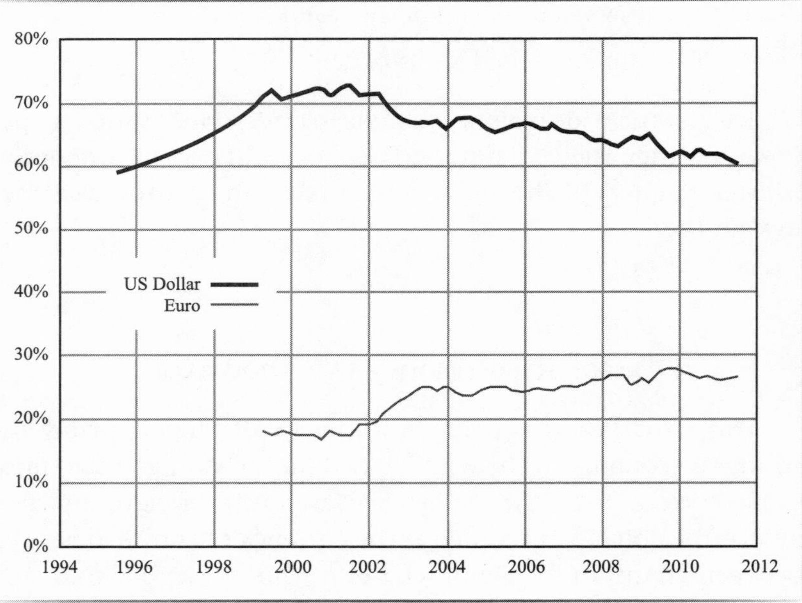

Figure 1.5. The U.S. dollar and the European euro are the primary reserve currencies for the banks of the world. Because large transactions between nations for commodities like energy and food are made using these reserve currencies, their stability has a big effect on the global economy.

This means the health of the dollar and the health of the euro have a great impact on many of the economies of the world—and this is where the problems begin. The debt linked to the reserve currencies is one of the factors contributing to our time of extremes.

Factor 2: Debt, Debt, and More Debt

It's no secret that the global economy is in crisis or that debt is a big part of the problem. Rarely a day goes by when we're not reminded by the media of the debt crisis in Europe or the staggering debt that the world is accumulating. While debt has always been a critical factor for governments and nations to address, following the financial crisis in the United States in 2008, during which tremendous amounts of money were dedicated to averting a global banking collapse, the debt of the U.S. and the world began to spiral out of control. In 2012, for example, the global debt was a record $48.8 trillion, over two times greater than the $19.9 trillion owed only ten years earlier, in 2002. By autumn of 2013, global debt had increased to a staggering $51.5 trillion, following what appears to be a trend of escalation that will continue into the foreseeable future.[11] This situation has placed us in uncharted territory. Never before have the largest economies of the world, like those of the United States, the eurozone, and Japan, for example, been carrying so much debt that it equalled or exceeded their annual income, or *gross domestic product* (GDP).[12]

The way in which this crisis is being addressed at present is for countries that have debt to add more money to their money supply to ensure there's enough to pay the bills and keep the wheels of commerce turning. While the term often used to describe this practice is *printing* money, these days only a relatively small amount of money is actually created as the physical, hold-in-your-hands kind of currency. The creation of money is more about monetary reserves and expansive monetary policies, such as the quantitative easing programs (QE1, QE2, QE3, and so on), designed to create the effect of adding money to the system.

The good news is that this solution is having a steadying effect on the world's economy for now. Each time the money is created, Social Security checks are covered, federal employees are paid, and life appears to continue as usual. The flip side is that there's another effect that makes this solution unsustainable in the long run.

When more money is created, whether it's dollars, euros, or yen, it means that more money is in circulation and each unit is worth less. In other words, because there's more of it available, the currency becomes diluted and weaker. Just as is the case for anything that's diluted, this means it takes more of the same currency to pay for the same things than it did in the past when the currency was stronger. The bottom line is easy to imagine: when our debt goes up and more money is created to cover our obligations, the value of our money goes down.

This devaluing of the dollar has been a big factor in the higher prices Americans have seen at gas pumps, in grocery stores, and at prescription-drug counters. Between 2000 and 2011, for example, the price of corn, one of the world's most important food crops, rose from $75 per ton to over $310 per ton.[13] Between 1998 and 2008, the price of gasoline increased from an average of $1.02 per gallon to an average $4.02 per gallon—a whopping 294 percent![14]

These factors—devaluation and debt—are also contributing to problems in parts of the world that rely upon the reserve currencies for the necessities of everyday life. The weakening of reserve currencies due to growing debt has put the cost of food, energy, and housing beyond the reach of household budgets in nations where the annual income is only a fraction of what it is in more affluent Western countries.

The record-setting debt of the world, and the resulting weakening of major currencies, is a key factor contributing to our time of extremes.

Considering the extreme conditions of our climate, the extreme demands for energy, and the extreme pressure being placed on our economies—all of which are amplified by extreme population levels—it's fair to say that we're living in a time of tremendous volatility. As my friend at the convenience store in the Introduction observed from his corner of the world, life is certainly no longer "business as usual."

Maybe Peggy Noonan, a columnist with *The Wall Street Journal,* has said it best: "We are living Days of Lore. Days of big history." Clarifying what she means by "big history," she continues, "We are living through an epoch scholars 50 years hence will ask about and study. . . . They will see us, you and me, as grizzled veterans of something big."[15] I think there's a lot of truth to Noonan's remark. Everywhere I travel in the world, there's a sense that we are, in fact, living in a time of something big.

In my opinion, if we can get a handle on: (1) why so many seemingly separate shifts are happening, (2) why they're happening now, and (3) where they're leading us, then we'll have taken a giant leap toward making sense of the change and our place in it. In doing so, we could also create a renewed sense of hope and optimism for ourselves, our families, and our communities. This hope could become the common denominator for people coming from different cultures, spiritual and religious traditions, and ways of life, and it also gives us a reason to think beyond our differences to the realities that are transforming us all. The key to our survival is to acknowledge the facts of what we're up against: the things that are changing and what the changes mean in our lives.

Never in the modern world have we attempted to meet the growing needs of so many people through shrinking supplies of so few resources, with climate change supercharging the demand.

Temporary Extremes or the New Normal?

Until recently, there's been a tendency to think of the kind of extremes I've just described as anomalies that are separate and unrelated. The result of such thinking is that we end up attempting to put out the fires of one problem here and another one there. While we can do so with varying degrees of temporary success, we never really get to the core issues at the heart of the extremes.

This approach brings to mind the image of holding a balloon full of water, noticing a leak in one place and trying to stop it just as another leak appears in another place. When we think of climate change, for example, we've been led to believe that if we were to stop using fossil fuels and embrace a clean, green, and sustainable lifestyle, we would somehow fix the warming that's part of our time of extremes. While I *definitely* believe in and support the development of clean, green, and sustainable forms of energy, and we *definitely* put less strain on resources with energy-saving lightbulbs in our homes and offices, and riding our bicycles to work and school is *definitely* healthier than driving, there is a consequence to making these lifestyle changes in the belief that they're *the* answer.

For a growing number of people and policymakers, focusing on these commendable shifts in the way we live has become a diversion from a stark and uncomfortable reality: the records of the earth itself tell us that the changes we're trying to stop are actually characteristics of a new normal. Rather than acknowledging the scientific facts, such as those in Figure 1.1—which describe climate cycles of the past, what we can realistically expect today, and how we can *adapt* to the changes—their thinking suggests that we can return to the old normal, such as the climate of the 20th century. The problem with this thinking is that the focus becomes one of stopping and reversing the changes, rather than creating the resilience to adapt to them.

We've been led to believe we can fix the problems, rather than adapting to the extremes that have become the new normal.

This is one of those places where the type of conversation I'm having with you can sometimes become uncomfortable and, for some people, difficult. The reason is because it means acknowledging the fact that the extremes are real, and where they come from. If we embrace the history of the earth itself, for example, it clearly shows that we're living at the time in a repeating cycle when big shifts in climate have been triggered in the past. Mainstream media, popular science, and traditional classrooms and textbooks have been reluctant to acknowledge the accuracy of the ancient calculations that describe such changes, specifically those of the 5,125-year cycles described by the Mesoamerican calendar. That is, until recently.

In a paper published in 2004, Lonnie Thompson, Ph.D., a glaciologist with Ohio State University's Byrd Polar Research Center, describes a sudden shift in climate 5,200 years ago that gives us insights into the shift we're experiencing today. Thompson reveals that discoveries from a number of different sources, in a number of different locations across the globe, all point to a startling conclusion. From pollen in lake-bed core samples in South America and methane in ice cores in Greenland and Antarctica, to tree-ring data from the United Kingdom and plants preserved in the ice caps of the Peruvian Andes, the story told by the records of the planet is unmistakable: the climate changed dramatically 5,200 years ago, and the impact to life on Earth was immense.

It's not so much the fact that a big change occurred that's making the headlines; it's *when* the change occurred. We're generally used to thinking of climate shifts as things that happened when dinosaurs roamed the earth and people, once they appeared, lived in caves. What makes Thompson's discoveries so powerful is that, in the overall scheme of history, 5,000 years really isn't such a long time ago. To give this revelation a bit of perspective, the study reveals that the change happened within recorded human history, just 3,000 years before the time of Jesus, during the early Bronze Age.

"Something happened back at this time and it was monumental," Dr. Thompson says.[16] Describing the significance, he continues, "The evidence clearly points back to this point in history and to some event that occurred. *It also points to similar changes occurring in today's climate as well* [author's emphasis]."[17]

From studies like Thompson's we can gain insights into the changes that we're living through today, and perhaps more important, insights into how we may adapt to them in our lives. I've personally spoken at conferences where the organizers themselves believed that the facts about our time of extremes should not be shared publicly. The reason given to me for holding back this information was even more disturbing than what the actual data is showing. "We don't want to scare people," is what I've been told.

I understand the intent of such comments, and honestly believe it comes from a sense of responsibility and feelings of genuine caring. However, I also believe that while pacifying people's anxiety may have worked for some situations in the past, it no longer serves us to follow this line of thinking today.

When I hear such statements, it reminds me of a dysfunctional family trying to deal with individual outbursts of rage that tear the members' lives apart without first acknowledging the underlying trigger. The fact is that this thinking doesn't work for a family, and it won't work for the world. Our time of extremes has placed us in uncharted territory. If ever there was a time when we needed to be honest with ourselves about what we're up against, I can't think of a better one than right now!

Tipping Points of Convergence

From the studies of respected "think tanks" like the Worldwatch Institute, founded in 1974 to independently research critical global issues, and the World Resources Institute, founded in 1982 to analyze environmental policy; to UNESCO's Millennium Ecosystem Assessment Synthesis Report, drafted by 1,300 scientists in 95 countries, it's clear that the best minds of our time have gone beyond the warnings of the past to alert us to dangerous trends of unsustainability. We're now living in the time that they warned us of in the past, and the magnitude of the changes we're experiencing is our cue to sit up and take notice.

In 2005, *Scientific American* published a special edition, "Crossroads for Planet Earth," which confirmed that ours is no ordinary time. One section describes the human race as "now entering a unique period in its history."[18] The purpose of the magazine issue was to identify a number of global crises that, if left unchecked, hold the potential to end human life and civilization as we know it today: everything from new diseases with no known cures and energy-intensive nations exhausting Earth's finite resources, to never-before-seen levels of global poverty and habitual disregard for the health of oceans, rivers, and rain forests. The conclusion was unanimous: we simply cannot continue living as we have in the past if we expect to survive even another 100 years.

Earth cannot sustain our habits. Over 1,000 scientists from various disciplines have honed this idea into a report released by the World Economic Forum, aptly titled *Global Risks 2013*.[19] The bottom line is that the conditions of climate change and the teetering global economy pose the possibility of a "perfect storm" of crises that will impact the world for a long time to come.

The point that these organizations and others are bringing into public awareness is that each of the scenarios identified in their reports is catastrophic, and all are happening now. The contributors to these special bulletins and reports are certainly not alone in their assessments of our situation. They, along with other science-based researchers—who range from independent authors to members of the intelligence communities of the United States, including the Pentagon and CIA, which see the crises as threats to stability and security—have sounded unmistakable alarms loudly and clearly.

The alarms are telling us that we're *already* in trouble—nature is already at a tipping point of losing the oceans, forests, and animals that make life as we've known it possible. When we factor in the reality of broken economies, vanishing resources, climate change, and the loss of entire industries—along with the jobs they provided for our families and communities—then the individual extremes take on a new meaning.

The tipping points of no return in different areas of our lives are leading us to a time of *convergence*. While different reasons have been given as to why so many crises are occurring in such a brief period of time, there seems to be a general consensus regarding the big picture: something extraordinary is unfolding in our world.

How do we begin to define something so big that it has been anticipated for thousands of years, has the potential to alter every life on Earth, yet can't be encapsulated in a single word or idea?

It may be precisely because the implications of our time of extremes are so vast that there's been a reluctance to even acknowledge that we're in the midst of something so big. Maybe the conditions, challenges, and crises we face, along with our communities, our nations, and our world, are best summed up by evolutionary biologist E. O. Wilson. He states that we're living what he calls a "bottleneck" in time, when the stress upon both our resources and our ability to solve the problems of our day will be pushed to their limits.[20]

Having discovered that respected organizations are pointing to the same critical issues and reaching the same general conclusions, we can clearly see that we're in the midst of a rare convergence of factors that is creating a transition for our world. The question is: *Where does the transition lead?*

Are we headed for a world of destruction? Or are we headed for a world of transformation? Our failure to recognize the big picture and where the trends are leading us may ultimately be the worst problem we face.

Fortunately, this problem is solvable.

Will the convergence of tipping points make our time of extremes one of destruction or transformation? The choice is ours.

Us/Them vs. We

When we look closely at the biggest shifts in our world, we see a common theme that brings the reason for so much change front and center, and into crystal clear focus. It's simply this: the only things that are collapsing are ways of thinking and living that are no longer sustainable. The fact that so many facets of daily life are breaking down so quickly tells us where the thinking of the past no longer works. And from peak debt to peak oil, the simultaneous buckling of big systems tells us that now is the time to rethink the very beliefs that have driven our choices in the past.

Facts such as these have led many experts to view our time of extremes as a time of *crisis* as well. But the word *crisis* doesn't necessarily mean that something bad is happening. It can also mean that something *big* is happening.

I used to have an aversion to the word *crisis*. Recently, however, I've come to appreciate it for one reason: if we say we're "in" a crisis, it means that we still have time to fix the problem. If we say that the crisis is "over," it implies there's nothing more we can do. So the fact that we're still in the midst of the crises of climate change, economic volatility, and energy production means we have a chance to adapt. These are consequences that we face today for a past way of thinking. Because the world has changed, these issues are asking for our immediate attention.

Never have so many people been asked to think so differently and to solve so many big problems in such a short period of time.

We live in a world where everything is connected. We can no longer think in terms of *us* and *them* when it comes to the consequences of the way we live. Today it's all about *we*. It was precisely to create a greater sense of we-ness that we developed the Internet that links us together, the transportation industry that moves people between continents and nations, our financial markets that operate 24/7, and the cell-phone networks that allow us to text our loved ones on the other side of the world at 3 A.M. The purpose is to connect us. But this has become like a double-edged sword: our global connections allow us to share everything from our music, art, culture, and celebrations—the good—to the not-so-good problems of scarce energy, food, and money.

During a recent trip to Cuzco, the high-elevation ancient capital of Peru, nestled in the Andes Mountains, I witnessed the grand opening of a McDonald's restaurant. It was located just a couple of doors down from the historic 400-year-old cathedral in the city's central square, which houses some of the oldest New World relics of the Catholic Church, predating the Spanish conquest. There's little beef in the area, but the local staple of alpaca (an animal related to the llama) is plentiful. So the Andean version of the Big Mac is actually made of two patties of alpaca meat in a sesame-seed bun covered by that famous special sauce.

I witnessed the same thing happening in the Tibetan capital of Lhasa, located at an altitude of 12,000 feet above sea level, where the local meat, yak, is substituted for the beef used in the West. The Tibetans in the area love to joke about the Big Yak burger that has replaced the traditional Big Mac. The point is that globalization has made McDonald's, Starbucks, and KFC, for example, familiar sights in remote places of the world today, just as they've been for decades in the biggest cities of the United States and Europe.

The same oneness that makes it possible to share such commercial pieces of culture, as well as fashion, music, and art, also makes it inevitable that big problems in one part of the world will affect the lives of entire communities in other parts of the world. This means that the effects of climate change, for example, are showing up as price increases that reflect the smaller harvests from drought-stricken fields of the world; the slowdown in the global economy is showing up as the closure of factories and the loss of jobs in our local neighborhoods; and the rise in global debt is translating into weakness in our local currency and the record-low interest that we're being paid on our CDs and retirement savings accounts. Through these simple examples it's clear that we can no longer separate the world "out there" from what's happening at our family dinner tables, in our classrooms, and in our offices.

Our oneness also means that we can no longer separate spirituality from our everyday lives. During the media session and interviews before a public seminar, it's common for the interviewer to ask me if I'm going to talk about the "science stuff" or the "spiritual stuff." My answer to the question is generally not what the interviewer is hoping to hear. "Where do you draw the line between spirituality and our everyday lives?" I reply.

It's an important question, because the artificial separation between science and spirit is precisely what keeps us stuck in the thinking that prevents us from adapting to today's crises.

"What could be more spiritual," I ask, "than applying the deepest truths revealed by science as the real-world solutions in our everyday lives?"

The Crisis of Change Itself

When big changes happen in our lives, we tend to view them initially as crises. The previous mention of climate change is a perfect example. When the climate of the world began to shift, it caught many people off guard. Although the teachings of different indigenous traditions around the world have warned us for centuries to expect these changes to occur, and the geological history of Earth clearly shows us that we are "on course" for a cyclic shift in climate, the average folks going about the business of their everyday lives simply weren't expecting it. And it's no surprise that they weren't. In the memories of the people living today, the weather patterns of the last century or so had become familiar, regular, and predictable. The temperatures and growing seasons for our farms and gardens had become as sure as night follows day. Then, suddenly, they all changed.

My wife and I experienced this change personally in the high desert of northern New Mexico. The area is known for its low humidity, an abundance of sunshine, and generally mild weather. Although rainfall is rare throughout much of the year, the New Mexico desert has traditionally experienced what the locals call the monsoon rains in the summer months. Like clockwork, beginning in July each year, the warm, moist air from the Gulf of Mexico makes its way north to collide with the cold, dry air coming across the mountains of Colorado and New Mexico. Each afternoon, when these air masses meet, they create a remarkable display of lightning and massive thunderstorms. Such downpours of rain continue throughout much of the summer. They did, that is, until recently.

New Mexico and much of the Desert Southwest is in the midst of a full-blown multiyear drought. For the first time in the memory of residents who've lived in the area for many generations, local ranchers are being forced to sell off their cattle and local farmers to abandon their crops because they can no longer sustain them. For the people and economy of New Mexico, the shift in the weather is a crisis that's forcing them to change the way they think and the way they live.

Caught by Surprise

June 30, 2012, will go down in the record books as the night that took the weather experts by surprise. While meteorologists saw the converging patterns of heat and moisture on their radar screens, even they were in awe of the size and severity of the storms that the patterns formed. "The widespread nature of the [radar] image we saw is a very rare occurrence," said Stephen Konarik, a meteorologist with the National Weather Service. "We would not have been planning on that magnitude of event."[21]

The cost of the damage from the storm system that stretched from the Upper Midwest of the United States to the Eastern Seaboard that night was about three-quarters of that from Hurricane Irene (August 2011), one of the worst in U.S. history. Even with the help of approximately 600 utility workers and emergency crews that came from as far away as Texas, Michigan, and Florida, residents would remain without power well into the following week. A local noted how the storm caught everyone off guard, stating, "I guess it was a real surprise to everyone, apparently even them."[22] By *them,* he meant the weather forecasters.

While the severity of such storms may come as a surprise to meteorologists and forecasters, to those living close to the cycles of nature it does not. Almost universally, ancient texts and indigenous traditions have warned that now is precisely the time when we can expect to experience tremendous change on many levels of our lives, including global climate and local weather. They've known that change was coming, for a simple reason—because it *always* does.

As described in my book *Fractal Time* (Hay House, 2009), every 5,000 years or so the cycles of the sun and the position of Earth in space conspire to bring about massive changes in our world, such as the one highlighted by the geological studies described earlier in this chapter. The fact that such changes are now documented scientifically adds to the credibility of our ancestors' wisdom. And because the changes are based upon cycles that are predictable and simple to calculate, it's not difficult to identify when the last great change occurred, and to then calculate when it will appear again. The essence of the changes described by those who have experienced them in the past follows a worldview that is straightforward and intuitive. It's essentially a map of relationships that gives meaning to our time of extremes (see Figure 1.6 on the next page).

This map helps us make sense of the underlying reality for the crises we face today: *When the world changes, we are changed.* We are changed as people. We are changed as communities and societies in the presence of our changing world. And when we see the magnitude of what's unfolding right now, we can be absolutely certain that we're in the midst of a big change in our lives, as are our loved ones, friends, and neighbors. We can also be certain that the changes we're undergoing are happening quickly. As we find nature being pushed to the limits of what is possible to sustain life, the extremes are pushing us as individuals, families, and communities as well. They're pushing us in ways that are sometimes obvious and sometimes subtle.

The extremes of life are forcing us to think differently about ourselves and reconsider how we sustain our jobs, careers, health, and relationships. In order to make sense of the seemingly senseless hardships affecting every facet of society, we're being pushed to look beyond the wisdom handed down to us by our parents, and theirs. This is where the message at the core of our most cherished spiritual traditions—our unity with the world and nature's cycles—is now taking on new meaning, and new relevance, in our everyday lives.

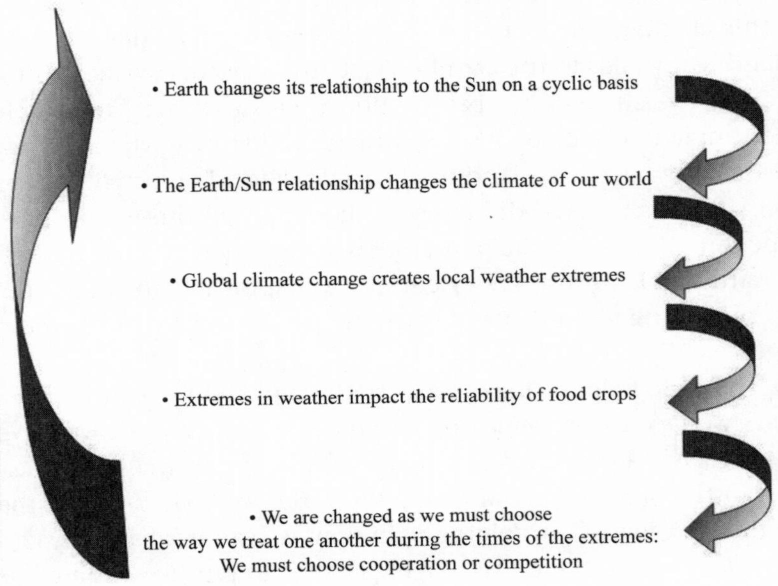

Figure 1.6. This simplified illustration shows how the cyclical changes in Earth's location in space (tilt, orbit, angle, and wobble) translate to the cyclical changes that drive human civilizations. Source: *Deep Truth* (Hay House, 2011).

While our ancestors generally understood the relationships illustrated in Figure 1.6, I'm not suggesting that every single member in every age-group of every indigenous tribe possessed this knowledge. What I am suggesting is that the general theme of cyclical change being driven by Earth's location in space, and how this would impact our planet and our lives, seems to have been an accepted principle in our ancestors' worldview. And it's easy to see why. Once the wisdom-keepers, ranging from the Maya of the Yucatán and the scribes of ancient Egypt to the students of the Hindu yuga cycles, established the motion of Earth in the heavens, the rest simply made sense.

Until being confirmed by the modern science of the mid-20th century, however, this ancestral knowledge continued to be held only by people of indigenous cultures.

Now We Know!

We humans have a history of embracing change and an amazing track record for successfully turning the extremes of crisis into transformation. Geology tells us that 20,000 to 30,000 years ago the climate of our world changed suddenly—and in a big way. From the preserved bodies of woolly mammoths discovered with remnants of their last bite of food still in their mouths, to the fossils of tropical plants discovered in Antarctica, the geologic record of the earth confirms that the climate changed dramatically in the past in ways that gave our ancestors little time to adapt. There was nothing in their memory that could have prepared them for what was happening or told them what to do. We know that they did adapt to the unexpected change and that their ability to do so paid off. Not only did they survive, but their numbers increased and their descendants—our ancestors—migrated throughout the world to populate the land at even greater levels than before the freeze.

More recently, we've demonstrated our ability to pull together as a global family to overcome some of the greatest changes of the modern world. Our ability to rebuild the world economy after the stock market crash of 1929 is a perfect example of this kind of unity. The unprecedented renaissance that took place in Europe and Japan after the destruction of World War II is another example of what I mean here. The point is that when we've faced big problems in the past, we've characteristically risen to the call and created the level of cooperation that was needed to meet the challenge. In times past, however, there was a key difference.

Throughout the greatest shifts in our world, we have typically dealt with a single crisis, like a collapsed economy, the devastation of a war, or a pandemic disease. So we know we're good at meeting the challenge of one crisis at a time. What makes our present-day challenge so very different is that we're dealing with multiple crises converging into the same window of time. It's this fact that makes our era of extremes so different from times past.

Unless we think very differently than we have previously, we know with reasonable certainty where the trajectory of the world's extremes is leading. To successfully meet the challenge before us, we must answer three key questions. As individuals, as communities, as nations, and as a global family, we must look squarely into the mirror of our lives and ask ourselves:

- *How can we solve the issues we face if we're not honest about them?*
- *Are we willing to accept new discoveries that reveal the deepest truths about our relationship to ourselves and the world?*
- *How do we adapt to a changing world through applying the principles of modern science and spirituality to everyday life?*

In December 2012, I had the opportunity to pose these very questions to an indigenous healer living in the jungles of Mexico's Yucatán Peninsula. Once we got past the barriers of language and translation, the answers came quickly. He began by unrolling a tapestry that he borrowed from a local vendor.

A man after my own heart! I thought. I viewed his woven tapestry as the jungle equivalent of the PowerPoint slides that I use to illustrate ideas for my audiences throughout the world. The image on the brightly colored weaving clearly showed the Mayan Tree of Life. Pointing with his finger, he highlighted the 13 levels of heaven (the upper world) above the ground, the 9 levels of the underworld below ground, and the branches and roots of the *ceiba* (silk cotton) tree, the sacred tree that connects the worlds.

While the idea of an upper world and an underworld (or many of them) may at first seem to reflect the Christian idea of heaven and hell, there's one important distinction. In the Mayan tradition, the levels of the underworld are not viewed as bad places reserved for people who've done something wrong. Nor are the heavens only for good people who do righteous deeds. Rather, the healer described both the heavens and the underworlds as parts of a continuous experience.

He said that we all experience both the heavens and the underworlds as part of our great life journey, which is based upon cycles. Driving the cycles of experience in all the worlds and everything in our lives is a force that cannot be represented in a picture. It cannot be represented at all. Because it encompasses everything that exists, it's beyond description. The name of the force in Yucatec Mayan is *Hunab Ku.*

This knowledge formed the foundation of the healer's answer to my question. He explained that the key to the wisdom of his ancestors and their knowledge of change is that they did not separate themselves from the world, as we have done today. They did not separate one experience from another. They did not separate art from science or spirituality from everyday life. From the movements of the stars to the cycles of weather, all aspects of life were viewed as part of the mix, as facets of that one continuous experience. Because of this worldview, Mayan wisdom-keepers were able to gain powerful insights into nature's cycles of time and change.

I listened carefully to what my new friend was saying. It's been said that the events of history repeat themselves. It may be that the knowledge of the past repeats itself as well, showing up time and again, and appearing in our lives precisely when it's needed. It's this kind of holistic view, describing the interlocking continuity of all life, that's now reappearing as the conclusions of the best science of today. Both science and indigenous wisdom remind us that we're part of all that we see. This means that we're a part of the solutions as well. The key is that we must first shift our perspective so we can recognize our connection.

It's this kind of thinking that constitutes the difference between reacting to our time of extremes and living with resilience that allows the extremes to become our path to transformation.

CHAPTER TWO

No Shortage of Solutions:

A Crisis of Thinking

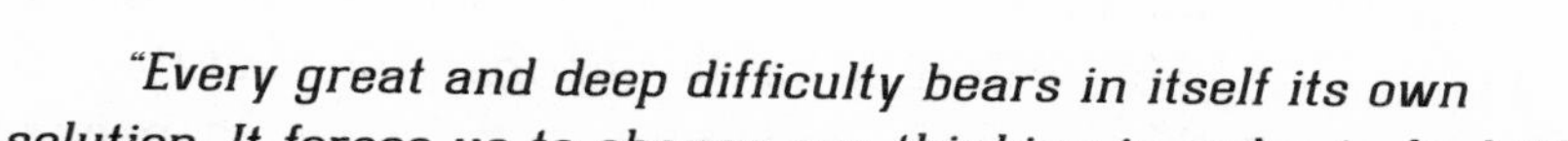

"Every great and deep difficulty bears in itself its own solution. It forces us to change our thinking in order to find it."

— Niels Bohr (1885–1962), Nobel Prize–winning physicist

It's been said that we humans are creatures of habit. Maybe Warren Buffett, paraphrasing 18th-century writer Samuel Johnson, summed it up best when he said, "The chains of habit are too light to be felt until they are too heavy to be broken."[1] If we're honest with ourselves, these words are probably just as true today as when Johnson spoke a variation of them over 200 years ago. We *are* creatures of habit, and it's for this very reason that change of any kind can be hard for us. It's often easier to hang on to the familiar ways of the past—even when those comfortable habits are no longer good for us—than to face the uncertainties that the "new" can bring to our lives.

Peter Drucker, whose writing has contributed to the model for modern business, says, "Everybody has accepted by now that 'change is unavoidable.' But this still implies that change is like 'death and taxes': It should be postponed as long as possible and no change would be vastly preferable. *But in a period of upheaval, such as the one we are living in, change is the norm* [author's emphasis]."[2] My grandfather would have agreed.

Before he died at the age of 96, Grandpa would talk to me for hours about the world and the way it was in his time. He was born in Eastern Europe at the beginning of the last century, and as I recounted in *Deep Truth,* he always began his stories by telling me how different the world of his day was from our world today. While I knew that what he was saying was certainly true, each time I listened to him share his memories I understood even more just what he meant. My grandfather would tell me of a world that I could only imagine: one where horse-drawn wagons still had the right of way when they encountered the newly invented automobiles, and where many homes had no electricity and telephones were rare. It was a world in which there was no network of superhighways, and indoor toilets were a luxury.

Grandpa always said that the world stopped making sense to him just after World War II. It was during that time that the new discoveries in science, and changes in everyday life, happened so quickly that he couldn't keep up with them. When the postwar technology wave produced innovations like jet planes, pocket radios, bar-code scanners, and fax machines, it all simply looked crazy to him. Because he could no longer relate to the changes occurring around him, he felt left out, like an outsider in his own world. My grandfather never caught up with modern technology. The shift that happened after World War II was the beginning of a crisis for him that lasted until the end of his life.

Designed to Change

There's a common thread that binds the world my grandfather knew following World War II and the world we live in today. Both are the product of tremendous change occurring in a very brief period. People in both worlds had to shift their modes of thinking and living—and in ways that they had not been prepared for. Perhaps most important of all, neither world was meant to last forever. The technology of both was *designed* to change. For example, the now unthinkably low fuel efficiency of the 1960s "muscle cars," some of which got less than 10 miles per gallon (mpg), was *meant* to give way to the more efficient engines of today, which commonly run at 35–40 mpg or more. The portable eight-track tapes of the 1970s were *meant* to give way to the smaller cassette tapes, and then to the CDs that followed them, and eventually to the pure energy of the electronic 0s and 1s of today's digital era.

On a larger scale, the 19th-century power grid of wires and cables that still connects our homes, families, and nations today was *meant* to be temporary. It was never meant to last into the 21st century. When inventor Nikola Tesla designed the system that allows alternating-current power to be carried over long distances, he did so to provide the people of the world immediate access to the comforts that electricity could bring into their homes and businesses. It was meant to serve them temporarily while he perfected another system that would broadcast energy without burdensome cables and wires, in much the same way that a TV signal is broadcast. For political reasons, Tesla lost his funding and was never able to complete his system of wireless electricity. One of the greatest electrical geniuses of modern times, Nikola Tesla died in 1943, and his "temporary" power grid remains with us today, over a hundred years longer than it was meant to last.

These familiar forms of technology are examples of thinking that were never meant to be the ultimate destination of timeless solutions. Rather, they were meant to be the bridges that would get us to our next steps. It's this subtle yet profound realization that has helped many people feel a little better about our world as it looks like it's turning upside down. As described in Chapter 1, the trigger for much of the change today is that the past ways of thinking and living are no longer sustainable. It's not so much that they are wrong or bad; it's just that we've outgrown them. They no longer fit into our world.

Much of the world we've known was meant to be a bridge to a better way of life, rather than a final destination that was to remain unchanged.

The Blueprint for a Vision

On May 25, 1961, President John F. Kennedy stood before a special session of the United States Congress to make an announcement that would forever change the destiny of America and the course of human history. With these words, the world shifted: "I believe that this nation should commit itself to achieving the goal, before this decade is out, of landing a man on the Moon and returning him safely to the earth."[3]

With this statement, Kennedy set into motion the massive effort of coordinating the technology, corporations, research, and funding that would be needed to accomplish his goal. Only the building of the Panama Canal during peacetime, and the super-secret Manhattan Project in wartime, could compare to the depth and scope of Kennedy's mandate to go to the moon.

In what is arguably one of the most impressive displays of military and civilian cooperation ever achieved, Kennedy's vision became a reality. It happened precisely as he had stated, and in less time than he had imagined. In the eight years between Kennedy's speech and humankind's first step on the moon, the plans were created, the propulsion systems were built, the bugs were worked out, and the space capsule that would carry precious human life went from the drafting tables to the launchpad. On July 16, 1969, the massive Saturn V rocket, measuring 363 feet long and weighing 6.5 million pounds, left the launchpad at Cape Kennedy carrying three men to the moon. Five days later, astronaut Neil Armstrong announced the landing with the now-immortal words: "That's one small step for man, one giant leap for mankind."[4]

When people talk about this astonishing feat, one of the first questions they typically ask is, "How could it have happened so quickly?" How could the materials have been created, the technology developed, and the systems completed in less than ten years? The answer to this question is the reason I'm sharing the story here. The success of the mission and the timing were possible because two key factors came together in just the right way.

First, the big pieces of the technology were already in place. While the integration of so many systems and components was a monumental task unto itself, in large part the theories, materials, and communications already existed. That's why the second factor was so important. While much of the technology was already available, no one in a high position of authority had ever made it a focus to bring everything together. When the leader of the most technologically advanced nation on Earth did so through his speech, his words gave the scientists and administrators permission to fall into line. Giving them a mandate opened the floodgates of innovation and resources for the exploration of space and more. *In other words, Kennedy made our journey to the moon a priority.*

We find ourselves in a similar situation today. Rather than sending humans to the moon, however, our mission pertains to what's happening right here on planet Earth. Just as the technology was already available in the 1960s for space travel, today we already have the knowledge and the means to alleviate the human suffering that's become the hallmark of our time of extremes. We already have the ability to feed every man, woman, and child living in the world.[5]

- **Fact:** The agriculture of the world produces 17 percent *more* calories today than it did 30 years ago, enough for at least 2,720 kilocalories per person per day.[6]
- **Fact:** Malnutrition and hunger are not caused by scarcity. Rather, they're the result of poverty; harmful economic systems; conflict; and to a lesser but growing degree, the droughts, floods, and unpredictable weather patterns resulting from climate change.[7]

We already have affordable, clean, and sustainable forms of energy that can be made available to every household that needs them. The global shift to such energy appears to be emerging in gradual stages, rather than instantaneously.

- **Fact:** The first stage of the world's energy changeover is occurring through the use of liquefied natural gas (LNG), which burns cleaner, produces 50 percent less CO_2, and is more affordable than conventional coal and oil. While it's not the ultimate solution to satisfying our growing need for energy, it shows a shift in thinking and is a step in the right direction.[8]

- **Fact:** The technology that makes additional forms of "alternative" energy viable is slowly and steadily improving. This includes solar, geothermal, and wind-power technology that can locally supplement conventional power sources, as well as create local resilience to regional energy problems.[9]
- **Fact:** Sources of energy that appear exotic by today's standards are gradually being implemented to replace fossil fuels altogether and add to a mix of clean and sustainable alternatives that can provide for the needs of our growing population.

We already know how to alleviate the abject poverty of the world that has been the source of scarcity and suffering.

- **Fact:** The United Nations Millennium Development Goal to reduce the world's most extreme poverty (of those living on less than US$1.25 per day) is working. The first goal, to halve the proportion of the world's population who is living in such poverty between 1990 and 2015, was actually met in 2010, *five years ahead of schedule*. This tells us that real change is achievable and lays the foundation for a push toward an even greater effort.[10]

It's obvious from facts such as these that the elements for big solutions already exist. As of this writing, what's lacking is the kind of vision that President Kennedy provided in 1961, *the shift in thinking* that makes such goals a priority.

The key to awakening our dreams is to make the object of our vision a priority in our lives.

No Shortage of Solutions

The examples in the previous section tell us that meaningful change is achievable and doesn't have to take generations to show up in our lives. The UN had the resources and the motivation to bring about a meaningful reduction in poverty for the world in less than 20 years, for instance. So while we know that such change is possible, no one has, as yet, made it a priority to mobilize the vast resources at our disposal and implement similar changes on a grand planetary scale. In the event that such a visionary declaration was made, the existing solutions could quickly bring an end to the many and diverse forms of suffering in our families and communities. In the absence of such a declaration, we find ourselves bearing witness to a world where the solutions that could bring hope remain hidden away.

It's not unusual for an audience to gasp in awe when I say that the big problems of the world are already solved—that is, the problems that technology *can* solve. Just as the technology for our successful mission to the moon already existed when Kennedy made his speech, the solutions to the big problems in our lives—such as social change, creating sustainable communities and cities, and more—already exist.

Although a number of visionary leaders and thinkers have created organizations and written excellent books to demonstrate what's possible in our lifetimes, it's beyond the scope of this book to do justice to them all. For this reason I've chosen a few examples from different fields that illustrate how much effort has already been directed toward the kind of change I'm talking about. We don't need to reinvent the wheel when it comes to knowing where to begin. Other people have already done so, and some have devoted their entire lives to doing the legwork so that we don't have to.

While I'm not suggesting that any of the following is the *only* plan of its kind, I'd like you to see the depth and quality of the solutions that are available to us: the plans that have been formulated and the implementation that has been drafted. The ball is rolling.

Now the question is: *What are we waiting for?*

Plan B

One of the leading voices in the effort to educate and mobilize the general public toward a sustainable shift in the way we think and live is the former head of the Worldwatch Institute, environmental analyst Lester R. Brown. "We are in a race between tipping points in nature and our political systems," Brown says.[11] In a bold attempt to head off the suffering of our collapsing civilization, he released a series of books designed to illustrate just how bad things were and how much worse they might get. The books all have the same title with different subtitles to show their individual emphases.

The first in the series, *Plan B: Rescuing a Planet Under Stress and a Civilization in Trouble* (Norton, 2003), describes the red-flag statistics that began telling us we were in trouble. His third book, *Plan B 3.0: Mobilizing to Save Civilization* (Norton, 2008), reflects an even greater sense of urgency about the dangerous trends further developing in our world. Since the time that his first *Plan B* book was published, many of the factors that were only warnings then have now become the reality of our world.

For example, Brown identified how critical times in nature—such as the time when a species' population is shrinking—mark the point of no return for that particular system. Brown then described how a number of related ecological systems on Earth are approaching similar points today.

One of the things I like best about the *Plan B* series is that it contains realistic action steps that we could put in place immediately to address the issues facing us. Examples of these items include:

- Designing cities that support people and the way people live, rather than supporting industries and commuter-based economies
- Implementing features that can immediately raise the energy efficiency of homes, offices, commercial buildings, and public transportation

- Establishing an economy based on a cyclic use of materials rather than the one-way, linear model that dominates today
- Making a shift in government spending (in the United States) that includes reallocating a portion of the massive military budget for use in the building of new, sustainable infrastructure

Brown's *Plan B* series is a sobering yet necessary assessment that offers the hope of action plans, while also highlighting the problems. Without a doubt, Brown's work is making a powerful mark on the way we think of our world. For many organizations, agencies, and individuals, the *Plan B* series has become a bible for identifying potential solutions.

Social Change 2.0

Just as Lester Brown identified the important issues and offered viable solutions for the big picture of global change, David Gershon has done much the same for the institutions that drive such change and societies themselves. Gershon is an accomplished author of a number of consciousness-raising books, including *Low Carbon Diet* (Empowerment Institute, 2006), which won the bronze Independent Publisher "Most Likely to Save the Planet" Book Award in 2007. In *Social Change 2.0* (High Point/Chelsea Green, 2009), he does a masterful job of drawing upon his expertise, with a background that extends from academia to serving as an advisor to the United Nations and the Clinton White House.

From these personal experiences, Gershon has been able to identify the reasons why so many attempts to solve social problems, ranging from inner-city to global issues, have hit a dead end. It's because the solutions are based upon ideas that have proved to be faulty. From his perspective of *systems theory,* Gershon then describes how the social crises that we see today are the signals telling us, "We are being called to reinvent not only our world, but also the process by which we achieve this reinvention."[12]

One of the many reasons I was drawn to Gershon's book is that, like Brown, he offers his readers real-world alternatives to traditional models of social change. These are the time-tested and proven methods that speak to the needs of today's societies and the transformation they're undergoing. He shares examples of what he's learned in a way that could become a template for creating positive change in almost any social setting, from a small community to an entire nation. After describing his work in facilitating the positive conversations between local officials and community members in a number of large American cities, for example, he shares meaningful steps for applying what he's found in a variety of situations. His principles and action steps include:

- Making changes in communities that are relevant to people's lives
- Organizing citizens to take greater responsibility for issues like health, safety, and beautification, among others
- Empowering local civil servants to take greater responsibility and accept greater accountability for the changes that are affecting their neighbors and families
- The design and implementation of a whole-systems approach to community change

When something is true in our lives, I am not surprised to see that truth show up time and again in many places. This is certainly true for *Social Change 2.0.* There is an overlap between many of the ideas that Gershon identifies in his book and the principles of Brown's work, as well as the futuristic communities envisioned by innovators such as Paolo Soleri, which are designed to integrate sustainable architecture with the ecology of the land the structures are built upon.

Arcology and Earthships

In 1970, something amazing and beautiful began to happen in the arid desert north of Phoenix, Arizona. A visionary architect began to build a community unlike any other anywhere else on Earth. The man's name was Paolo Soleri (1919–2013), and the kind of community environment that he envisioned is a perfect example of the urban housing that's needed in our time of extremes. It's perfect because it's designed to help large numbers of people adapt to the shifts taking place in our world, both natural and human-made. A student of renowned architect Frank Lloyd Wright, Soleri named his community Arcosanti. He based it upon a principle that is best described in the community's own words: "Arcosanti is an urban laboratory focused on innovative design, community, and environmental accountability. Our goal is to actively pursue lean alternatives to urban sprawl based on Paolo Soleri's theory of compact city design, Arcology (*arc*hitecture + ec*ology*)."[13]

Using a combination of otherworldly aesthetics and solid engineering principles, Soleri based the design of Arcosanti on the theme of working *with* the land and the elements of nature, rather than by forcing the land to accommodate our ideas about homes, schools, and offices. What this means in real life, for example, is that a rock cliff located in the place where a home will be built becomes the wall of a living room rather than being sheared down to the bedrock to accommodate sheetrock and plywood.

One of the fundamental ideas of *arcology* is to adapt to whatever it is that nature offers. In the case of Soleri's community, one of those elements is sunlight. Arizona's deserts are known for their abundant, high-quality light, which lends itself to solar-energy technology of all kinds. Arcosanti was designed to be a self-sufficient and sustainable community of 5,000 people who would derive all their energy needs from various forms of solar power. The Two Suns Arcology module of the Arcosanti village is a system of collection, transmission, and consumption of solar energy, which incorporates both active and passive solar energy to provide for the village's needs. A massive system of terraced greenhouses accumulates the heat of the sun, which is then redirected to other buildings for their heating and cooling needs. I've had the opportunity to experience some of Soleri's constructions, and I remember wondering at the time why we weren't incorporating ideas like his into the homes and cities of the modern world to begin with.

Another visionary design for self-sustaining communities also has its roots in America's Desert Southwest. It's a community in the high desert near Taos, New Mexico, that was established in the 1970s. It was during that decade that architect Michael Reynolds began building an entire community that was "off the grid," requiring no public utility connections for electricity, sewage, or water. The construction was based upon the use of traditionally discarded materials, such as aluminum cans, glass bottles, and rubber tires for the walls. These were covered with stucco plaster to form beautiful and very organic-looking structures. He named the homes and offices he was constructing *Earthships,* in part because he literally used earth—the local dirt—in their construction.

The use of the soil came about in different ways. One of these was called *rammed earth.* It's precisely what it sounds like: the piling and ramming of soil against specially prepared foundations and walls of buildings, effectively making them partially buried. The insulating and acoustic-deadening effect of rammed earth is unmatched in traditional construction. These homes and offices are warm and quiet!

The second way the dirt was used involved packing it into old rubber tires to form some of the walls, especially on the northern exposure, where there was no warmth from direct sunlight. The density of the packed earth made each tire into a perfect round brick with a space of dead air at the center, providing an enormously high insulation effect against the heat and cold of the desert extremes.

Each Earthship uses the south-facing glass walls to allow the desert sunlight to radiate into the building and heat the clay brick or flagstone floors during the day. After the sun goes down at night, the bricks continue to radiate their heat evenly and effectively throughout the house. I've been in Earthship homes where the indoor temperature in December hovers around 80°F, and remains stable well into the night. Each home is equipped with a self-contained system to collect the used water from the home and filter and recycle it to water the trees, flowers, and vegetable gardens that are grown outside, as well as in the building's atrium.

Whether these specific designs are ever used on a larger scale is a question that remains to be answered. The reason I'm sharing them here is because these communities, and others that are already functional in other parts of the world, are the laboratories that inform us as to what's possible when it comes to rethinking our neighborhoods and even entire cities.

As we rebuild after the devastating effects of climate change, such as the EF5 tornado that leveled the city of Moore, Oklahoma, in May 2013; and category 3 Hurricane Sandy that destroyed entire communities on America's Eastern Seaboard in October 2012, the sustainable principles demonstrated by these visionary communities may provide the flagship models for how we construct the cities of the future.

Global Shift

Everyone learns a little differently. For precisely this reason, many very good teachers have written very good books regarding our time of extremes. While the perspectives of some books are oriented toward the big picture and how the changes in our lives translate to changes in the world, others acknowledge these relationships while focusing more on integrating change in our personal and spiritual lives. Edmund J. Bourne, Ph.D., has written one such book, *Global Shift: How a New Worldview Is Transforming Humanity* (New Harbinger, 2008). Two elements of this book drew me to it and made it one of my favorites on this subject.

The first element of the book that I like is how Bourne integrates leading-edge science with indigenous traditions, spirituality, and the realities of everyday life to paint a picture of the new world that's emerging. Rather than asking us to accept a single perspective as *the* perspective, he paints an honest portrait of the real world as one in which people are searching for a new worldview that makes sense, and most important, that works.

Within the context of an emerging worldview, he dedicates an entire chapter of the book to taking action. I found this chapter rich in ideas and resources that could help us embrace the promise of the book's title. Among the familiar suggestions that I'd expect to see in such a book, such as lifestyle changes, environmental conservation, and community charities, Bourne also identifies things we can do in our financial lives that reflect the economic shifts happening in our daily realities. These suggestions include:

- Socially responsible ways to invest our money
- Innovative ways to invest in our communities
- Conscious ways to invest in the world's financial markets

While it's not likely that we would implement all the changes in Bourne's book at once, by the end of it we've gained a solid grasp of the magnitude of the shift that's unfolding in our lives, and we have ample ideas for solid actions that could make our experience of the global shift a little smoother.

It's clear that no single source of information or single idea is *the* answer to the critical choices that we're making in our lives today. Rather, there are many different solutions to many facets of many issues that are all appearing at the same time. Bourne sums this up beautifully, saying, "None of us can solve the immense problems the Earth and its people face alone."[14]

My reason for sharing examples of thinking like Bourne's, and the others previously mentioned, is to show that the ideas already exist and the wheels are already in motion to help us handle the global shift. As Bourne writes, "Each of us, by engaging in a few simple actions to help the environment and disadvantaged people, can make a contribution and potentially influence others we know to do the same."[15]

I've met people who think of our era as a time of frightening urgency as well. Once they recognize the extremes, their reaction is that we must act and do something immediately. *Now!* While it's a natural reaction to want to spring into action as soon as possible, my feeling is that we're living in what I like to call the zone of *graceful urgency.* It's *graceful* in the sense that we still have the time to do what it takes to avoid the tipping points of climate change, peak oil, and peak debt, and the dire consequences so many of the experts are predicting. There's *urgency* in the sense that now is the time to respond. Whatever we're going to do, whatever shifts we're going to make in our world, and whatever changes we're going to implement in our lives, now is the perfect time for those adaptations and innovations.

We already have solutions to big problems, such as food, energy, and a sustainable economy. Our problem is a crisis in thinking.

What Will It Take?

It's clear from the studies, reports, and messages from organizations and authors described in the previous section that we have the foundation for real solutions that can make the world better and our lives easier. It's also clear that we have the ability to implement those solutions now. So the obvious questions are: *Where are these solutions today? Why aren't we using them now? What will it take before we do?*

The answer to our questions is illustrated in President Kennedy's visionary plan to go to the moon. Something else had to happen first, beyond giving the mandate to put a man there. *Before* he could go to the American people with his ideas, *before* the technology could be designed, *before* any trajectories from the launchpad to the moon could be calculated, *before* any spacesuits could be designed or the Tang breakfast drinks could be sealed into space-worthy pouches—*before* any of these things could even begin to happen—something else had to happen first. That "something" is what's missing in our lives today.

It's a shift in thinking.

It's fair to say that the greatest crisis of our time of extremes, *beyond* the crises of debt, energy, and food, is a crisis of thinking. It's our thinking that would make the lifesaving solutions we already have a priority in our daily lives, and motivate us to implement those solutions in the world. The thinking we need would come from a deep-seated desire to contribute *to* the world, rather than from a sense of scarcity and taking *from* the world; and from cooperating *with* one another, rather than competing *against* one another.

This very style of thinking is now supported by the new discoveries and the best science of our time. So, to answer the question of *What would it take to bring the solutions that already exist into our lives?* let's begin at the beginning: *Where did the thinking that has led us to the greatest crises in 5,000 years of history really come from?* The answer may surprise you.

Rethinking the False Assumptions of Science

There's a story buried deep in our culture that plays a huge role in our everyday lives. It's the usually unspoken story of *us:* who we are, where we come from, and how things seem to work in our world. I'm not suggesting that this story is necessarily something we routinely think about, or even one that we're conscious of. It's not a story that we share at the breakfast table with our families each morning or contemplate while we go about our rituals to prepare for the day. For many of us, it's a story that's buried so deeply in the way we think and act that we accept its consequences automatically without a second thought. Although it may be buried, it remains so present with us that it guides our choices and affects the way we respond to our loved ones, co-workers, and friends—and to the world—each and every day.

It's a story of separation.

Since the birth of modern science nearly 300 years ago, the story of our lives has been that we're little more than specks of dust in the universe and biological sidebars in the overall scheme of life. We've been led to believe that we're separate from one another. We've been taught that we're essentially powerless when it comes to the healing of our own bodies or our ability to influence peace in our communities and beyond.

Our story of separation includes Charles Darwin's belief that life is a struggle and we must fight for the good things that come to us in life. As children, many of us were conditioned to think this way through the mantra that we live in a "dog-eat-dog" world. The very phrase embodies the belief that the world is like one big, limited, finite pie, and therefore we must struggle and fight for our slice of the pie or miss out forever. This is the basis for the popular worldview of scarcity or lack, and the need we perceive for violent competition between people and nations. *It may be no coincidence that during the time we've held this view, the world has found itself facing the greatest crises of war, suffering, and disease in recorded history.*

Is it any wonder that we often feel powerless to help our loved ones and ourselves when it comes to life's great crises? Is it any wonder that we often feel just as helpless when we see our world changing so fast that it's been described as "falling apart at the seams"? At first blush, there seems to be no reason for us to think any differently or to believe we have any more control over ourselves or where our lives are heading than this worldview indicates we do. After all, there's nothing in our traditional textbooks or traditional way of seeing the world that allows for anything else. That is, until we take another look at certain discoveries made during the last years of the 20th century.

Although the results of paradigm-shattering research have been published in leading technical journals, they're often shared in the complex language of science, masking the power of their meaning from those outside the scientific community. Average nonscientific, nontechnical people don't feel the impact of the new discoveries because they're being left out of the conversation.

The latest discoveries in the fields of biology, physics, archaeology, and genetics are forcing scientists to rewrite the story of who we are and how we fit into the world. In biology, for example, the publication of more than 400 studies showing that nature is based upon a model of cooperation, rather than Darwin's "survival of the fittest," has turned the thinking of evolutionary science upside down. In light of such discoveries, and others, some key assumptions of the past—*now recognized as the false assumptions of science*—can no longer be taught as fact. Examples of these include the following:

- **False Assumption 1:** Nature is based upon survival of the strongest.[16]
- **False Assumption 2:** Random events of evolution explain human origins.[17]
- **False Assumption 3:** Consciousness is separate from our physical world.[18]
- **False Assumption 4:** The space between physical things is empty.[19]
- **False Assumption 5:** Advanced civilization began 5,000–5,500 years ago.[20]

While knowing about such discoveries would be interesting at any time in our lives, they're absolutely vital to us in this time of extremes because the way we solve the problems of our lives is based upon the way we view ourselves in relationship to the world. When we think about everyday life—the way we care for ourselves and our families, how we solve our problems, and the choices we make—it's plain to see that much of what we accept as common knowledge is rooted in core beliefs based in these false assumptions.

Rather than following the scientific imagery portraying us as insignificant beings that originated through a miraculous series of biological "flukes" and then survived 5,000 years of civilization as powerless victims separate from the harsh world we've found ourselves in, the new science suggests something radically different. In the late 1990s and early 2000s, peer-reviewed scientific studies revealed the following facts:

- **Fact 1:** Advanced civilization is at least twice as old as the 5,000–5,500 years estimated by conventional timelines.[21]
- **Fact 2:** Nature relies upon cooperation and mutual aid, not competition, for survival.[22]
- **Fact 3:** Human life shows unmistakable signs of design.[23]
- **Fact 4:** Our emotions directly influence what happens in the sea of energy we are bathed in.[24]
- **Fact 5:** The universe, our world, and our bodies are made of a shared field of energy—a matrix—that makes the unity known as *entanglement* possible.[25]

Albert Einstein is reported to have said that "insanity" is doing the same thing over and over again in the same way and expecting different results. I think there's a lot of truth in this statement. To attempt to resolve the challenges we face in our time of extremes by looking at them through the eyes of the same beliefs that led *to* the crises makes little sense. To do so now, particularly while knowing that those beliefs are false, makes even less sense.

To meet the challenges of our time of extremes, we must be willing to think differently about ourselves than we have for the last three centuries. And to do so means that we must cross some of the traditional boundaries that have isolated the discoveries in one area of scientific study from those in another. When we do, something wonderful begins to happen.

The Broken Chain of Knowledge

There is a chain of knowledge that links our modern world with the past. Each time that chain is broken, we lose access to valuable information about the world and ourselves. We know that the chain has been broken at least twice in recorded history: once with the burning of the Great Library of Alexandria during the Roman conquest of Egypt, and then again with the edits of the

Bible by the Christian church hierarchy during the 4th century C.E. As a scientist, I am of the opinion that the closer we can get to the original teachings that existed *before* the knowledge was lost, the more clearly we can understand what our ancestors knew in their own times that we could apply in ours.

For the bulk of my adult life, I've searched the places least disturbed by the modern world to find sources of ancient and indigenous wisdom. My journey has taken me to some of the most amazing sites remaining on Earth. From the magnificent monasteries of the Tibetan Plateau and the humble monasteries in the mountains of Egypt and southern Peru, to the Dead Sea Scrolls and the oral histories of native peoples throughout the world, I've listened to stories and studied records. As different as each of the traditions I've encountered appears to be from the others, there are common themes weaving them into a collective fabric that displays our past. Those themes are reflected in the wisdom shared by the Mayan elder I met in Mexico's Yucatán jungles in fall 2012. In summary, he described how our ancestors did not separate . . .

- . . . themselves from the world around them.
- . . . art, science, and everyday life.
- . . . the present from the past.

While such wisdom is certainly not scientific, the themes that the wisdom conveys have, in fact, been confirmed by the best science of our time. In light of such confirmations, the question that comes to me again and again is this: *If our ancestors had such a deep understanding of the earth and our relationship to it, and modern science is only just now able to validate this relationship, then what else did they know that we've forgotten?*

The Question at the Root of Each Choice

A single question guides us throughout each day of our lives. For some people, the question is subconscious, while for others it's not. Either way, our answer to this question is the key to every decision we've ever made in our lives, or will make from this moment forward. Our answer provides the basis for each and every choice we've ever arrived at and is at the heart of every challenge that's ever crossed our paths. The question is such a simple one that many people make the mistake of discounting its meaning in their lives. The question that holds such power for us as individuals is simply this: *Who am I?* And because there are so many of us in the world today making big choices, the question also becomes: *Who are we?*

For over 5,000 years, the ancient and indigenous people of the world answered this question in a way that worked for them. Their worldview gave them the reasons to live in harmony with the earth, rather than to attempt to master it. It gave them reasons to work together as communities and form regional councils that worked to share the resources of the planet, rather to attempt to own them.

With the birth of the scientific method, during the time of Sir Isaac Newton, all of that began to change. Since then, for over 300 years, science has tried to prove empirically what the indigenous traditions of our past accomplished intuitively. During this period, the story of separation and the need for competition has become so deeply ingrained in our worldview that we sometimes fail to realize what a huge role it plays. Nonetheless, it's the thinking of the past that's led to the crises we face in our lives today.

To answer the question of who we are means we must first answer six fundamental questions regarding our relationships to ourselves and the world. They must be answered by every civilization, every society, every religious organization, and members of groups from each spiritual tradition in order to meet the needs of those who participate in the organization or follow the group's teachings. The questions address the most fundamental issues of existence.

Figure 2.1 on the next page illustrates how these ideas fit with one another, forming a pyramid of thinking. The questions they pose make sense intuitively and form a hierarchy of increasingly complex relationships. Beginning with the most fundamental question of all, from the bottom of the pyramid they are:

1. Where does life come from?
2. Where does human life come from?

3. What is our relationship to our bodies?
4. What is our relationship to our world?
5. What is our relationship to our past?
6. How do we solve our problems? [We ask this last, because the way it's answered depends upon the thinking that answers the previous questions.]

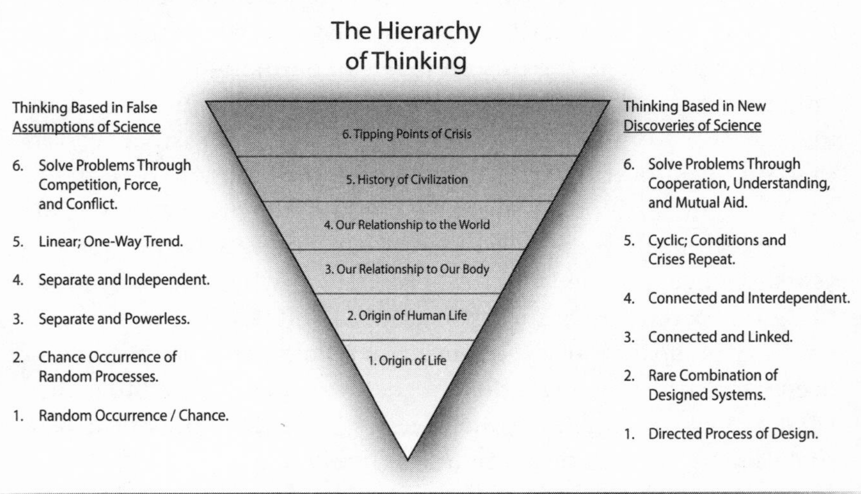

Figure 2.1. An illustration of the pyramid of thinking. The way we answer the six fundamental questions shown vertically in the center of the pyramid forms the lens through which we see ourselves in the world and think of ourselves in life. The false assumptions listed to the left are based upon 300 years of science and the belief in separation. To the right are the new assumptions based upon the best science of today, which reveals a world of unity and our role in it. It's the principles of this lens that determine how we go about solving problems in our lives, in our families and communities, and even between nations. Source: *Deep Truth* (Hay House, 2011).

On the left side of the pyramid, we see the false assumptions of science. These six assumptions encapsulate an entire paradigm of thinking that has formed the foundation of our story in the modern world. It's these very beliefs of separation and competition that have been at odds with leading-edge discoveries that began appearing at the end of the 20th century. With the acceptance of these now-obsolete beliefs, Darwin's ideas of competition make perfect sense.

The problem is that the new data no longer supports the old theories.

The way we think of ourselves in the world creates the lens through which we solve our problems.

Dangerous Thinking

It's common for participants in my seminars to ask why it matters that the assumptions of the past are wrong. Charles Darwin's ideas offer a perfect example. They were first introduced in the mid-1800s, and we're now in the 21st century. Honestly, why is it important?

These are good questions, and the answers surprise many people. It's precisely because so many of the false assumptions of science came into being when they did that they've had the impact they had on our world. Because so many of these false assumptions were introduced in the late 1800s and early 1900s—precisely when the foundation for our modern way of life was put into place—it's not surprising to see these principles reflected in so many aspects of our world today. During this time, the propositions put forth by the science of the day, such as the belief that there is no field of energy that connects the world (everything is separate from everything else) and the belief that nature is based upon competition and survival of the strongest, were quickly accepted and applied to the thinking about war, economies, and the way we solve our problems.

In ways that are sometimes subtle, and sometimes not so subtle, these false beliefs are still with us today. For example, studies from experts, such as University of Illinois archaeologist Lawrence H. Keeley, author of *War Before Civilization* (Oxford University Press, 1996), contribute to the acceptance of war as a normal expression of human behavior. Based on his scholarly exploration of our past and his interpretation of the evidence he's found, Keeley's opinion is that war is a natural state of human affairs. "War is something like trade or exchange," he says. "It is something that all humans do."[26] This type of thinking, which embraces competition, struggle, and "survival of the strongest" as natural elements, is reflected in the administrative structures of the big systems that are in crisis today. The world's economic system, the business models of many modern corporations, and the way in which we manage vital necessities of food and energy are all examples of modern consequences of an obsolete way of thinking.

These false beliefs are with us in ways that are less subtle as well. Some of the greatest suffering of the 20th century was justified by the ideas of survival of the strongest. The thinking implied in all forms of genocide, and directly spelled out in some, is linked to Darwin's observations of nature, the way he portrayed it in his writings, and how these writings were interpreted by others. This thinking is mirrored in philosophical works such as the infamous "Little Red Book" (officially titled *Quotations from Chairman Mao Tse-Tung*) and in *Mein Kampf,* the book that detailed Adolf Hitler's worldview. Both books were used as justification for brutal killings that took a combined toll of at least 40 million in the last century.

Nature's Model: Cooperation

In the opening address at the 1993 Symposium on the Humanistic Aspects of Regional Development, held in Birobidzhan, Russia, co-chair Ronald Logan offered a context for viewing the new discoveries of cooperation in nature as a model for successful societies. Logan cited the work of Alfie Kohn, author of *No Contest* (Houghton Mifflin, 1992), describing what Kohn's research reveals regarding a beneficial amount of competition in groups. After reviewing more than 400 studies documenting cooperation and competition, Kohn concludes: "The ideal amount of competition . . . in any environment, the classroom, the workplace, the family, the playing field, is none. . . . [Competition] is always destructive."[27]

The natural world is widely recognized as a proving ground for experiments in unity, cooperation, and survival among insects and animals. From nature's lessons we're shown, without question, that unity and cooperation are advantageous to living beings. Such time-tested strategies from the world around us may ultimately lead us to develop a new blueprint for our own survival. To apply a strategy of cooperation, however, an additional factor must be accounted for in our world that does not appear in the animal kingdom. As individuals, and as a species, human beings generally must know "where" we are going and what we can expect when we get "there," before we are willing to change the way we live. We need to know that the result is worthwhile and something to look forward to.

Clearly, we don't know all that there is to know about how the universe works and our role in it. While future studies will undoubtedly produce greater insights, it's sometimes best to make choices based upon what we know in the moment—so that we can live to refine them later.

Will We Embrace What Science Has Revealed?

A powerful voice in the scientific community, Sir Martin Rees, professor of astrophysics at the University of Cambridge, suggests that "the odds are no better than 50/50 that our present civilization will survive to the end of the next century."[28] While we've always had natural disasters to contend with, a new class of threats that Rees calls "human induced" now have to be taken into account as well.

Emerging studies, such as those reported in *Scientific American*'s "Crossroads for Planet Earth" edition, echo Rees's warning, telling us, "The next 50 years will be decisive in determining whether the human race—now entering a unique period in its history—can ensure the best possible future for itself."[29] The good news the experts almost universally agree upon, however, is that "if decision makers can get the framework right, the future of humanity will be secured by thousands of mundane decisions."[30] It's in the details of everyday life that the "most profound advances are made."[31]

Without a doubt, each of us will be asked to make countless decisions in the near future. I can't help thinking, however, that one of the most profound, and perhaps the simplest, will be to embrace what the new science has shown us about who we are and our role in the world. If we can accept, rather than deny, the powerful evidence that the individual sciences are showing us, then everything changes. With that change we can begin anew.

While for some people the possibilities hinted at by new discoveries are a refreshing way to view the world, for others they shake the foundation of long-standing tradition. It's sometimes easier to rest on the false assumptions of outdated science than to embrace information that changes everything we understand. When we do, however, we live in the illusion of a lie. We lie to ourselves about who we are and the possibilities that await us. We lie to those who trust and rely upon us to teach them the latest and greatest truths about our world.

When I share this irony with live audiences, often the response echoes the wisdom of science-fiction author Tad Williams, who wrote: "We tell lies when we are afraid . . . afraid of what we don't know, afraid of what others will think, afraid of what will be found out about us. But every time we tell a lie, the thing that we fear grows stronger."[32]

When the discoveries of today tell us that the teachings of the past are no longer true, we must make a choice. Do we continue teaching the false principles and suffering the consequences of wrong assumptions? If we do, then we must answer an even deeper question: *What are we afraid of?* What is it about knowing the deepest truths of who we are, our origins, and our relationship to one another and the earth that's so threatening to our way of life?

Figuring this out may become the greatest challenge of our time in history. It forces us to answer the big question that is uncomfortable for some people and threatening for others: *Can we face the truth that we have asked ourselves to discover?* Do we have the courage to accept what the best science of today reveals about who we are in the universe, and how we fit into the world? If the answer is yes, then we must also accept the responsibility that comes with knowing we can change the world by changing ourselves.

Our willingness to accept the deep truths of life is the key to whether or not our children will survive our choices and have the opportunity to explore the *next* deep truths discovered in their lives.

Reluctance to reflect new scientific discoveries in mainstream media, classrooms, and textbooks keeps us stuck in the thinking that has led to the greatest crises of human history.

The Catalyst: People and More People

Clearly, the biggest catalyst for change in our world is the sheer number of people who now share the earth, and finding the ways to meet their daily needs. In 1968, biologist Paul Ehrlich and his wife, Anne, released their sobering assessment of what we can reasonably expect from the growing numbers of people in our global family. Three sentences early in their powerful book *The Population Bomb* (Sierra Club/Ballantine, 1968) say it all: "The battle to feed all of humanity is over. In the 1970s, hundreds of millions of people will starve to death in spite of any crash programs embarked upon now. At this late date nothing can prevent a substantial increase in the world death rate."[33]

The authors have stated that the purpose of their book was first to create an awareness of the problems stemming from the world's growing population, and then to call attention to the suffering that was inevitable if the growth trends and demand for resources continued. While the book was criticized for its unsettling predictions of human suffering and mass starvation, the authors believe that their book actually achieved the goal that led to its writing. "[It] alerted people to the importance of environmental issues and brought human numbers into the debate on the human future," they stated recently.[34] In a follow-up article, "The Population Bomb Revisited," they responded to the criticism by saying, "Perhaps the most serious flaw in *The Bomb* was that it was much too optimistic about the future."[35]

In addition to natural cycles of change that we have no control over, arguably the single greatest factor driving our time of extremes is the very topic that the Ehrlichs described in 1968: Earth's growing population. While the epic suffering and death they predicted has in fact occurred, it's happened over a span covering four-plus decades rather than the compressed period of the 1970s and '80s they originally projected. The sheer number of people now living in our world, the resources needed by each and every one of them each and every day, and their desire for the energy-intensive lifestyle popularized by Western culture are perpetuating a self-sustaining loop of conditions amplifying our time of extremes. We see an example of such a loop developing between the growing populations of countries like India and China, which together account for about 38 percent of the people in the entire world, and their emerging demand for energy.

As more and more people in these two countries enjoy new levels of prosperity from globalization, booming industry, and higher-paying jobs, they're following the Western model of what that kind of success has looked like in the past. They aspire to have the same luxuries of multicar families and commuter-based communities that have been identified with affluence in the West since the boom of the post–World War II 1950s.

It's these ideas of affluence and the way they're expressed that create a vicious cycle that demands more energy to power more homes, more climate-controlled office buildings, more public transportation, and more private automobiles, which in turn create more opportunities for more people, and so on. The sheer number of private automobiles produced on a global scale gives us an idea of just what such demand means. As recently as 2006, the world's automobile industry produced about 50 million new vehicles each year. In the space of just six years, however, that number increased to over 60 million. In other words, in just 10 years, 10 million new vehicles per year—approximately 165,000 each day—were added to the roads of the world![36]

The problem is that the energy needs created by this modern phenomenon are still being met by the energy thinking of the last century. Gasoline remains the preferred way to power automobiles.

This is where the cycle is pushing against unsustainable limits. Gasoline comes from oil. From the increased emissions of greenhouse gases and the health-threatening pollution that it produces to the effect of higher-priced fuel on the world's economy, the implications of a growing demand for oil are immense.

Whether it was the environmental protests of the 1960s or the scientific warnings of the 1970s, concerns regarding the world's population and the fact that the growing number of people is the trigger for greater demands upon shrinking resources are certainly no secret. It may be precisely *because* we've heard about the problem for so long, without any meaningful signs of a solution, that we sometimes feel absolutely overwhelmed even thinking about it.

Feedback Loop 1: More People/More Energy/More People . . .

The statistics for the world's population tell us that the number of people living on Earth hovered under 500 million for nearly 11,500 years. When we look at how that number has grown in such a relatively short period of time after being so stable for so long, the question is: *Why?* What could have driven up the number of people living on Earth so quickly? While various factors play a role in answering this question, including the warming of the climate following the last ice age and the discovery of agriculture to sustain communities, one factor stands out from all the others. That factor is the undeniable link between people, energy, and food.

The question is, which came first? Was it the growing size of Earth's population that triggered the search for more food and a fuel source that could meet people's energy needs? Or was it the discovery of an abundant and efficient source of energy that led to the ability to grow more food and the rise in our population? Depending upon which researcher we ask or what study we reference, there appears to be evidence supporting both scenarios.

The dynamic relationship between energy and people is beautifully summed up by Canadian ecologist Paul Chefurka. "It's obvious at a glance that food, oil and population are tightly related," he says, "but the nature of their relationship is open to interpretation."[37] Describing the perspectives that are possible, he states, "If you were an economist you could say that as the number of people grows, we go out and grow more food and find more oil to meet our growing needs. Conversely, if you were an ecologist you might say that increasing supplies of oil and food allow our population to grow. Or you could say (as I do) that they all exist in a complex feedback loop."[38]

Regardless of what we conclude has driven the rise in population and energy consumption, the fact is that the discovery of cheap and accessible fuel sources is directly linked with the largest increase in human population in the history of the world. The first doubling of the world's population, in 1804, illustrates this relationship, as it coincided precisely with the rise of coal as a global fuel source.

Coal was so abundant and inexpensive in Europe and North America in the 19th century that it quickly became the standard for heating homes, as well as for use in industry. While it was certainly used as early as the mid-1700s, the mining and processing methods and railroads needed to pull the coal from the ground and move it in large quantities to where it was needed were still being developed. It wasn't until the mid to late 19th century, and even into the first half of the 20th century, that coal became the energy of choice. By the end of World War II, however, the use of other fuel oils, such as crude oil and oil products, became safe, efficient, and cheap. Although this led to a decline in the use of coal specifically as the preferred energy source, it furthered the relationship between people and energy.

Today, we find ourselves at a crossroads similar to that involving coal and oil in the last century. This crossroads is triggered by the shrinking reserves of cheap oil and the new forms of energy that are filling the void. This includes harnessing renewable forms of energy, as well as tapping into mammoth-sized reserves of natural gas that are turning the energy equation of the world upside down. The key here is that the use of inexpensive energy that's easy to access correlates strongly with the rise in population.

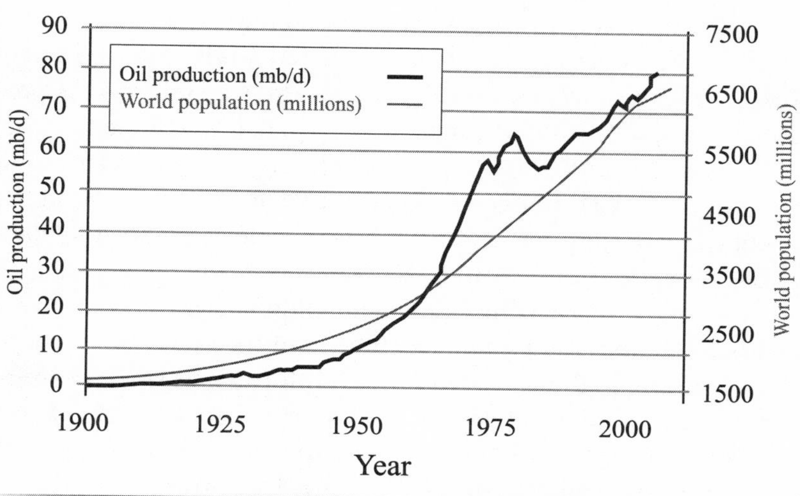

Figure 2.2. The growth of the world's population is closely tied to the availability of cheap energy. We see this relationship clearly in the parallel between the rise in the world's oil production at the turn of the last century and the dramatic increase in population at precisely the same time. Source: International Energy Agency.

The use of cheap energy gave our forebears more time for leisure activities because their focus shifted away from survival. And it's this higher standard of living that led directly to the explosion in population. To put such growth into perspective, between 1926, the year Elizabeth II was born, and 2013, the queen of England witnessed the population of the earth rise from 2 billion to 7 billion. The marriage between people and cheap energy that began 200 years ago continues as our global family now is projected to reach 8 billion to 10.5 billion by 2050.[39]

Feedback Loop 2: More People/More Food/More People . . .

In the same way that the world's population is linked to energy supplies, the food needed to feed our global family is also directly linked to energy. When we think about the way our food is produced today, intuitively this relationship makes tremendous sense. As the population of the world has increased, the demand for food has followed. With the development of farm equipment powered by cheap oil in the 20th century, farmers could produce more food in shorter periods of time to feed greater numbers of people.

As a young boy growing up in the Midwestern United States, I clearly remember the signs along Interstate 70, a part of the country's emerging highway system, which informed us when we were crossing the border between states. During our frequent drives between Missouri and Kansas, in addition to the colorful plaques that told us we were crossing a state line, there was an additional sign that proudly displayed how much the agriculture of the state contributed to our country. The sign was updated each year to reflect the shifting conditions of weather and the availability of water. It became a family game to guess what the numbers would be before we got to the sign, and the winner would buy the family a soft drink at the next rest stop.

In the early 1960s, the sign read: ONE KANSAS FARMER FEEDS 26 PEOPLE. In 2010, the same sign read: ONE KANSAS FARMER FEEDS 155 PEOPLE. The information in Figure 2.3, from the United Nations Food and Agriculture Organization (FAO), confirms on a global scale what the Kansas sign was showing on a local scale. The world's ability to produce greater amounts of food with fewer farmers is a trend that seems to be well established. It's also the source of what appears for some people to be a conflict of information.

On the one hand, the data tells us that we've got enough food for every mouth on the planet. On the other hand, we're inundated with requests for aid to feed the masses of people suffering from starvation in multiple countries on a daily basis. *Clearly, the problem is not with the amount of food available; it's in getting the existing food to the people who need it.* The term for this dilemma is *food insecurity.*

Entire organizations have been created in an effort to bring an end to this issue.

In 2010, the FAO released their annual report identifying the state of the world and progress made toward creating greater food security. They estimated that nearly a billion people in the world were chronically undernourished, despite the first decline in the rate in 15 years.[40] Most of the people identified as undernourished in this study lived in developing countries. The conclusion of the report is similar to what you or I would conclude even without having the statistical data to support it: the levels of undernourishment in the world are "unacceptably high."[41]

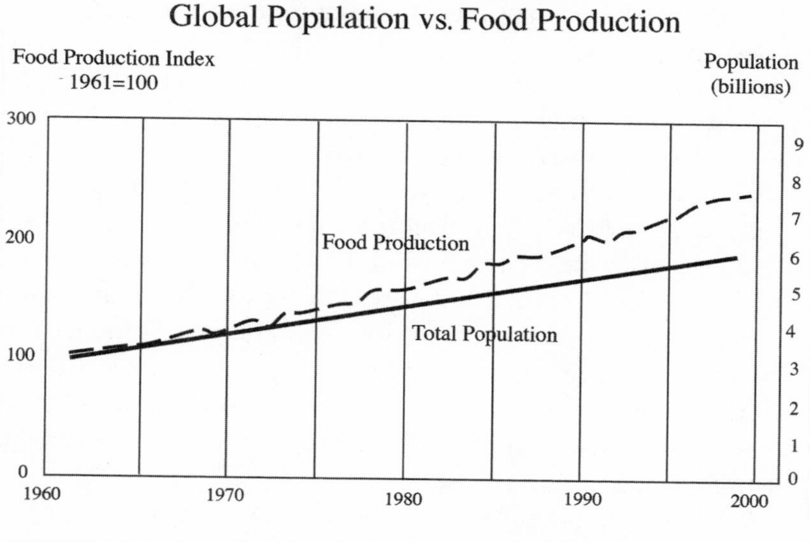

Figure 2.3. There is a direct link between the increasing population of the world and the need for more food to feed our global family. This relationship is clearly shown in this graph and also illustrates the fact that food shortages are not due to production problems. Source: United Nations Food and Agriculture Organization.

So while the number of people being fed by our Kansas farmer has increased about 496 percent since the 1960s, the cost of the food produced has increased in percentages measured in the *thousands!* For example, in 1960 the average cost of six ears of corn was about 25 cents. In 2011, the price for the same six ears of corn was $3.00—an increase of 1,100 percent in 51 years! Similarly, the cost of potatoes in 1960 was about 39 cents per pound. In 2011, that price had increased by 1,129 percent to $4.99 per pound. Even adjusted for inflation, such a rise in food costs is staggering.

One of the biggest factors contributing to the price surges comes from the cost of the energy needed to produce the food. When we think about it, this makes sense as well.

It takes a lot of fuel to produce our food. It takes energy to drive the tractors to plow and prepare the land and plant the seeds. While the crops are growing, it takes fuel to create the electricity to pump water from the well to the irrigation systems to keep the plants alive. It takes fuel to run the tractors and huge combines at harvest time to gather the produce. It takes fuel to run the conveyors that move, sort, and prepare the produce for market; and of course, it takes fuel to power the vehicles that get the produce from where it's grown to our local market.

While advances in technology have helped with the efficiency of farm equipment, the improvements are relative. A tractor made in 1980, for example, averaged around 14.4 miles per gallon of fuel, while those produced in 2000 were only a little better, averaging about 16.5 mpg. Because it takes so much energy to produce our food, it's not surprising that as the end of cheap fuel has arrived, the end of cheap food has arrived as well. Figure 2.4 below illustrates this relationship in a way that is clear and, for some, startling. The implications are immense.

As the growing number of people in the world demand greater amounts of food, and the cost of the energy to produce the food increases, we are now living a time when staples, such as rice and corn, are beyond the reach of a large portion of the world's poorest populations.

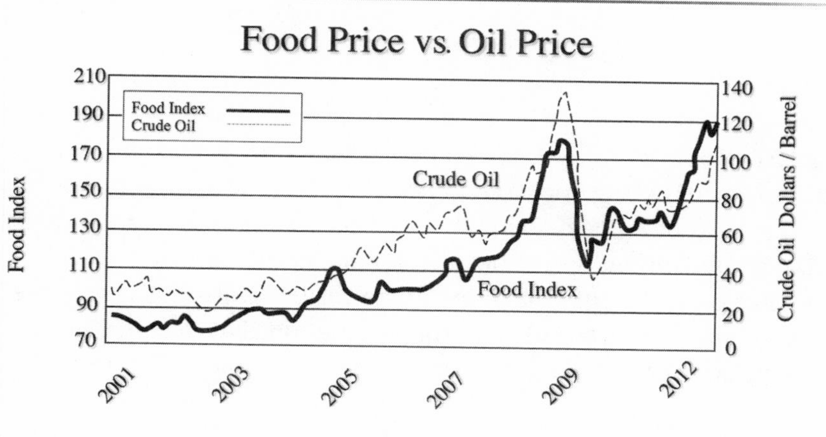

Figure 2.4. As the world's reserves of cheap oil continue to shrink, the higher-priced fuels used to produce agricultural crops are reflected in the cost of the world's food supply. The image above clearly shows this relationship. The implications of using cheaper or alternative fuels are obvious. In the absence of such steps, higher fuel costs effectively render the food unavailable to many people. Source: Adapted from IMF—Primary Commodity Prices.

It's obvious that the relationship between population, food, and energy is a complex one. It's also clear that it's difficult to separate one facet of this relationship from the others. When we talk about finding successful solutions to related issues, such as those we've explored in this chapter, one of the keys is to go directly to the common denominator that links the problems together. In our time of extremes, it's easy to narrow the list of possibilities to the single factor that the others hinge upon: our thinking. The crisis in thinking that permeates our lives is based in a reluctance to accept the discoveries revealed by the best science of our day, such as the role of cooperation in nature, and what they mean in our lives.

To transform our time of extremes, we must have the courage to heal the crisis of thinking.

When the converging crises described by experts and pundits are filtered through a worldview based in the false assumptions identified earlier in this chapter, many believe that we're on a one-way collision course with an inevitable outcome of decline and destruction. While scientists and media commentators are very good at predicting such outcomes—the tipping points of things like peak oil and peak debt—the fact many experts are missing is that those tipping points need never appear in our lives.

Before every tipping point of no return, nature gives us the opportunity to turn crisis into transformation. This fact is the good news that makes the name of this book, *The Turning Point,* possible.

CHAPTER THREE

THE TURNING POINT:

Nature's Answer to Life's Extremes

"If you do not change direction, you may end up where you are heading."

— ATTRIBUTED TO LAO-TZU (C. 604–531 B.C.E.), CHINESE PHILOSOPHER

In 2008, Tom Stoppard, the renowned Czech-born British playwright, was feeling our time of extremes in a big way. For Stoppard, the sense that so many big things were happening in our world all at once left him overwhelmed and confused—feelings that led to a self-diagnosed case of writer's block. During an interview with Reuters, the creator of such classic plays as *The Coast of Utopia* and *Rosencrantz and Guildenstern Are Dead* confessed that he felt so overcome by global extremes that he didn't know which direction he should take his work.

"So much is in the foreground now, huge, important subjects, that you kind of goggle at them," Stoppard candidly described his dilemma in the interview.[1] "Shall I do global warming or shall I do Iraq, maybe I'll do Afghanistan, and nothing gets written," he confessed.[2] He eventually overcame his writer's block and went on to create more innovative plays, such as *Dark Side,* written to celebrate the 40th anniversary of Pink Floyd's seminal album *The Dark Side of the Moon.*

Stoppard is not alone in his sense of overwhelm. I'm sharing his story as an example of what many people say they're feeling nowadays: they're stunned by so many big events happening all at once. Conference participants throughout the world have shared with me a similar sense of helplessness and hopelessness, as well as awe at how fast their lives and the world are shifting.

It's certainly easy to feel overwhelmed by the magnitude of change. It's also hard to see how anything we do as individuals could possibly make a difference to the world. While I have no doubt that it's possible for one person to bring big change to the world in a positive way, I also know that it often takes a lifetime, or even the sacrifice of a life, to do so. From Mother Teresa to Mahatma Gandhi, Nelson Mandela, and John Lennon, poignant examples exist of how one person in the limelight of the world stage can open a door of possibility, vision, and imagination for others. What may not be so obvious, however, is what had to happen before these people could be such powerful beacons of possibility. Before they were able to shine their messages to the world, they first had to be honest with themselves about their dreams and the choices they would make to bring them to life.

The Speed of Change

Whether we're feeling the impact of global warming upon our weekly grocery bill or the burden of global debt in the form of the loss of jobs in our community, it's good to be honest with ourselves about what's realistic for our lives and what's not. People tell me all the time that they want to change the world. The question is: *How?* Realistically, what can we do as individuals in the face of so many simultaneous crises? How can we turn our time of extremes into a time of transformation? And how do we share our personal transformation with our communities and loved ones?

This is where being honest with ourselves comes in.

There are two facts I would invite you to consider:

- **Fact 1:** Honestly, the world's probably not going to change in the time it takes to read this book.
- **Fact 2:** Honestly, the way you respond to the world can definitely change in the time it takes to read this book.

There's an additional fact that makes facts 1 and 2 true. It's a fact based in the science of the natural world and how nature adapts to change.

- **Fact 3:** Nature always makes room for new possibilities and positive change.

When it comes to this third fact, our time of extremes is no exception.

Many experts and media pundits view the converging crises in the world as inevitable stepping-stones tracing a one-way path to irreversible decline and destruction. While scientists and media commentators are very good at predicting such outcomes, most experts are missing out on the good news that justifies the title of this book. There's a time in any crisis when it can lead to positive transformation; when simply surviving can become joyous thriving. In our lives that time is called the *turning point.* In our world, that time is *now!*

In other words, although it appears that we're on a collision course with the effects of climate change, peak oil, and peak debt, just as the United Nations and others suggest, these and other crises can be avoided if we act now. The question is: *Will we embrace the turning points that lead to the greatest transformation of living and thinking that the world has ever seen?* The facts suggest we're about to find out!

There's a time when every crisis can be turned into transformation; when simply surviving can become thriving. That time is the *turning point.*

Tipping Points: Small Triggers of Big Change

There are times in life when the principles underlying things that seem small and insignificant can make a big difference and lead to big change. A boiling pot of water on the kitchen stove is a perfect example. While we've all seen water boil, we may not have realized precisely what we were seeing as it happened. And, if we didn't realize what we were watching on the stovetop, then we were probably missing one of nature's most powerful agents of change when it comes to our lives as well. Here's how it works.

When we place the pot on the burner, the water doesn't boil instantly. Instead, it's a process. What we see at first is a change so slight that it may even look like nothing's happening. So we watch and we wait. Degree by degree, the water gets warmer. Our thermometer reads 195°F, then 200°F, then 207°F. At precisely 211°F, something extraordinary begins to happen. While the water still looks pretty much like it did when we turned on the heat, there's something happening on a subtle level. If we look closely, we see that a few small bubbles have formed on the inside of the pot. *With the rise of just one more degree, from 211°F to 212°F, we see a big change.* All of a sudden bubbles appear everywhere in the pot and the water erupts into full-on chaos. Now our water is really boiling, and we can begin cooking our rice or pasta, steeping our tea, or doing whatever it was that led us to boil the water to begin with.

The key here is that a small difference was all it took to push the water to the boiling point. Although the lower temperatures were necessary steps to get to that point, it was only when the temperature bumped up that one last small amount that the conditions in the water changed and the water began to boil. That one last degree illustrates the process I'm describing. It's called the *tipping point,* and it changes everything.

While the term *tipping point* has been around for a long time in mathematics and some other circles, it suddenly burst into our everyday vocabulary in the year 2000 following publication of Malcolm Gladwell's book of that name. *The Tipping Point* is a powerful exploration of what triggers change in society and how those changes can ultimately shift our everyday world. Gladwell defines a tipping point as the "moment of critical mass, the threshold, the boiling point."[3]

A small shift can tip the scales of balance in a big way.

Tipping points are often used to describe the point of no return when evolving conditions reach a place or a time that they no longer support the status quo. It's at this point that the original condition no longer exists, and a new one appears. This is precisely what happened in our example of boiling water. At 212°F, the molecules began to behave in a new way that reflected the new conditions.

For the purposes of this book, a tipping point can be thought of as the culmination of conditions that creates a point of no return. And when we talk about a point of no return, it's generally not in a good way.

Turning Points: Nature's Answer to Life's Extremes

We see tipping points all around us. In the mainstream media, they're used to describe conditions that range from how much longer the world's economies can hold up against the mounting strain of debt, to how many people in the United States can remain out of work before the taxes that run the nation become insufficient, or how far the relations between Israel and Iran can deteriorate before war becomes inevitable. By and large, however, the most common use of the term in recent years is with regard to climate change and what it means to us.

How much can global warming increase before we reach the tipping point where Earth can no longer sustain life? How far can the climate-induced rising food and energy prices increase before the average household can no longer afford them? While we'll discuss these tipping points, and more, in greater detail later on, the focus here is the idea of tipping points themselves, and the good news that comes with them. So let's get to that good news.

As mentioned earlier, before we ever reach a tipping point of no return, nature allows for a shift that leads to a new outcome. The place where the shift appears is the turning point. The fact that turning points exist stands in sharp contrast to what we've been led to believe about ourselves and the world. In the real terms of everyday life, it means that there's *always* a way out of a difficult situation; there's *always* an opportunity to change the path leading to one outcome to a new path with a new outcome.

While this fact would be appealing at any time in our lives, it's vital to recognize it today, when we're led to believe that our future holds frightening tipping points in terms of jobs, food, and energy.

Regardless of how much we believe we've mastered the forces of nature or insulated ourselves from the elements, the fact remains that we're a part of the natural world. We always have been and always will be, and today is no different. To see just how deeply we are linked to nature, we need look no further than the power of lunar cycles to influence the menstrual cycle of a woman's body, the power of day and night to influence our cycles of sleep, or the power that the lack of natural light has on the incidence of depression and suicide in places where sunshine is scarce.

Even in a world of high-rise offices and apartments, where it's common for people to go for days without touching the earth under their feet or feeling the rays of the sun bathing their skin, it's clear that we're deeply enmeshed with the rhythms of nature. And it's because we are so deeply connected to nature that it makes perfect sense for nature's mathematics to be *our mathematics* as well.

This is good news, because when we find ourselves headed toward an unwanted tipping point, nature gives us a way to set a new course with a new outcome. In mathematics, nature's key to change is commonly called an *inflection point.* In everyday life, it's our now-familiar turning point. The power of the turning point is that it allows us to *turn away* from what is generally an unwanted outcome.

A Turning Point of Hope

We've all seen examples of turning points in our lives or those of friends and family. They can happen spontaneously, or they may be created intentionally. It's entirely possible that we've experienced both kinds without recognizing what we were seeing. So how do we know when one appears?

A familiar example of a turning point would be when a friend or family member undergoes successful surgery to correct a dangerous condition in his or her body. Whether it's the removal of a life-threatening tumor or the repair of a vital organ, when such things happen, it's commonly said that the surgery has given our loved one a "second chance." In other words, rather than continuing the course of deterioration that was leading to the tipping point of no return—the failure of his or her body—it's the turning point of the procedure that offers the new lease on life.

I witnessed an example of just such a turning point in my family when my mother chose to undergo surgery for a cancerous tumor in one of her lungs in 2000. Apparently she had unknowingly contracted tuberculosis when she was a young girl. It was never diagnosed at the time, and her body had healed itself with no medical intervention. The doctors said that the scar created by a TB wound can become cancerous if a person lives long enough for the tissue to calcify. Evidently this is what had happened with my mom.

While she and I have had many conversations about our bodies' awesome ability to heal, and Mom has certainly been to enough of my seminars to see the evidence of spontaneous healings, she was very clear about how she wanted to deal with her own condition. In a late-night conversation on the phone, Mom simply said, "I know those healings are possible, but they're not for me. I just want this thing out of me!"

I heard her loud and clear. I supported my mother's choice and helped her find the best facilities and doctors possible to honor it.

As we made the rounds to evaluate hospitals and university research centers, Mom had the opportunity to personally interview each potential surgeon. She asked her questions to get to know each doctor, and I listened with another set of ears to what the best voices in the field of lung surgery were telling her. At the end of each conversation, I would ask one additional question. After all of Mom's concerns were addressed, I'd shake hands with the doctor, look him or her in the eye, and ask, "What role do you believe that God or a higher power plays in your work?" With only one exception, my question became the cue to end the handshake, as one by one, each doctor would turn and walk out of the room.

It was at the very last interview with the very last doctor on our list at a university teaching hospital in Albuquerque, New Mexico, that one surgeon didn't leave. Instead, when he heard my question, he gripped my hand even firmer and let out a big belly laugh that surprised me.

With a gleam in his eyes, he looked directly into mine, and with a thick European accent that I couldn't quite identify, he answered my question by asking one of his own. "Who do you think works through these hands to perform the miracles in the operating room?" he said as he raised his arms for us to see. He let out another laugh, hugged my mom, turned, and walked out of the office.

I looked at Mom and said, "I think you've just found your doctor!"

Mom's surgery was a complete and total success. She has been cancer-free ever since, and has also made changes in her life that help her to stay that way. I'm sharing the story here as another example of how a choice in life can become the turning point that leads to good things. For my mother, knowing with absolute certainty that her body was free of the tissue that threatened her life was the turning point that gave her the freedom to change her routines of diet, exercise, and the way she'd been taught to think and live. It was the choice to do something that matched her belief system, however—having surgery—that was the key that made these other types of changes possible.

Our personal turning points must fit into our own worldview of possibilities.

Nature's Rule: Keep It Simple!

Nature is based in simplicity. It only becomes complex when we make it complex. The principles of life and our world can be described with simple ideas using simple words. And it's precisely because nature *is* so simple that natural relationships can be described using simple mathematics. A fractal pattern is a perfect example of what I mean.

In the 1970s, a mathematics professor at Yale University, Benoit Mandelbrot, developed a way for us to see the simple patterns of nature that make the world, and everything in it, possible. He called his new way of seeing things *fractal geometry,* or *fractals.* Before Mandelbrot's discovery, scientists used another kind of geometry to describe the world: Euclidean geometry.

The old way of thinking was that nature *is* so complex that it can't be described using one system of numbers. For that reason, most of us have grown up learning a form of geometry that only approximates nature's patterns. It's the geometry that uses perfect lines, perfect squares, perfect circles, and perfect curves. This is why our first drawings of trees may have looked like lollipops on sticks when we were young artists.

The problem is that nature doesn't use perfect lines and curves to build mountains, clouds, and trees. Instead, it uses imperfect fragments—a zigzag line here and a wobbly curve there—that, when taken all together, become the mountains, clouds, and trees. These imperfect fragments are fractal patterns. The key is that in a fractal, each fragment, no matter how small, looks like the larger pattern that it's a part of. The term that describes these repeating patterns is *self-similar.*

It is because nature is made of a few self-similar patterns that appear on many different scales that a CT scan of the blood vessels feeding into the arteries of our bodies looks like a satellite image of tributaries feeding into the Amazon River. It's for the same reason that the energy of an electron orbiting around a nucleus looks so much like a planet orbiting around the sun. Nature is made of these simple, self-similar patterns that appear again and again at different levels of magnitude.

With nature's simplicity in mind, when Mandelbrot programmed his formula into a computer, the output was stunning. By seeing everything in the natural world as small fragments that look a lot like other small fragments, and combining these similar fragments into bigger patterns, the images that were produced did more than just approximate nature. *They looked exactly like nature!* And that is precisely what Mandelbrot's new geometry shows us about our world. Nature builds itself from simple patterns.

Figure 3.1. In the 1970s, Benoit Mandelbrot used a computer to produce the first fractal images. The fern leaf on the left and the landscape on the right are both computer generated by shifting the values of the same simple formula $z = z^2 + c$. Source: *Fractal Fern:* Dreamstime: © Tupungato; *Fractal Terrain:* Wikimedia Commons: Stevo-88.

With these ideas in mind, it's not surprising that geometry shows us the idea of a turning point so beautifully as well. In Figure 3.2, we see the illustration of a turning point. It's shown as the place where a line that's moving in one direction changes shape and begins to move in a new direction. If we follow the line in the illustration from the top toward the bottom of the graph, it forms a shape that dips briefly, levels out, and then begins to trace a new path downward.

The point where the line on the chart changes its shape represents the place in the real world that is the subject of this book: the turning point. Because the change is possible for the line, we can know with certainty that change is possible for us as well. Our lives are based on the same natural laws. The graph in Figure 3.2 shows us precisely how it happens. While the change on the graph appears as a simple shift in a line, in our lives the change that occurs at a turning point can mean the difference between success and failure, abundance and lack, and even life and death.

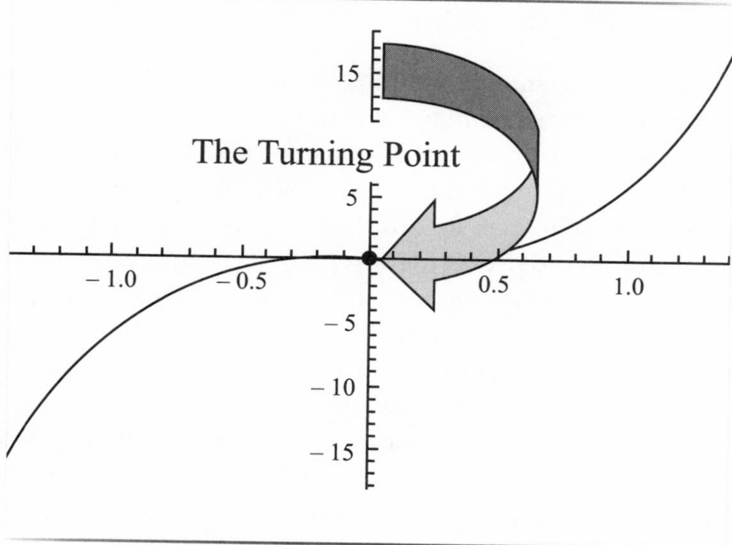

Figure 3.2. An illustration of nature's turning point. It's the place where energy moving in one direction, toward one outcome, can change to a new direction, and lead to a new outcome. Because we are part of the natural world, turning points are available for us as well.

An easy way to think of the turning point is to consider the shape of the curves themselves. If our two-dimensional graph were to magically become three-dimensional, from the upper right portion of the drawing to the turning point, the curve is like a cup. It has a concave shape. In other words, it could hold water if it were available. From the turning point down to the lower left part of the graph, the line changes shape, as if a cup has been turned upside down. This convex shape could not hold water.

The place where the change occurs is the turning point. It's this area between the two cups where science now confirms what different mystical traditions have told us for centuries: there is power in the place between!

Nature's simplicity promises that turning points are simple as well.

Mystery in the Space Between

In many indigenous traditions, it's understood that the mysterious space between things holds the power of new possibilities. In North American native traditions, for example, it's the space between day and night that's believed to open the door to all paths and new outcomes for our lives. When we think about what the time between day and night represents, we see clear parallels between the native traditions and the power of the turning point.

Two times each day, something remarkable happens with respect to Earth's location in space and the effect it has upon us. When the evening sun disappears from the sky as it sets on the horizon, the doorway to a mysterious period of time briefly appears. Although the sun is no longer visible, the sky is still light. It's not really daytime any longer, yet it's not quite night. It's this space between day and night that was called the *crack between the worlds*. The crack between the worlds appears again at dawn, when the sky is no longer the darkness of the night, yet hasn't become the light of day.

From the descriptions of ancient Egyptians and Peruvian shamans to those of healers from America's Desert Southwest, the theme of these turning points is the same. Twice each day, nature gives us a time when our prayers may be offered with the greatest potential to shift our lives. In the language of their time, our ancestors shared the power of what nature shows us in Figure 3.2. Turning points are the way nature allows for change.

The beauty of knowing that a turning point exists is that it holds the opportunity for us to change *before* we experience something that we don't want in our lives.

Turning Points: Sometimes Intentional, Sometimes Spontaneous

Nature recognizes two types of turning points. They come from different sources and show up in different ways in our lives. As mentioned earlier, a turning point can be *spontaneous,* such as the time between day and night described previously, while other turning points are *intentional.* In other words, it's possible to create a turning point when we need one. This is good news. It means that we can create our own turning points in our lives, as well as in our world. We can create them for issues of health, finance, relationships, and career. We can create them frequently, or on rare occasions. Each time we do, we embrace nature's fail-safe mechanism, which allows us to avoid the hurt, heartbreak, destruction, and suffering that all too often appear as the result of failing to recognize one of nature's windows of opportunity.

Now that we know *what* turning points are, the best way to understand *how* they work is through real-life examples. The dramatic weight loss of Bill, a man who tipped the scales at over 300 pounds not long ago, perfectly illustrates what I mean.

An Intentional Turning Point

Unfortunately, the beginning of Bill's story is something heard far too commonly. He was unhappy about his weight and had tried popular diets without success. Nothing he did seemed to work for him. Bill's wife, who was also overweight, did find success with a weight-loss program that she'd discovered. When Bill couldn't get similar results, the difference in their lifestyles made their relationship a struggle, and she asked for a divorce. The combination of not being able to lose the unwanted weight coupled with the potential loss of his marriage led to a predictable outcome. Bill felt hopeless, lost, and depressed. "I began to hate myself for what I was," he says, "and started realizing that I had a lot more I could look forward to."[4]

Bill rekindled a connection that he had made previously with a weight-loss support group. Just like the boiling water at the beginning of this chapter, the changes in his life and weight appeared slowly. As he saw the pounds disappearing, gradually at first, and then faster, he increased the intensity of his workouts. Within seven months, Bill had lost 100 pounds and dropped ten pants sizes. He felt great! He was healthier than he'd been in a very long time and translated his personal success at transforming his body into becoming a minister in his church, where he could help others.

It was during this same period that Bill was severely injured in an automobile accident. Before help could arrive, he found himself trapped inside his car with multiple injuries, including broken ribs, a broken shoulder, and damage to his face. Following his rescue, he was in critical condition for three days and then was hospitalized for three more weeks during his recuperation. It was his will, stamina, and improved physical condition working in harmony that set the stage for his successful recovery.

The doctors and paramedics agreed on one thing: if Bill had had the accident before his life change, the sheer weight of his body in the car would have reduced his chances for rescue and even survival. What's important about this story is that it was Bill's *choice to do something* about his weight that was the turning point in his life. Because he made the choice to lose 100 pounds, Bill's turning point was an intentional one.

We can create a turning point with a single choice.

A Spontaneous Turning Point

In 1928, a Scottish scientist working with bacteria cultures in a laboratory noticed that something unusual had happened while he was away on vacation. During the time he was gone, some of the cultures had changed in a way that was unexpected. Just before leaving, he'd set aside some used petri dishes still containing the bacteria to free up work space for a co-worker. When he returned, he noticed that mold had grown in some of those dishes. While the appearance of the mold itself was not really so unusual, it's the way the bacteria were reacting to the mold that caught his attention. The thin film that such bacteria typically create as they spread across a surface had been killed in the places where mold was present.

In other words, the mold had killed the bacteria.

The man's name was Alexander Fleming, and the mold that had "contaminated" his petri dishes and killed the bacteria contained the powerful antibiotic *penicillin*. Penicillin was the first discovery of a medicine of its kind that would kill only the harmful bacteria in the human body without killing the good bacteria or the body itself.

Immediately, penicillin became the drug of choice for conditions ranging from skin grafts that are susceptible to staph infections, to sexually transmitted diseases and myriad infections caused by animals and insects. As powerful as this "miracle drug" was in its time, however, penicillin was found to be limited in the way it could be used and how effective it was. It wasn't long before even more powerful forms of penicillin were developed to overcome the limitations. Many of those forms continue to be used today. They include *ampicillin, amoxicillin,* and *dicloxacillin*.

Fleming's discovery is a perfect example of a spontaneous turning point. It is spontaneous because he didn't set out to intentionally create the antibiotic before he left for vacation. It happened unexpectedly. It was his willingness to accept and embrace what he had witnessed, however, that made the turning point possible. If he had simply ignored the mold, cleaned the petri dishes, and continued with the experiments he had started before his vacation, we would be living in a very different world today. Fortunately for us all, this wasn't the case and he embraced a turning point for himself, and for the countless numbers of people throughout the world who have benefited from his discovery.

We can embrace a turning point that spontaneously appears in our lives.

As different as these examples of turning points appear to be from one another, they both describe real events that changed lives in two very different ways. In the case of Bill, the turning point of his weight loss was one that he created *intentionally* as the result of a choice that he made. For Alexander Fleming, the turning point of using the mold as a healing agent was *spontaneous;* he noticed something unusual and recognized the meaning of what he had witnessed.

These two examples illustrate the ways in which turning points tend to show up in our lives. While there's nothing unusual about the fact that they exist, the key to their power is what we do when they appear. The two factors that can give meaning to a turning point are:

- Having the wisdom to recognize one when it appears
- Having the strength to accept/embrace what it shows us

Now that we know *how* turning points show up in our lives, the question is, *where* do they come from?

Where Does a Turning Point Come From?

The source of a turning point can only be one place. It stems from *us* and the meaning that we give to a direct and personal experience. The key here is that it is *our* experience. It's not something that people from our workplace say they learned from their favorite reality-TV program, something that our religious organizations tell us we should be feeling, or something that our families say *is so* because they've always accepted it. A turning point can only become real for us when we're the ones who have the experience. It's the result of something that moves us so deeply that we must shift our beliefs to match the facts of our experience.

Such turning points commonly come to us in one of two ways, or a combination of the two. Either:

- A discovery changes the way we think and what we believe.

or

- A paradigm-altering event changes our worldview.

It's through precisely these kinds of experiences that great teachers often help their students cross the gap between their limiting beliefs and the possibilities of their own power. They do so by showing them something or by creating a paradigm-altering experience for them. Either way, the student must then incorporate the lesson into his or her own thinking and beliefs.

The Himalayan spiritual master Jetsun Milarepa, an 11th-century yogi, for example, led his students into a state of consciousness that allowed them to move their hands *through* the solid rock that formed the walls of the caves that were their "classrooms." By doing so, the students discovered for themselves that they were limited not by the walls of the cave itself, but by their beliefs about the walls. I've experienced these teaching caves personally during my pilgrimages to the Tibetan Plateau. I've placed my hands into the impressions that the masters' hands left in the stone. Even the remnants of such demonstrations have a powerful effect upon those who see them for themselves. In more recent times, a similar effect has been used to teach the students of martial arts about their beliefs as well.

We've all seen the demonstrations of martial artists breaking through a stack of concrete blocks with a single blow from a bare hand. While this kind of demonstration is definitely dramatic and amazing to see, what's not often obvious to those watching is that the feat is less about the artist's sheer strength and will to break the block, and more about belief and the power of the martial artist's focus.

From personal experience, I can share that the secret to breaking the concrete blocks or the stacks of wood that are sometimes used is where the student places his or her attention. The martial artist is trained to identify a point in space just slightly *below* the bottom of the lowest block. This point is the key to the entire demonstration. The martial artist isn't thinking about how hard he or she will have to strike or how thick the block is. In fact, other than using the bottom of the block as a reference point, he or she isn't thinking about the block at all.

The whole point of the exercise is that for just an instant, the thoughts, feelings, emotions, and beliefs within the martial artist's body, mind, and soul are totally focused on a single point in space and time, the point just below the block. That's the rendezvous point in space where his or her hand will complete a motion. In that moment of focus nothing else exists, including the concrete block.

Such a demonstration actually meets the criteria for both previously identified turning-point sources. The act itself is a paradigm-altering event that changes the way the person feels about his or her relationship to the world. And the fact that the marital artist accomplished the feat becomes the discovery providing the factual evidence that the feat is possible. Both criteria create the need for a shift in thinking.

One Summer, Two Global Turning Points!

We've all experienced turning points in our lives, although some are more memorable than others. In the summer of 1969,

I experienced two turning points that changed my life, and they both happened within less than a month of each other! I was on break from school that summer and working on a ranch in southern Missouri. The near-100°F temperature, combined with the near–100 percent humidity that's typical at that time of year in this region, pretty much assured that every outdoor activity would be a miserable experience. This was especially true for my main job of "bucking" wire-bound bales of hay onto the back of a slow-moving truck.

Walking alongside the vehicle, I was tasked with lifting each 60-pound bale from the ground and catapulting it into the truck to be stacked just as the truck arrived at the next bale, where my co-workers and I would repeat the sequence. This went on for hours at a time. I looked forward to dinner each evening not only to find relief from the dust, insects, humidity, and heat, but also because it was the only opportunity to watch the evening news and connect with the rest of the world.

Turning Point 1: To the Moon

There was a tiny black-and-white television in the dining room where everyone at the ranch would gather for meals. The TV was in one corner of the room, and the volume was usually turned so low that we could only guess what the people in the grainy images were saying. One night, however, that changed. As the drone of voices at the table fell silent for the dinner prayer, the words that were coming from the TV were unmistakable. "That's one small step for man, one giant leap for mankind," the voice said.[5]

I felt the wave of two very different realities pulse through my body as I listened—one from the world that separated us from one another before the announcement, and one from the world where that separation disappeared, if only briefly, afterward. The words were from Neil Armstrong, and his voice was traveling from the ladder of a fragile spacecraft on the surface of another world, across space, to the television networks around the earth, and to the little TV in front of me.

The first human had just set foot on the moon, and through the recording, I was reliving the moment it happened. This was the moment that humankind's collective view of itself from countless generations past suddenly gave way to a new and expanded vision of hope and possibility. It changed me forever. It changed the way I felt about the world. It changed the way I felt about the people in the world.

On that day, we were a global family beyond North and South Americans, Europeans, Asians, Australians, and Africans. In that moment, we were human beings, and we'd just accomplished something that until that day had been only the stuff of dreams. Suddenly it all became real. We were on the moon, and I felt it in my body. That moment was a turning point for me, and I remember it vividly to this day.

Turning Point 2: Three Days of Peace

Just when I thought that I couldn't possibly regain the awe that I'd just experienced, the unthinkable happened. The TV stations that had been showing the images of Neil Armstrong on the moon just a few weeks before were now carrying another story that the whole world was watching as well.

As I stepped over and turned up the volume on the TV set, it was clear that the story had the attention of the tired workers with me at the dinner table. In a twist of fate that couldn't have been choreographed any better in a utopian novel, the television was showing some 500,000 young people living together peacefully at the Woodstock Music Festival in New York. And it was happening during the same summer as the moon landing! *What are the chances?* I thought, reflecting on the irony.

The power and synchronicity of what I was seeing on the television was both surreal and deeply moving. The news reports were describing how the 50,000 or so people originally anticipated by the festival organizers had unexpectedly turned into a half million! The bottom line was that the facilities could no longer handle the sheer number of people safely. The organizers did the only thing they could do: they declared the festival a free event, and then did their very best to provide food, water, and medical and sanitation services to the rain-soaked audience that had turned the New York State Thruway into a virtual parking lot on their way to get there!

While it had long been known that both the landing on the moon and a gathering of so many people were possible, the unknown factor was how such events would turn out. The fact that Woodstock ended up being the largest and most peaceful gathering of its kind in modern history was a paradigm-altering moment in the minds of people throughout the world. With so many young people gathered in such a small area with so little supervision against the backdrop of heated emotions regarding the Vietnam War, the widespread belief had been that chaos would turn the event into a dangerous disaster. But what transpired that weekend showed mainstream Americans that their fears were unfounded. Throughout the three days (which turned into four days) of music, nudity, sex, drugs, rain, and mud, the reality of the festival became the theme for a generation: peace and love.

The fact that humans went to the moon, walked on the surface, and returned safely altered the paradigm that had held the vision of people bound to this world only. That this event happened during the same summer as Woodstock is a striking fact that future generations will study and marvel at. In the span of just a few weeks, we showed ourselves that we have the technology to visit other worlds and the wisdom to live peacefully on this one without the need for law enforcement or a higher authority forcing us to do so.

As different as the events were from one another, both Woodstock and the moon landing proved to be powerful turning points in my life, as well as in the lives of countless other people. And while we know that millions watched both events unfold on TV, I can only describe the reason why they were so life-changing for me. Both scenarios challenged the world's thinking, ideas, and beliefs that had been in place before they occurred. And both scenarios showed me what was possible.

While the preceding examples illustrate the way turning points can show up in our lives—either intentionally or spontaneously—by identifying additional examples that are familiar to us all, perhaps we can get a sense of when they've occurred in the past and just how powerful they can be. In Figure 3.3, I've identified some key turning points that come to mind as such examples.

Two Kinds of Turning Point

Category	Familiar Example
• A Paradigm-Altering Event	• The election of Barack Obama as the first black president of the United States • The terrorist attacks of December 7, 1941, and those 60 years later on September 11, 2001 • The first successful landing of a human on the moon and his safe return • The fact that climate change is altering the way we can live on Earth
• A Discovery OR Revelation	• The discovery that DNA carries the instruction codes for life • The discovery of a way to generate electricity and bring it into our homes, schools, and workplaces • The discovery of vaccines that have nearly eradicated life-threatening conditions like polio and tuberculosis • The discovery that nature is based upon a model of cooperation and mutual aid rather than competition, as Darwin hypothesized

Figure 3.3. Examples of two kinds of turning point. In both examples—as an event that changes our lives or as a discovery that changes the way we think and act—we find ourselves faced with facts that we must either discount or embrace. Once we know that the facts exist, it's our choice that determines where our turning point leads.

Whether a turning point is spontaneous or intentional, the key to taking advantage of it is to understand that once one occurs, it opens the door to entirely new possibilities and outcomes. In light of the kind and number of crises that we face in our lives today, it may be that our ability to recognize critical turning points, or to create them when needed, will become the key to transforming our lives.

What Happens After the Turning Point?

The key to unleashing the power of a turning point is to embrace the possibilities that it brings after we recognize it exists. Figure 3.4 gives us a picture of what I mean. It's divided into two regions labeled the "Old Paradigm" and the "New Paradigm." The place where one ends and another begins, the turning point, is shown with an arrow. Because this turning point represents a break in an existing flow of events, it's what happens *after* the break that paves the way to a new outcome.

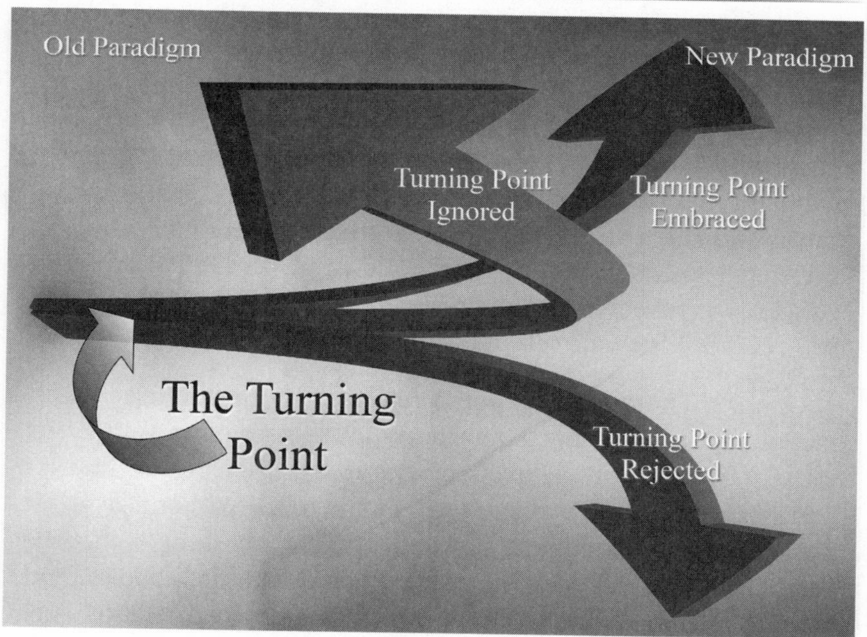

Figure 3.4. It's what happens *after* a turning point that tells the story. In this illustration, the turning point, noted by the light-colored arrow to the left, becomes the source of three very different possibilities: it may be *embraced, rejected,* or *ignored.* The possibility noted at the upper right is the acceptance and embracing of the turning point and what it has revealed. The possibility at the lower right is the rejection of the turning point and the attempt to cling to the idea of a reality that no longer exists. The third possibility is to ignore the turning point. This is represented by the arrow in the center that points to the past. Source: Dreamstime: © MIK3812345.

At a turning point, three choices, each leading to one of three paths, become available. Each path creates a different scenario that leads to a very different outcome. These scenarios can be summarized as follows:

PATH 1: **We recognize the turning point and embrace it.** In this scenario, the new information becomes the reason to think and act differently. It gives our minds the facts that we sometimes need to justify making a big change in our lives. It's our willingness to embrace what the facts show us that can trigger a new way of thinking. In the previous example of Bill and his choice to create health in his life, it was an emotional crisis that led to his turning point. He felt hopeless, lost, and depressed. "I began to hate myself," he said. In the depths of the crisis, the turning point appeared.

He described his signal of hope as the realization of another possibility. Once again in his own words, he explained, "I started realizing that I had a lot more I could look forward to."[6] His realization was the turning point. Rather than denying his feelings of hopelessness or surrendering and following them to a destructive conclusion, he embraced his realization that more was possible. Bill's choice is how he selected Path 1 at his turning point.

PATH 2: **The turning point is rejected.** Those who reject information revealed by new discoveries find themselves on Path 2. Because they reject what the discoveries reveal, they believe that it's possible to think and live the way they did in the past and go about their business as usual. The problem with this thinking is that the conditions have changed, either in the world or in their bodies. And because of the change, it's impossible to maintain the status quo. Their choice places them at odds with the reality of the world. In Bill's case, for example, the failure to lose weight would have led to additional health issues and, ultimately, could have cost him his life.

PATH 3: **The power of the turning point is ignored.** This path is perhaps the most difficult to witness, especially in the lives of our family members and loved ones. The reason is because those who choose this path often do so believing they're doing the best thing for themselves, even when new information tells them their belief is not supported. A perfect example of this scenario is illustrated in the conflicting information regarding the role of fats in our diet—a view that is now reversed 180 degrees from the views of the past.

There was a time not so long ago when all dietary fat was demonized as being the cause of a host of health problems, including obesity and diabetes. In this extreme thinking, some people eliminated every fat you can imagine from their diets, including coconut, avocado, butter, and even extra-virgin olive oil. In their firm belief that their choice would lead to better health and greater longevity, they followed their new dietary regimen with a rigidity that would rival that of a military boot camp. I know, because I was close to people in my family and workplace who followed such a diet and did their best to convince everyone else to do the same as well!

Problems appeared when follow-up studies showed that the absence of fat in the diet actually contributes to health problems such as cancer, depression, and a weakened immune system. Better methods of testing proved that recommendations of the past actually denied the body the essential nutrients that are now called *good fats*. Examples of such good fats are the omega-3 fatty acids that have been linked to reducing inflammation and lowering the risk of other conditions like heart disease and cancer.[7]

For people experiencing this path, it's fair to say that there's a conflict between what they've believed to be true in the past and what the new information now tells them. Sometimes the "disconnect" between reality and belief is so great that people simply can't find a way to incorporate discoveries into their existing way of thinking. My experience of people dealing with such a conflict is that it's not so much that they reject the new information as it is that they simply ignore it. In their family customs, or the beliefs embraced by their spiritual or religious community, there is simply no room for what the discoveries reveal.

This place between the acceptance of the new discoveries and the outright rejection of them even in the face of new facts is sometimes called the *zone of dissonance*. The term *cognitive dissonance,* coined in 1956 by psychologist Leon Festinger, Ph.D., is defined as the "discomfort experienced when simultaneously holding two or more conflicting ideas, beliefs, values or emotional reactions."[8]

In Figure 3.4, we saw this zone of dissonance as the place between the embracing and the rejection of the turning point. Once people find themselves in the dissonance zone, they are held only by the power of their beliefs. There is nothing that stops them from moving into either of the polarities of acceptance or rejection at any time.

The choice we make at the turning point determines what it means in our lives.

While creating a turning point may make sense when we see it depicted as a graph, the question is: *How do we make one occur in the real world?* Once again, an example is probably the best way to answer this question. So let's begin with the story of a man who created a turning point by first discovering what was most important to him in his life. In doing so, he discovered a personal turning point and the new life that was waiting for him beyond it.

A Real-World Turning Point

Ken Kuhne knew he was a successful man. He had proved it through his life, his family, and his business. As the owner and operator of Biomes Construction, a company dedicated to building nontoxic and environmentally friendly homes, he believed his business was a perfect fit for the ecologically minded communities of northern New Mexico's high desert.

In spring 2008, however, things changed. It was obvious to Ken that the world was shifting in big ways and that the shifts meant big changes for the housing industry and his business. Even before the devastating crash in the economy during October of that year, he was wondering how he could respond in a positive way to the crisis that was already causing the world's fragile financial markets to buckle. In Ken's own words, he woke up one night thinking "about what the most important things were, and that's basically feeding and watering yourself. I need to help people grow their own food supply."[9]

Ken's vision was clear. The question was, how would he go about fulfilling it? His answer was intuitive and simple. It was then that Ken made the choice to honor what he knew best as a builder, while combining his skills with the needs emerging in today's world. In the past, Ken had constructed homes for people. But that was not what the world needed now. So he began to build a different kind of home. Rather than building a place for people to live, he began building homes for *plants* to live in.

Ken designed and built modular raised-bed gardens to provide a unique, sustainable, and affordable way for people to grow their own food. His raised-bed, self-watering, and weatherproof gardens are part of a success story that continues to this day. Aptly named Grow Y'Own, Ken's gardens have become so popular throughout northern New Mexico and beyond that I would be surprised if Ken ever goes back to building homes for people again.

I can share Ken's story firsthand because he's my neighbor. I've known of his work for years, and my wife and I are proud owners of two of his raised-bed systems. Both Ken and I have seen our community go through hard times in the past for varying reasons. The drought in the early 1990s, for example, was the worst seen until the present day. Now it's the influence of climate change, coupled with the economy of the world, that's having a similar effect.

Ken's story is an example of a personal turning point, and one he created intentionally. It was Ken's willingness to contribute to what his friends, family, and neighbors need today, rather than trying to find a place where his skills have traditionally fit in the past, that made his turning point a success. It's from stories like Ken's that we can learn to take these ideas from the realm of theory directly into our lives life today.

Changing the Question

In Chapter 2, we explored the pyramid of thinking that determines how we view ourselves in our lives and in the world. We also identified the new discoveries that show where the thinking of the past is now known to be incomplete, and in some cases, wrong. While all of the discoveries indicated in Chapter 2 (see Figure 2.1) helped revolutionize the way we answer the question *Who am I?* two of them contribute directly to our shift in thinking and the way we can create our own turning points.

- The universe, our world, and our bodies are made of a shared field of energy that makes the unity known as entanglement possible.
- Nature relies upon cooperation and mutual aid for survival, not what Darwin called "survival of the strongest."

These scientific discoveries, and others, give us the reasons to shift the way we think of ourselves. In the old way of thinking, the question upon which we based our choices and problem-solving was:

What can I get from the world that exists?

Today, within the context of the new discoveries and our time of extremes, it makes sense to change the question. Our new question is:

What can I give to/share with/contribute to the world that's emerging?

As Ken's example illustrates so beautifully, it's our answer to this question that changes everything. The way we answer *What can I give to the world that's emerging?* is the key to developing new jobs/careers, new relationships with other people, and perhaps most important, new relationships with ourselves. Our answer changes the very reasons we approach life in the way that we do. It changes the way we think of ourselves in the world—and the way we think of our own worth in the world.

Just to be clear, this powerful question is not based upon our worldly qualifications. It doesn't ask us what we *think* we're capable of doing or what it is that we're licensed or certified to do. It's not asking us what field our degree is in or how much money we need.

Rather, it's asking us to do a self-assessment. And in our time of extremes, it makes perfect sense to do so.

Knowing that the world is changing in big ways, we can recognize that our role in the world is changing as well. *What can I give to the world that's emerging?* is an honest question to ask ourselves, as it invites us to acknowledge the realities of our shifting world.

If you haven't already done so, this is an opportunity for you to experience in your own life what Ken did in his. While there are many variations with respect to how we may make such an assessment in our lives, the following guidelines offer a simple template that's a place to begin.

1. **Ask yourself how your world has changed.**

- Identify the familiar routines of the past that no longer exist today.
- Identify new routines that have replaced those no longer used.
- Identify responsibilities that are new in your life.
- Identify the relationships that no longer seem to "fit" in your life.

2. **Ask yourself what's important to you in this moment.**

- What's missing in your life?
- What's missing in the lives of your friends, family members, and co-workers?
- What needs now exist for you and your world that did not exist ten years ago?

3. **Ask yourself what you can offer.**

- How can your knowledge, skills, and passions be used to fill the needs of today?

I invite you to give each of these questions the time and attention it deserves. Write your answers on a piece of paper and store them in a place where they're safe and out of the way. Come back to them in a couple of days, look them over, and update your responses. It's not unusual to discover that entirely new answers seem to come from nowhere after you stop thinking about the questions for a while.

There are no right or wrong answers to these three questions. The way they're answered is not part of a test or hidden agenda. They are honest and direct, and hold the key to putting big energy into equally big changes in your life, just the way Ken Kuhne did in his.

New discoveries give us the reason to change the compass of our lives from *What can I get from the world that exists?* to *What can I give to the world that's emerging?*

How Do We Know When It's Time for Change?

Once we know how easy it is to create and embrace turning points, the question becomes: *How do we know when it's time for one?* I'm asked this question often. In addition to the many times I've answered it in various ways for other people, I've also had to answer it for myself. And while it's a good question to ask, it's one that's not always easy to answer. The reason is because it's usually about relationships. Whether we're assessing our job, our family, our romantic partner in life, or a belief system that we've held dear, the need for a change is almost always tied to the most intimate relationships in our lives.

In the following story, while the name of my friend has been changed to honor his privacy, the details can help us all understand the key to making big choices in our lives and knowing when it's necessary or advantageous to create a turning point.

Working as an engineer in the aerospace industry during the Cold War years of the 1980s, I had the opportunity to see firsthand the effects of job stress on my co-workers, their families, and their relationships. The long hours in the office, followed by days, and sometimes weeks, of travel to install software on Air Force computers around the country, definitely did not add up to a regular nine-to-five kind of job. It was commonplace for the team of men and women I worked with to arrive at a computer facility and find that sleeping cots, blankets, and endless amounts of coffee and the menus for order-in meals were already waiting for us. It took only one such installation for me to discover why: Once our credentials were cleared and we were locked into the security of a computer vault, no one could leave until the new software was installed, debugged, and up and running. Sometimes the job was complete in a matter of hours. At other times, the job took weeks. Under such conditions it doesn't take much effort to imagine the stress that these work environments created for individuals, marriages, and families.

It was during one of these on-site installations that a co-worker discovered his wife could no longer deal with his long hours away from home and days with no communication. During a dinner break that we took together one evening, Gary confided to me that the most important relationship in his life, his marriage, was in trouble. Quickly the conversation revealed that the problems he and his wife were having were not *just* because of the long hours. Rather, the long hours were a catalyst that brought up the deeper issues that pushed an already-strained marriage to the brink of collapse.

Looking at me from across the table piled high with carryout boxes and fortune-cookie wrappers from days of Chinese food meals, Gary asked the one question I'd hoped he wouldn't, because I knew I couldn't answer it.

"What should I do?" he said.

It was a tough question for me because I knew both him and his wife as friends. I also knew that regardless of what I heard from him in the course of our conversation, there was a single truth that I could be certain of: Only Gary and his wife could know everything needed to answer his question. Only they knew what had happened between them. Only they knew the nuances of the conversations, the promises and trusts that had been forged and then broken, leading up to our conversation. I shared my insight, thinking that doing so would end the conversation. But it didn't.

Chuckling at a fortune-cookie message that he refused to let me see, Gary looked up and asked another question that I was much more comfortable with: "What would you do if you were me? Would you try to work things out, or would you leave the marriage?"

"Wow!" I said. "That's not an easy question! I can't possibly tell you what I'd do. I couldn't know until I was in the moment of the decision. But what I *can* tell you is how I'd make my decision. I *can* share the questions I'd ask to get clear and find out what's true for me."

I knew that my answer wasn't what Gary was hoping for. But I also knew he was curious. After all, he was an engineer. His job was to discover what it takes to make things work. I assumed that his curiosity applied to his marriage as well.

"Well, I guess I'll have to settle for that," he said, sitting up in his chair. "So what is it? How would you make your decision?"

What came next was information I felt very comfortable offering. The reason is because I was sharing with my friend the same questions, the same criteria for decision making, that I'd already posed to myself countless times in my life. Three questions always help me to get clear on what I'm experiencing, to know what possibilities exist, and to recognize what my options are in any situation. From romance and marriage, to jobs and family, these three questions have never failed me.

I'm describing them here because I believe they may help you as well with the big decisions you make in your life, especially knowing when it's time for a change. It's common for the outcome of these questions to become a turning point themselves.

In true engineer form, I reached for a pen from my jacket pocket and a scrap of paper. I scribbled the questions and reached across the table to hand them to Gary. My only instructions were to answer each question honestly.

Knowing When It's Time for a Change

1. **Am I happy in this relationship?**

- While there are always exceptions, most of our choices are about a relationship. Our relationship doesn't have to be with another person, however. It can be with ourselves and linked to a job, a way of life, a diet, or even a habit.
- Once this question is clearly stated, the answer generally "pops" into our heads quickly. Our job is to honor ourselves by truthfully acknowledging the reality of what has been revealed.

2. **Is this a healthy relationship?**

- This question may be the simplest, because you already know the answer. For example, do you medicate symptoms, such as high blood pressure, high cholesterol, chronic rashes, and a weakened immune system, each of which has been linked to the unresolved emotions of frustration, anger, resentment, and hurt?[10]
- Do you find yourself searching for diversions, such as excessive amounts of food, alcohol intoxication, or other relationships, to help you avoid the person or place with which you're not happy?

3. **Is it likely that things will improve?**

- This question is probably the most difficult of the three to answer. And you cannot know the answer if you have not already tried to make changes.
- Have you had an honest and direct sharing with your supervisor, co-worker, family member, intimate partner, or yourself about what's not working for you?
- Have you sought objective and professional insights from therapy, counseling, or coaching?

Once you have the answer to these three questions, the next step is where the real work begins. If you've answered two of the three questions with a no, then it tells you that it's probably time for a change in your life. While I'm not suggesting that you hinge the future of your marriage or the fate of the human species upon your answers, I *am* suggesting that they are invaluable tools to help you know how to make some of the biggest decisions you will ever make.

For example, I've lost track of how many times, in the face of a challenging situation, I've asked myself if I'm dealing with a temporary "speed bump" of difficulty on the road of life, or if the road I'm on (the situation, job, relationship, diet, or habit that's causing turmoil) has turned into a brand-new highway taking me somewhere I don't want to go. The three questions in the previous list, "Knowing When It's Time for a Change," have helped me know the answer. And it's these questions that helped Gary make his choice as well.

In Gary's case, although *he* chose to work things out with his wife, while we were away installing software his wife made a different choice. When Gary returned to his home, his wife was gone. His children were gone. His furniture was gone. His dogs were gone. Gary was left to deal with a very different world from the one he had known only a week earlier.

When we're moved to examine our relationships, it's often because we intuitively know the answer to our questions already. The longer we delay in making choices for ourselves, the fewer options we have as the range of possibilities is narrowed by the choices that other people make.

CHAPTER FOUR

GETTING THERE:

Turning Points of Personal Resilience

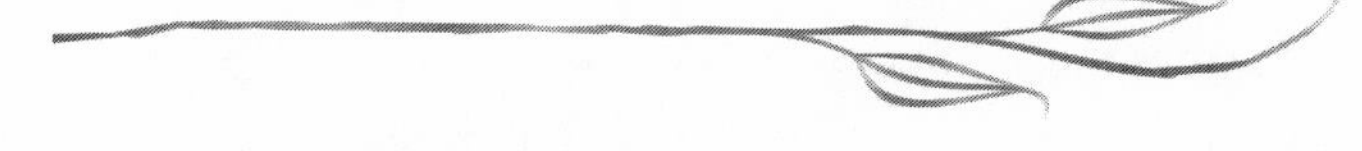

"Personal transformation can and does have global effects. . . . The revolution that will save the world is ultimately a personal one."

— MARIANNE WILLIAMSON (1952–),
SPIRITUAL TEACHER, AUTHOR, AND LECTURER

On September 11, 2011, the tenth anniversary of the 9/11 attacks on America, *Time* magazine created a special edition dedicated to honoring the way in which individuals, families, and the nation hard-hit by the tragedy have been able to carry on with life and living. Its title says it all: "Beyond 9/11: Portraits of Resilience." If there was ever a question as to the role that resilience has played in America's recovery, the first sentence of the special edition put it to rest, calling resilience the theme of the nation in the 21st century.[1] Through intimate stories shared by citizens and leaders alike, *Time* sought to "define what it means to meet adversity, and then overcome it."[2]

While we often hear about the resilience that allows us to move beyond the hardships of life, could there be more to the word than that? Is there a form of resilience that can be cultivated with a bigger picture in mind? Is it possible to *live each day in a resilient frame of mind* that softens the impact of dramatic change, rather than trying to *achieve* resilience after the fact? The answer to this question is a resounding *yes!* It's the reason why I've written this chapter.

Cultivating resilience is part of a trend that's gaining a foothold within communities throughout the world. In choosing the path of resilience within ourselves, our families, and our communities, we can create positive turning points in our time of extremes. In addition to minimizing the hardships that can come with unexpected change, many people have discovered that the building blocks of personal resilience are a great way to live as well, and one that makes sense in light of today's world.

It's possible for individuals, families, and communities to create turning points of resilience that minimize the impact of abrupt change and shorten the time it takes to recover when hardship does occur.

Resilience: What Does It Mean?

Resilience means different things to different people, varying by culture, by age-group, and even by the way the word is used. The requirements for resilience in the daily routines of a couple just starting their life together, for example, are very different than those for partners who have been married for 50 years. For teenagers in the Western world, who are dependent upon their parents for the basics of everyday life, resilience means something very different than it does in a tribal setting, where young people often form their own communities to care for themselves and others of a similar age. The principles that create resilience under battlefield conditions are tailored to a very different set of needs than those identified by organizations like the Post Carbon Institute, which explore what it takes to live sustainably in the era after peak oil. Clearly, resilience is one of the qualities in life that we must adapt to our specific circumstances.

While much of the research on this topic is offered with respect to whole communities and society, the place where resilience begins is with us. At the very core, this conversation is all about people. Our world of extremes is inviting us as individuals and families to think and live differently to meet our needs—and in some cases, leaving us little choice other than to do so.

So let's begin at the beginning. What does it take to create, develop, and sustain a resilient lifestyle—to live in a resilient way?

In the modern world, resilience is often used to describe someone's ability to recover from something that has already happened, such as a devastating setback in life or a traumatic loss. "The couple has shown tremendous resilience in healing from the loss of their son in the war," for example, is a comment that, unfortunately, has become far too common. "The resilience that my friend has shown after his wife left the marriage is an inspiration for us all" illustrates another way we often hear the term used today. In recent years, it's become customary to hear "resilience" mentioned when describing the attitude and physical fortitude of entire communities, even nations, as they recover from the devastation of hurricanes, tornadoes, earthquakes, and terrorist attacks.

Resilience is not limited only to human experiences, however. It can be applied to any system, living or not, where dynamic change is involved. Over a period of millennia, the complex ecosystems of the Amazon rain forests, for example, developed *resilience* in adapting to dynamic shifts in Earth's climate. Today's sophisticated computer programs are *resilient:* they can detect and fix software glitches that keep them from doing what they were designed to do. From the immune system that keeps us healthy and the nervous system that keeps us safe, to the way we produce vital hormones and generate new blood cells that keep us alive, our bodies have multiple and interconnected systems that we depend upon, and each one has its own form of resilience.

While the American Psychological Association defines resilience as "the process of adapting well in the face of adversity" and "'bouncing back' from difficult experiences,"[3] the Stockholm Resilience Centre identifies resilience as the "capacity of a system to continually change and adapt yet remain within critical thresholds."[4] It's the theme reflected in this second definition that best illustrates our expanded view of resilience. We're talking about a way of living and being that gives us the flexibility to change and adapt to new conditions, which is the key to transformation in our time of extremes.

As universal as the phenomenon of resilience is, interestingly I've found that many cultures have no single word in their language that actually reflects what it means. The only way that someone speaking in one of these languages can share the idea of resilience is to string together a number of related words in their native tongue that will approximate what the single word means in English. During a book tour through central Europe, for example, I was describing the principles that would become the core of *The Turning Point* book when I discovered how such a disparity in words can play out in the real world.

During my onstage presentation, I was working with a translator using consecutive translation: meaning, I would speak, then he would translate, then I would speak, and so on (as compared to a simultaneous translator where the translator is in another part of the room speaking directly through the headsets of those in the audience listening). Suddenly, the entire presentation came to an abrupt halt when my translator found himself in a lively conversation not with me, but with members of the audience. Surprisingly, they were debating the way he had just translated the word *resilience.*

While I had assumed that there would be an equivalent word for my ideas in every language, it was then that I discovered this is not the case. Just the way English speakers have to put together the separate words *life* and *force* to approximate the Hindu word *prana,* there was no single word for *resilience* in the language my interpreter was using. I also learned that it's good to meet with the translators *before* presentations to iron out such potential wrinkles.

While the idea of resilience and what it means may vary for people of different age-groups and cultures, the way it shows up in life does not. We find the elements of resilience in two places:

- The way we think
- The way we live

Through one, or a combination, of these two expressions, some form of resilience is found in every facet of our experience. From our emotional ability to cope with the stress of big change, to the physical ability of our bodies to resist illness and disease, and the ability of our minds to resolve the psychological impacts of trauma and loss, many forms of resilience clearly exist. It's also clear that they play a big part in our lives each and every day. For the purposes of this book, I will address two general forms: the personal resilience that will be explored in this chapter, and the community resilience that will be covered in the next one.

Our ideas of resilience are reflected in the way we think and the way we live.

Personal Resilience

Even with decades of research and thousands of studies published in hundreds of professional journals, there's still no single theory of resilience. There are, however, facets of resilience that seem to fall into general categories that we can use as a springboard for our exploration. Professional organizations have taken the myriad studies of different kinds of resilience and adapted them to the specific needs of their communities. We can find specialists trained to help us with everything from physical resilience in endurance sports, for instance, to psychological resilience in business or emotional resilience in difficult relationships. The common denominator in all of these communities is *trauma,* and we don't have to look very far to find sources of this in our lives.

With cable television programs blaring 24/7 news cycles filled with gruesome details of war, warnings of threats to the security of our homes and schools, bloody incidents of neighborhood shootings, and an alarming increase in the number of teen suicides linked to ridicule and bullying perpetrated through social media, our society is routinely filled with trauma. Each traumatic incident creates the need to heal from the damage it leaves in our lives, families, and communities. Although our social traumas stem from different sources, the characteristics that help us first to cope with the experiences, and then to find the resilience needed to transform ourselves beyond the experiences, are remarkably similar.

There are a number of excellent resources available to guide us in this process. One that I've found to be especially useful in real-world situations is the National Victim Assistance Academy (NVAA). Under the auspices of the Office for Victims of Crime Training and Technical Assistance Center, this academy is a federal program designed to support professional service providers who assist people traumatized by crime. The training programs they've developed help victims transcend hurtful experiences through specific steps that create skills of resilience.[5]

One of the reasons I like the NVAA framework so much is that it addresses a broad landscape of physical, emotional, and spiritual needs, from the way we personally cope in stressful conditions to the way we deal with other people in times of stress. A representative summary of the key factors for resilience the NVAA has developed includes:

- Knowledge of ourselves
- A personal sense of hope
- The ability to cope in a healthy way
- Strong interpersonal relationships
- Finding a personal meaning in life

Let's explore each of these factors a little more deeply to get a better idea of why these five characteristics are so important and how they fit into our lives.

A framework for personal resilience includes qualities such as: self-knowledge, a sense of hope, healthy coping skills, strong relationships, and a sense of meaning in life.

Knowledge of Ourselves

Located within the innermost chamber of the ancient Luxor Temple in Egypt, a place called the Holy of Holies, there's an inscription that reminds those who pass through the doors of the secret hidden within their own existence. The phrase "Man, know thyself" is followed up with the benefit that comes from doing so. The full text reads: "Man, know thyself and thou shalt know the gods."

Those first three words, embedded within many of the ancient Egyptian texts, are the same ones found at the entrance to the Temple of Apollo at Delphi in Greece. In Delphi, however, the words are simplified to read: "Know thyself." From the wisdom traditions of ancient Egypt and Greece to the deepest mysteries of the world's most cherished spiritual practices, there is nearly universal agreement that our ability to meet life's challenges hinges upon how well we know ourselves. This is where identifying the false assumptions of the past (and the new discoveries that tell us they're false) becomes especially useful.

For nearly three centuries, the accepted science of our world has told us that we're separate from ourselves and one another, and that the law of the land is based upon competition and struggle. From the time we're young, many of us have heard these ideas boiled down to the simple admonition that we live in a dog-eat-dog world. This often-subconscious belief remains at the very core of our most difficult relationships, those in which we still believe we must struggle to be successful. This is where the new discoveries that help us answer the question *Who am I?* also give us the reasons to change our thinking and our beliefs.

From the discovery of quantum entanglement, which confirms just how deeply we're connected to one another and our world, to the fact that cooperation rather than competition is the fundamental rule of nature, the more we find out about ourselves, the better equipped we are to deal effectively with the changes in the world. When we replace the false assumptions of separation with the deepest truths of our connection and the role of cooperation in our lives, our self-knowledge gives us the reasons to think more holistically and to act with greater certainty when it comes to the choices we make in our lives.

A Personal Sense of Hope

When we hear heartfelt and inspiring stories of people who have survived seemingly un-survivable situations, two of the first questions usually being directed to them are, "How did you do it? What kept you from simply giving up?"

It's worth exploring the way these two questions are answered, because of the similarity of the emotional impact. As different as specific traumatic situations may appear from one another, whether stemming from crimes or natural disasters, almost universally those who survive and recover in a healthy way say that they were sustained by their sense of optimism and hope.

I remember seeing the television footage of the American hostages being taken from the U.S. Embassy in Iran in 1979, and the effect these images had on my co-workers and me. At the beginning, we had shared the sense, reflected by many people in the world, that the situation would be resolved quickly. As the days and weeks of their captivity dragged on, however, it became obvious that there would be no quick solution, or relief, for those being held prisoner.

Even then, however, I don't think anyone—myself, my co-workers, and my circle of friends or the leaders of the nations involved included—had any idea that the situation that would become known as the "Iran hostage crisis" would last as long as it did: a total of 444 days. During the interviews that followed the freeing of the captives, we began to gain insights into what sustained them for over a year after their ordeal began. A number of the former hostages cited their spirituality and love for their families, both of which gave them hope, as keys to their survival. In a 2012 interview, retired Air Force colonel Tom Schaefer, one of the 52 American hostages, commented, "My bottom line was that my faith in God and belief in the power of prayer got me through it all."[6]

On December 4, 1991, another hostage situation came to a close, as Terry Anderson was released from his captivity at the hands of Hezbollah, a political party in Lebanon, which had begun nearly seven years earlier. Anderson, who was the bureau chief for the Associated Press in Beirut at the time he was taken, presently has the dubious distinction of being the longest-held American political captive in the Middle East to date. His ordeal of solitude, fear, and resilience lasted for a total of 2,454 days—just under seven years! In an interview following his release, Anderson attributed his strength and good health to his optimism and a sense of hope. The optimism was that he always believed his captors would spare his life. The hope of the freedom that awaited him when his situation was resolved was the key, he said, to the discipline of taking his captivity hour by hour, an exercise that he called mentally "doing time."[7]

Hope is more than an unfounded belief or the powerless wish of a better time. Hope is essential for our well-being. In 1991, psychologist Charles R. Snyder, Ph.D., and his colleagues developed the scientific approach to studying the often-undervalued role of hope in our lives, known as *hope theory*.[8]

Clarifying the importance of our experiences of hope, cognitive psychologist Scott Barry Kaufman, Ph.D., says, "Having goals is not enough. . . . Hope allows people to approach problems with a mindset and strategy-set suitable to success, thereby increasing the chances they will actually accomplish their goals."[9] It's clear that science is catching up with what people in desperate situations have known intuitively for centuries: our sense of hope gives us the reason to expect a better tomorrow.

The Ability to Cope in a Healthy Way

From the late 1970s through the early '90s, I worked in a series of scientific and technical environments during three distinct periods of crisis: the energy crisis of the 1970s, the atomic-weapons crisis of the Cold War, and the data-compatibility crisis between computer platforms during the late 1980s and early '90s. It was during this part of my life that I had the opportunity to witness firsthand how individuals and groups respond to the stress created by the responsibility of their jobs. From the fuel systems for NASA's Space Shuttle Program to the ability of military medical teams in the field to communicate with floating hospital ships hundreds of miles away, in each situation I was involved with, people's lives depended upon the products and services that the companies I represented provided.

In each situation and each industry, time and again, I heard my fellow workers say that they had problems coping with the stress of the demands that were being placed upon them. Clearly, beyond the development of the services that we were contracted to deliver, stress was the greatest challenge that each of us faced every day of our careers. On the projects that I supervised, a big part of my responsibility was finding ways to keep my teams healthy and together long enough to complete our assignments.

The word that my teams used to describe their experience was *overwhelmed*. They felt *overwhelmed* by the magnitude of the project, *overwhelmed* by how much needed to be done, and *overwhelmed* by their own doubts regarding their abilities to deliver. We've all felt similarly overwhelmed at some point in our lives, and I don't want to create the impression that there's anything wrong with the feeling itself. If we can accept that our sense of being overwhelmed, by anything in life, is an *indicator* of something that needs our attention, the experience itself can be viewed as a positive one that leads to a healthy outcome.

Without such a perspective, however, the people on my teams were responding to their experience in ways that were not only *un*healthy, but their responses were actually preventing them from doing their jobs. I began to notice team members taking more sick days, feeling depressed during the time they were in the office, and developing habits of distraction, such as compulsive eating and the increased use of tobacco. Not surprisingly, these are among the indicators of unhealthy coping responses described by organizations such as the Mayo Clinic, the National Institutes of Health, and others in their research regarding stress management.

The following is a composite list of unhealthy coping skills adapted from a cross section of stress-response studies. The symptoms themselves are self-explanatory. And while it's likely that we've all experienced each of these symptoms occasionally in the past with no problem, it's when multiple symptoms become chronic that they're probably telling us our stress has become a concern.

A Partial List of Indicators of Unhealthy Coping Skills

- Problems getting to sleep, staying asleep, and sleeping at the right time of day or night
- Pain; headaches; and the unconscious clenching of fists, the biting of lips, or tightness in the neck and shoulders
- Turning to food when we're not hungry or eating beyond fullness when we are hungry
- Feeling depressed, lethargic, and emotionally numb
- Crying uncontrollably at unexpected times for no apparent reason
- Inordinate responses of anger and negativity
- Using alcohol, smoking, and substance abuse to calm down

One of the keys to the success of the team members I worked with was to shift their perspective regarding the project itself and their role in it. They found that by breaking the big picture of their responsibilities down into smaller and more manageable pieces, and by doing their homework and preparing everything that they needed in order to accomplish each of these pieces in advance, they could focus on each job that landed on their desk with much less stress.

Not surprisingly, the steps I'm describing are also among the healthy coping mechanisms identified by experts. The following is a representative list of healthy coping skills. Greater detail describing how to implement these skills into your life is available at the websites of groups such as the Mayo Clinic, National Institutes of Health, the Institute of HeartMath, and others (see the Resources section at the back of the book).

A Partial List of Healthy Coping Strategies

- **Make sure you're healthy.** Sometimes a problem in the body can show up during the vulnerability created by stressful conditions.
- **Scale back on your commitments.** Learn to say no to offers of more responsibility than you can reasonably handle. Learn to break large jobs into smaller tasks with clear milestones to accomplish. Delegate elements of your tasks in ways that are honoring and empowering to your co-workers, friends, or family members.
- **Exercise on a regular basis.** The definition of exercise is changing. Studies have shown that only 10–15 minutes a day of constant movement (flow yoga, resistance training, or swimming, for example) relieves the body of circulating stress hormones without kicking up more stress hormones and the type of fat-storing hormones triggered by longer endurance exercises that "trick" the body into thinking it's in a survival situation.
- **Do your homework and prepare.** When we're prepared for our day, we experience less stress over whatever it has in store for us. Avoid stressful situations by preparing for meetings and trips, scheduling your time better, and setting realistic goals.
- **Make sleep a priority in your life.** Your body will interpret a lack of sleep as a source of stress. As with any stressful situation, the effects of not getting

enough sleep can show up as anxiety reactions, a gain in weight, and periods of crying and anger at unexpected times.

- **Connect with other people.** Either professionally, casually, or in combination, social connections offer an outlet to share frustrations, a sounding board for insights and solutions, and the opportunity for other people to help you in ways that they enjoy and are good at.
- **Learn to relieve your stress.** There are probably as many ways to relieve stress as there are people who experience it. While yoga, meditation, and massage work for some, taking a walk in nature or having a creative outlet, such as drawing, painting, and making music, works better for others. The key here is to experiment, discover what works for you, and then make this practice a priority in your life.
- **Professional help.** Some people are good at finding solutions to stress on their own. Others are more comfortable delving into such intimate experiences with professional guidance. If this is your choice, I recommend an objective and qualified counselor, therapist, or life coach with training in anxiety and stress management.

Clearly, our ability to meet the stress of life's challenges by doing things that bring us a sense of well-being is the key to our health and happiness. While our challenges may stem from different sources, the preceding skills apply to any life stressors, because they all depend upon our ability to cope.

Strong Interpersonal Relationships

It's been said that everyone needs a friend. Whether or not we call it friendship, science shows us beyond a doubt that: (1) we need human connections in our lives, and (2) having them is really good for us. As creative beings, we all find ways to have our needs met in one way or another. When it comes to interpersonal relationships, some people are more comfortable interacting in large communities, clubs, and organizations, while others are fulfilled by maintaining a relatively small, intimate group of personal friends. Some people have found that it works to have both. In whatever way we connect and relate, it's a good thing that we do. It's good for our health, as well as for our ability to cope with stressful situations.

In the previous example of my co-workers under stress, for example, it was the camaraderie they experienced through their interpersonal relationships on the job (which sometimes deepened into friendships) that provided them the emotional support for coping with the stress of doing the projects. Sometimes just being able to walk over to the desk of a co-worker to ask for a fresh set of eyes on a problem is all that it takes to relieve the stress of working with an issue that seems unsolvable.

In addition to the benefits of having strong personal relationships in the workplace, studies have shown that they're good for us in *life*. They're good for our immune systems, for our communication skills, for our self-esteem, and even for our life expectancy. While such benefits make sense intuitively, scientific studies are now confirming factually what we've always sensed about friendship, love, and well-being.

In a 2011 report published by the BC (British Columbia) Council for Families, entitled "Healthy Relationships: Their Influence on Physical Health," results from a number of studies from a number of disciplines were pulled together to illustrate the impact of the relationships in our lives.[10] In summary:

- People in relationships provide information, advice, services, and new social contacts to one another, enabling them to discover local and social services and know how to use them more effectively.
- Relationships provide people with a caring environment.
- Relationships provide a group identity.

- Relationships provide a buffer to stress.
- Relationships provide a purpose for living a healthy lifestyle.

Professional studies, such as the ones cited by this report, and the direct sharing from trauma survivors both show that stable and well-functioning relationships help us develop a larger meaning and purpose in our lives. When we have this sense of purpose, we seem to be more motivated to protect ourselves against disease, illness, or injury.

Finding a Personal Meaning in Everyday Life

One of the greatest factors contributing to resilience in life, yet possibly the least talked about, is the personal meaning that we give to our own existence. This is one of those places where the lines drawn between science, spirituality, religion, and the real world can become a bit fuzzy. Knowing that there can be no definitive answer to "What is the meaning of life?" each of us is left to develop our own sense of what the world is all about and how we fit into it and where we belong.

There are some people who believe we must know the technical stuff, including how life began, to find meaning in each day. The problem in this thinking arises with the sources of the knowledge themselves: science, religion, and direct experience. In the modern world, many people believe these are mutually exclusive ways of knowing. In other words, they feel we must choose only one way, such as science or religion. Although it's not such a popular notion, in reality all three ways of knowing can contribute powerfully to helping us find personal meaning in the bigger picture of life. Science, for example, can objectively confirm the facts that our spiritual teachings and direct experiences are leading us to believe are true.

In whatever way we find our answers, it's the significance we find in each moment of each day of our lives that gives meaning to everything else. It's only when we feel that we're part of something bigger than ourselves, and can identify where we fit and how we contribute to this "bigger something," that our existence in the world and life make sense. In the absence of such meaning, the events of life, including our family relationships, our loves, our jobs, careers, joys, disappointments, failures, and successes, all appear random and disconnected from one another and from us. As a friend of mine stated so clearly to me during a conversation about this very topic, "In a life without meaning, what would be the point?"

Whatever we believe is the meaning of our existence, Eleanor Roosevelt may have best summed up the healthy way to think about such things on a daily basis: ". . . the purpose of life, after all, is to live it, to taste experience to the utmost, to reach out eagerly and without fear for newer and richer experience."[11]

The Sixth Element of Resilience

In addition to the five characteristics of personal resilience previously identified in this chapter—self-knowledge, a sense of hope, healthy coping skills, strong interpersonal relationships, and the personal meaning that we find in life—there's a sixth element to creating resilience that's typically not included in the formal studies. Interestingly, however, it's this single element that we find at the core of the most respected and ancient wisdom traditions. It's also the window to the inner realm of our experience that leading-edge scientists now regard as the next great frontier in self-care. The sixth factor of personal resilience is the shift that we can create in our emotions to prepare our bodies for life's extremes in a healthy way. This avenue of resilience lives in the *heart.*

I remember clearly the central teaching regarding the biology of the body from my high school science classes. When I was in school during the 1960s and '70s, the brain was considered the master organ of the body. Unless you've had the opportunity to attend a school with a very progressive science program, there's a good chance that you learned from the same textbooks I did and were taught the same principles. Unless your children are fortunate enough to learn from leading-edge science programs and updated textbooks today, they're probably still being taught the same thing as well. The problem is that new discoveries tell us this old way of thinking is incomplete.

In the days when we didn't know what the new discoveries of the heart would reveal, it actually made sense to think of the brain as a master organ. After all, it *appears* to control everything. The brain is the command center for when and how 1,300-plus biochemical reactions occur and chemicals are released into our bodies. The brain regulates everything from when we wake up and go to sleep, to how much and how fast we grow, the strength of our immune system, and the functioning of the five senses that connect us with the world.

Yet while the brain is certainly a big factor in the way we function—and we couldn't do without it—we also know that the brain doesn't act alone. It receives the instructions from another organ in the body, the very organ that our ancient and indigenous ancestors always told us was the key to life. *The master organ of the body is the heart.*

The Language of the Heart

In each moment of every day, a conversation is taking place inside us that's one of the most vital we will ever find ourselves engaged in. It's the silent, often subconscious, and never-ending conversation of emotion-based signals between the heart and the brain. The reason this conversation is so important is that the quality of the emotional signal the heart sends to the brain determines what kind of chemicals are released into our bodies. When we feel what we would typically call *negative* emotions (for instance, anger, hate, jealousy, and rage), the heart sends a signal to the brain that mirrors our feelings. Such emotions are irregular and chaotic, and this is precisely what the signals they send to the brain look like.

If you can envision a chart of the ups and downs for the stock market on a wild and volatile day, you'll have an idea of the kind of signals we create in our hearts in times of such emotions. The human body interprets this kind of signal as stress, and sets into motion mechanisms to help us respond appropriately.

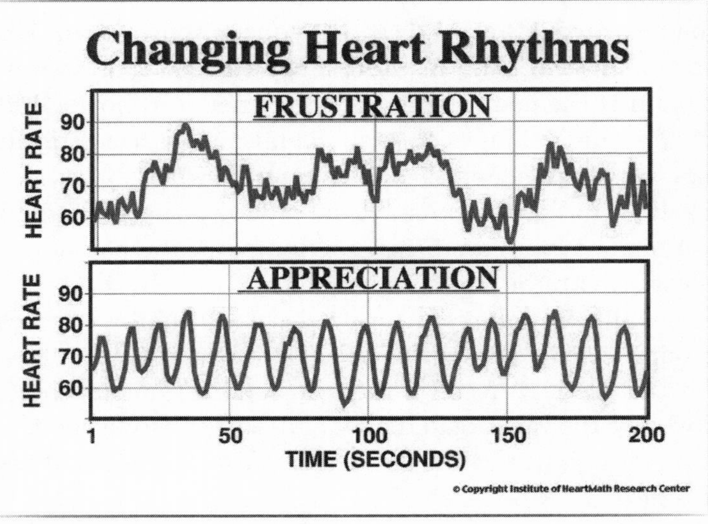

Figure 4.1. A comparison of the signals between the heart and the brain in two extremes of emotion: the "negative" emotion of frustration and the "positive" emotion of appreciation. Source: The Institute of HeartMath.

The stress from negative emotions increases the levels of cortisol and adrenaline in our bloodstreams, hormones that are often called *stress hormones,* which prepare us for a quick and powerful reaction to whatever is causing us stress. That reaction includes redirecting the blood supply from the organs deep within our bodies to the places where it's most needed in such times: the muscles, limbs, and extremities that we use to either confront the source of our stress or run as fast as we can to get away from it—our instinctive fight-or-flight response.

For our distant ancestors, this response would save them from an angry bear that had camped out in their cave, for example. When they felt that the threat was gone, their emotions shifted and the elevated levels of the stress hormones returned to the normal levels of everyday life. The key here is that the stress response is designed to be temporary and brief. When it kicks in, we infuse our bodies with the chemistry needed to respond quickly and powerfully to the threat. It's all about survival.

The good news is that when such high levels of stress chemicals are present, we can become superhumans. We've all heard stories of a 98-pound woman successfully tilting a full-size automobile off the ground long enough to save her child pinned beneath—and doing so without first considering if such a feat was even possible. In such cases, the fight-or-flight response is activated on behalf of the child, who would have died without intervention. In these instances, the extra-human strength of the mother is attributed to the surge of stress hormones pouring into the body from her feelings of *do or die*—feelings that originate in the heart.

The flip side of the good news is that while the benefits can be helpful during a short period of time, the stress that triggers the surge effectively shuts down the release of other chemicals that support important functions in our bodies. The release of vital chemicals that support functions of growth, immunity, and antiaging is dramatically reduced during times of fight or flight. In other words, the body can be in only one mode or the other: *fight/flight mode* or *healing/growth mode.*[12] Clearly, we were never meant to live day in and day out with constant stress as a way of life. Yet this is precisely the situation that many of us find ourselves experiencing today.

In our modern world of information overload, speed dating, multiple consecutive double cappuccinos, and the often-heard sense that life is "speeding up," it's inevitable that our bodies can feel that we're in a constant state of never-ending stress. People who cannot find a release from this kind of stress find themselves in sustained fight-or-flight mode, with all of the consequences that come with the territory. A quick look around an office or a classroom, or even a glance at our family members over Sunday dinner, confirms what the data suggests. It's not surprising to find that people with the greatest levels of sustained stress are also in the poorest health.

The rise in U.S. statistics for stress-related conditions, including heart disease and stroke, eating disorders, immune deficiencies, and some cancers, is less of a surprise when we take into account the relentless stress that many people experience in their daily lives.

The good news is that the same mechanism that creates and sustains our stress responses, often on a subconscious level, can also be regulated to help us relieve the stress in a healthy way—even when the world is in chaos. And we can do so quickly and intentionally.

Just the way our hearts send our brains the signals of chaos when we feel negative emotions, positive emotions send another kind of signal to our brains that is more regular, more rhythmic, and orderly. In the presence of positive emotions, such as appreciation, gratitude, compassion, and caring, the brain releases a very different kind of chemistry into the body. When we feel a sense of well-being, the level of stress hormones in our bodies *decreases,* while the life-affirming chemistry of a powerful immune system with antiaging properties *increases.* The shift between the stress response and a feeling of well-being can happen quickly.

Studies documented by the Institute of HeartMath (IHM), a pioneering research organization based in Boulder Creek, California, have shown that cortisol levels can decrease as much as 23 percent, and levels of DHEA, a life-affirming precursor to other vital hormones in the body, can increase 100 percent if we spend as little as three minutes using focused techniques designed to produce such responses.[13] The reason why I'm describing these phenomena in this part of the book is because the techniques that are found to have such benefits upon our health are the same ones that create the resilience in our hearts. This is the key to personal resilience in life.

The quality of our emotions determines the instructions our hearts send to our brains.

A Deeper Resilience from Within

The human nervous system is an awe-inspiring and intricate network of over 45 miles of living "wires" (nerves) that carry the effects of our heart/brain conversation to every other part of the body. While scientists have known for quite some time *how* the messages from the brain travel throughout the body, it was only in the last years of the 20th century that new discoveries revealed precisely *where* the signals originate. Not surprisingly, the role of the heart is central.

Now that we understand what the conversation between our hearts and our brains can accomplish, let's look at the mechanisms that make this conversation possible and how to change the "dialogue" in healthy ways. It all begins with the resilience that we create within the heart itself. One of the ways of determining our level of resilience is to measure the peaks and valleys of our heart rhythms.

While we're generally familiar with the moving graph of our heart rhythms that a doctor scrutinizes, we may not be fully aware of everything that the graph is showing. In addition to telling us information about the overall condition of the heart, the rhythms can also tell us about the health of our nervous system and even conditions that may lead to problems at a later time. The graph the doctor is looking at is probably an electrocardiogram (ECG), which is sometimes known as an EKG. The ECG device measures the electrical output of the heart and is completely passive. In other words, it's not sending any electrical information into the body. Rather, it's measuring the electrical impulses that the heart creates and sends throughout the body.

While the interpretation of heart rhythms could fill an entire book and represents a lifetime of study, I'm describing this here for a specific reason. There's an aspect of the heart that's the key to creating resilience. When looking at the sample ECG in Figure 4.2, even to the untrained eye it's clear that there are repeating patterns of large spikes created by each heartbeat. What's important to our discussion is that the distance from the top of one large spike (called an *R wave*) to the next is not always the same; it varies from beat to beat. While it may look like the space from one peak to the next is identical, when we measure the intervals we find that the distances between them change. And it's a good thing they do, because this is where our resilience in life begins.

The more the time changes between beats, the greater the resilience we have to life and to changes in our world. Because we're measuring the variable distances between heartbeats, the measurement is called just what we'd expect: *heart-rate variability* (HRV). HRV is measured in very small units of time called *milliseconds,* and the difference between one heartbeat and the next may be a matter of only a fraction of a second. In Figure 4.2, for example, the difference in time between R wave 2 and R wave 3, compared to the time between R wave 3 and R wave 4, is only 67 milliseconds. While this is a small amount, what's important is that there *is* a difference.

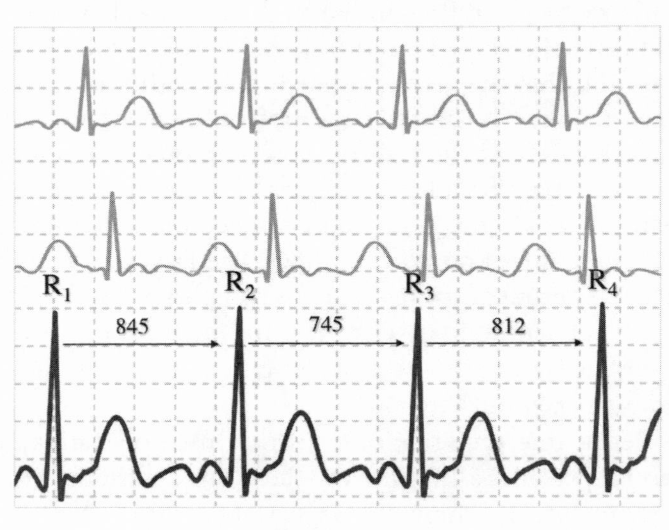

Figure 4.2. A portion of a typical ECG showing the cyclic peaks and dips of a typical heartbeat. The large peaks indicated by the arrows are the R waves of a single heartbeat. The distance from the peak of one R wave to the next changes from beat to beat. It's this difference that gives us our heart-rate variability. Source: Dreamstime: © Z_i_b_i.

Early in life, we have a high level of HRV. Now that we understand the purpose of HRV, it makes perfect sense that we would. When we are young children, discovering and adapting to the environment, our bodies need a way to adjust to what we find—and quickly. The first time our fingers discover what hot water from the kitchen faucet is all about, for example, or when we find out that not all dogs are as friendly as the one that lives in our house, we need to respond quickly. The heart's capacity to alter its rhythms—our HRV—and send blood to where it's most needed is necessary for our survival.

The signal that the heart sends to the brain creates a state known as *psycho-physiological coherence,* or more commonly, *coherence.* The beauty of knowing about coherence is that we don't have to guess when it happens. Easy-to-use sensors and software can tell us precisely what level of coherence we're in, as well as help us build the skills for even more coherence.[14]

Just to be clear, the heart and brain are always in some state of coherence. In the chaos of daily life and the presence of negative emotions, our coherence levels may be low. Through simple exercises, such as the one at the end of this chapter, we can shift key parameters in our bodies to create higher levels of coherence. There's a direct connection between the HRV in our bodies, our level of coherence, and the resilience we have when facing the extreme changes in our world. *The greater our level of coherence, the greater our HRV and our resilience will be.*

With this in mind, the previous discussion of positive and negative emotions and the role they play in our heart function takes on even greater significance. When we find the emotions that create greater coherence, we create greater resilience as well.

More coherence leads to greater resilience.

Three Steps to Personal Resilience: Attitude Breathing®

Many of the recent discoveries regarding heart coherence, heart intelligence, and how to use both in our lives have been made by the scientists at the Institute of HeartMath. Following the developmental work that evolved into the techniques used by IHM today, the founding of the organization began in the early 1990s. IHM is dedicated to exploring the power of the heart in unconventional ways.

While we know that the heart pumps blood to our bodies, for example, studies conducted by IHM suggest that our hearts are involved in much more than simply moving blood through our arteries, veins, and capillaries. From the emotions that create coherence between our hearts and our brains, and the link between coherence and HRV, to the quality of the pressure wave in our blood from each heartbeat, it's clear that we're only beginning to understand the full spectrum of the heart's functions.

I've had the honor of working with the founders, staff, and researchers at IHM for nearly two decades. In doing so, I've also had the opportunity to share the experiences of life, travel, and the demands of presenting our work together to diverse audiences throughout the world. It's through these experiences that I can now say that the years-long professional relationships have developed into deep and lasting friendships. During my association with IHM, I've seen the real-world expression of early-20th-century poet Khalil Gibran's heartfelt observation: "Work is our love made visible."[15] At IHM, love is made visible each day as the founders and staff reveal deeper insights into the power of the heart's intelligence, and the role it plays each day in our lives.

While the people at IHM will continue their study of the heart for years to come, we can benefit from what they've discovered so far. In my opinion, among their greatest contributions are the simple and proven techniques of creating heart/brain coherence. Through peer-reviewed research, IHM has shown beyond any doubt that two factors relate directly to personal resilience in our time of extremes.

- Our emotions can be regulated to create coherence in our bodies.
- We can use simple steps to implement this fact in our lives.

Working with some of the most prestigious organizations and innovative researchers in the world, IHM has developed a simple system known as *Attitude Breathing* that allows us to apply the discoveries they've made in their laboratories easily in our everyday lives. The researchers describe the benefit of this technique, stating, "The heart will automatically harmonize the energy between the heart, mind and body, increasing coherence and clarity."[16] They've distilled the shift in emotions that creates the greatest levels of coherence into the following three simple steps, which are adapted from *Transforming Stress* by Doc Childre and Deborah Rozman (New Harbinger Publications, 2005):

Step 1. Recognize an unwanted attitude—a feeling or attitude that you want to change. This could be anxiety, sadness, despair, depression, self-judgment, guilt, anger, overwhelm—anything that's distressing.

Step 2. Identify and breathe in a replacement attitude: select a positive attitude and then breathe the feeling of that new attitude in slowly and casually through your heart area. Do this for a while to anchor the new feeling.

Examples of Unwanted Feelings/Attitudes	Examples of Replacement Feelings/Attitudes
Stress	Breathe neutral to chill out and revitalize.
Anxiety	Breathe calm and balance.
Overwhelm	Breathe ease and peace.
Sadness or depression	Breathe appreciation and nonjudgment.
Guilt	Breathe compassion and nonjudgment.

Step 3. As you breathe a replacement attitude, tell yourself to take the "big deal" and drama out of the negative feeling or attitude. Tell yourself: *Take the significance out.* Repeat this over

and over as you use Attitude Breathing until you feel a shift or a change. Remember that even when a negative attitude feels justified, the buildup of emotional energy will block up your system. Have a genuine "I mean business" attitude and heart intent to really move those emotions into a more coherent state. It could take a few minutes of Attitude Breathing, but it's worth the practice.

As you keep practicing, you will start to create new neural pathways, and old trigger attitudes and resistances start to release.

(Attitude Breathing® was developed by the Institute of HeartMath. Copyright © 2013 Institute of HeartMath.)

Over the years, I've visited with many indigenous families from various cultures throughout the world. As different as their traditions have been from one another, a common theme runs through all of them. That theme is the power of the heart to change our bodies, heal our lives, and create unity in our families and communities. While modern science largely discounted the very essence of such traditions in the past, the results of studies from IHM and other organizations are giving new credibility to the wisdom of our most ancient and cherished spiritual traditions.

Although our ancestors certainly didn't use what we recognize as the scientific method to prove what they knew, their techniques of heart-based prayer, meditation, and healing appear to have been firmly rooted in their knowledge of the heart's ability to influence our bodies and our lives. When I began to understand this fact as a young adult, it affected me in two profound ways.

The first was that knowing about such relationships made any other discipline I could ever study pale in comparison. After all, what could possibly be more important than unlocking the mysteries of the single organ in our bodies that is designed to connect us with our everyday world and beyond?

The second effect was to stimulate my curiosity. If our ancient ancestors were so right about the power of the heart, what else did they know in their own times that we've forgotten in ours?

The steps to coherence are as simple as *focus, feel,* and *breathe.*

Transformation Begins with Us

It's been said that the United States is a nation of communities. As true as this statement is for America, I believe it's equally true for all nations of the world. Through my research into the world's ancient and indigenous traditions, and the opportunities I've had to share what I've found with audiences on nearly every continent, I've experienced the reality of this statement. From Tokyo to Lima, from Cairo to Bangkok, the biggest cities in the world are made up of many small communities, each able to sustain itself on some levels while needing to interact with other communities at other levels. These huge urban complexes are made of local communities where people with similar heritages, backgrounds, interests, and ways of life have found common ground in their need to connect.

On an afternoon stroll through New York City, the difference between Chinatown and Little Italy is pronounced as you make your way from one neighborhood to the other. Yet as different as they are from one another, you're still in the same city. While the community-centered nature of a city may be obvious, it's important to identify it here because of the role that individuals—their states of mind and resilience—play within the community. Psychiatrist M. Scott Peck, M.D. (1936–2005), summed up this idea clearly and logically when he said, "For the reality is that there can be no vulnerability without risk; and there can be no community without vulnerability; and there can be no peace—and ultimately no life—without community."[17]

We are communal beings by nature, and living in communities of any size helps us meet our physical, emotional, and spiritual needs, as well as providing us opportunities to lead healthy, joyous, and meaningful lives. Because communities fill so many of our needs, it's not surprising that they also provide a way for us to share our vision of a better world and what it takes to get there. I've known people who have devoted their entire adult lives to their own self-improvement. They've found the ways to heal the hurts of childhood; the abuse from unhealthy relationships; and even the health crises they face in later years that commonly accompany the issues of low self-esteem, poor diet, and loss of personal value. From early in life, they've done all of the work for themselves, yet wonder why the rest of the world doesn't seem to reflect the healthy values they've arrived at in their own lives.

This is where the value and the power of community come in. While we can spend a lifetime improving ourselves—and this can be a very good thing—having a community around us gives us a way to carry our work to the next level. In a community, we can share the benefit of our lifetime of work with others who are interested yet have not had the same opportunities that we've had to discover the rich truths of personal power and resilience.

While it's always been healthy in the past to find other people willing to learn together and share their innermost values as they pertain to everyday life, today it's vital. In this time of extremes, the resilience that we develop as individuals becomes even more effective, powerful, and potent when it can be applied by our families, friends, and neighbors. When we share our healing insights, we find the answer to the question of what it takes to create a way of life that reflects the values we've discovered through our personal journey.

In the foreseeable future, it will be the communities that choose to adapt to the extremes of the new normal that will fare better—meaning, they will be stronger and better able to help others transform their lives in our time of extremes.

CHAPTER FIVE

The Next Level:

Turning Points of Community Resilience

"For a community to be whole and healthy, it must be based on people's love and concern for each other."

— Millard Fuller (1935–2009),
founder of Habitat for Humanity

The Ethiopian village of Mudiyambo had relied upon cattle for their income, their food, and their livelihood for as long as anyone could remember. As the weather in Africa began to shift due to climate change, however, the rains came less often and the Horn of Africa became one of the most drought-stricken areas in the world. Entire herds of cattle were wiped out time and again, and the village was desperate. When a global relief agency offered to retrain the villagers to become agricultural farmers rather than cattle ranchers through a program called Transformational Community Development (TCD), the villagers' reactions were mixed. In the words of one of the agency leaders, "When we started TCD, the number of villagers who were interested to get training was very small. Others considered it a waste of time."[1]

With open minds, hard work, and a willingness to shift the thinking of the past, however, everything changed. The trainings began and the success was contagious. When the villagers who were originally reluctant to embrace the change saw with their own eyes how successful they could be growing vegetables in place of raising cattle, they began "asking our TCD workers to get this lesson and want[ing] to start [their own] agricultural activity," says the leader.[2]

The shift is complete, and the village is now an agricultural community with a healthy economy. And there were unexpected benefits that came with the shift as well. The people discovered that their new economy is even more sustainable than it was before the drought, and they are healthier due to their new diet that provides nutrients on a regular basis.

Mudiyambo is a powerful success story that government leaders are now hoping to duplicate in other villages throughout Ethiopia. It's also a beautiful example of how the personal resilience of a few people willing to change their way of thinking can become the path to transformation for an entire village. The success of Mudiyambo is a testament to the power of resilience and the role it can play on a larger scale in our communities.

What Is Community?

Just as we discovered in the last chapter that *resilience* has a number of different meanings, the word *community* means different things to different people as well. For some, the word immediately conjures up images of Woodstock-like gatherings and the 1960s-style communes that were popularized in movies such as *Easy Rider,* while for others it brings to mind isolated groups of men, women, and children in the rural setting of a self-sufficient village, sharing everything from children and partners to gardening and the chores of daily living. While it's certainly possible that these features may exist in some communities in the world, in most they don't. Today community is more about living, working, and sharing with other people in ways that make life, and bearing life's responsibilities, easier. With this idea in mind, it's easy to see why the types of communities run the gamut of expression.

I've known communities made up of six to eight families, for example, that share the common bond of a particular spiritual practice. These families pool their resources so they can buy a series of homes adjacent to one another within the same neighborhood cul de sac. They are literally next door to one another, and because they are, they're able to share child care, meal preparation, gardening, and the practices that form the core of their spiritual lives while holding down full-time professional jobs.

While these particular groups are fully functioning communities unto themselves, they also represent a local branch of a national community made of other groups of families that live in the same way in other parts of the world. Through messages delivered from a central office via fax, e-mail, and Skype, all of the local branches focus upon a common spiritual theme each week, such as compassion or forgiveness. In this way they remain active on many community levels at once, from their local spiritual community to the greater neighborhood beyond their immediate community, to their professional communities, and ultimately to their global spiritual community. This is just an example of one kind of community in a world of thousands or more similar communities. So when we try to describe precisely what a community looks like, we find there are as many variations as there are needs and ideas on the part of the people who form them. The reason is because community is all about life and the way we live it.

Communities are everywhere. They're in the middle of the biggest cities of the world, and they're also in the middle of the biggest expanses of open and undeveloped land on the planet. A community can be one person living alone on a mountaintop, or it can be a husband and wife and their two children living as our next-door neighbors. It can be the retired couple down the block sharing gardening tips with the soon-to-be-retired couple across the street.

A community can be a room full of people who meet together at the town hall when they need to make a decision regarding taxes, roads, or whether or not to allow drilling for oil in their county. Or it can be an organized group of people who get together to build a home with Habitat for Humanity.

A community can be two native women bartering for their family's dinner on a sparsely populated island in the middle of Lake Titicaca in Peru, or it can be the mega-community of over 25 million people living, working, and sharing life in the metropolitan area of Seoul, South Korea.

So you get the idea. There are countless expressions of the idea of community, as they form in order to fill a variety of needs.

As different as the communities may appear from one another in size and scope, however, the "glue" that holds them together is surprisingly similar. Whether it's a single person or a city of 25 million, two keys must be present for any community to be successful. The members of the community share:

- A common vision
- A common bond

It's through these two qualities that the needs of community members are met. And when a community's needs are successfully met, it is also these qualities that help sustain the community and prepare it for future challenges.

Regardless of a community's size or its reason for forming, the existence of a shared vision and a common bond are essential to its success.

Not Your Grandparents' Communities

While we're surrounded by communities today, they're often very different from communities as we've known them in the past. In the 19th and 20th centuries, for example, community was often the outgrowth of people who lived close to one another, fulfilling similar needs. Whether it was for food; security; or expertise in building, gardening, or sharing the responsibilities of raising children, people commonly looked to their nearest neighbors for the support they needed in their everyday lives. This has changed in the modern world.

In the large high-rise apartments of any major metropolis today, it's not uncommon for two families of similar size with children of similar ages to live in the same building, on the same floor, their front doors within feet of one another, and go for years without ever knowing each other's names or even what one another looks like. So while each family still has their needs met when it comes to the convenience of an apartment and city living, their intimate community of support and close-knit friendships may be spread out across miles of concrete-and-glass buildings, rather than forged with the people who are their closest neighbors. The reasons range from the impersonal nature of computers and cell phones to the mind-set of independence that has played such a powerful role in America and the Western world—yet this kind of relationship is clearly not what our grandparents had in mind when they talked about community.

Novelist and poet Margaret Atwood described how this dilemma has played out specifically for America, stating, "The United States has promoted individualism so much that the responsibilities of giving to a community, and vice versa, have been trampled by rampant individualism."[3]

From an even grander perspective, spiritual teacher Ram Dass has identified both why the impersonal nature of today's community exists as well as the consequences it has brought to our everyday lives. "Our inordinate concern with individuality has marked our group identity. I'm part of the problem," he confesses.[4]

"The '60s were about individual freedom, and we threw out the baby with the bath. We're dealing with the effect of imbalance; we're so focused on separateness that we've lost interconnectedness, the inherent gregarious nature of humanity where we need others to give us meaning. The web of violence in this culture is clearly connected to the breakup of these types of systems."[5]

I believe there's a lot of truth in what Ram Dass, Margaret Atwood, and a number of other authors and experts have said about the role of community in our lives today. While our communities serve their purpose on the grand scale, in everyday life we've lost a big part of what made our communities so successful in the past: *the personal connection of knowing our neighbors and being aware of their lives and their needs.* I also believe that this is precisely where our lives are about to change quickly and in a big way. The change is already happening, and it's being driven by our time of extremes.

In recognizing the principles that worked for the communities of the 19th and early 20th centuries, we may also discover the clues to where the evolution in community is leading us today. If we can create our future communities based upon the healthy things that worked in the past, yet model them without the drawbacks of the things that *didn't* work, then we're well on our way to creating new lifestyles that can accommodate the extreme conditions of our time. The term often used to describe such a rekindling of ideas from the past is taken from the popular 1985 movie of a teenager's experience of time travel: *back to the future.*[6]

Many people are discovering that the seemingly new ways of thinking and living that work so well today actually represent a step backward to when they were commonplace in times past. We may discover that the steps to our success in our time of extremes are actually the steps that take us *back to our own future.*

In a world of increasingly impersonal and digital relationships, community fulfills our need for personal connection through knowing our neighbors and being aware of their lives and their needs.

"We Are One" Means We Share Everything

We hear the mantra and see the words everywhere: WE ARE ONE. It's written on bumper stickers, silk-screened on T-shirts, printed on glossy book covers, and featured in magazine specials. The words emerged in the late 20th century in recognition of the fact that the human family is just that: one big, diverse family sharing one planet. Beyond the ideologies, politics, cultures, and religions that sometimes tear at our unity and make us feel separate from one another, the fact is, we're a single family unlike any other known to exist anywhere else ever.

It's precisely because we are a global family that the problems experienced in one part of the world are rarely *limited* to that part of the world. While this fact has always been true to some extent, the rise of globalism now makes our "oneness" the reason why community resilience is the key to our future. When we find ways of thinking and living that work in response to the crises in one part of the world, just as the surrounding villages in Ethiopia clamored for the training that proved to change lives, the same thing happens on a larger scale.

It's no secret that we're already a global society. With rare exceptions, such as North Korea's isolation from the rest of the global community, it's fair to say that the boundaries that have separated one country from another have become a bit blurred and are becoming even more so. We no longer live in a world of separate economies, for instance. The financial markets that drive the economy are global and trade continuously 24/7. We also no longer live in a world of isolated technology, energy, defense, or communication systems. The summertime produce found in our supermarkets in the dead of winter is grown on farms half a world away and then flown, shipped, and trucked in on a daily basis. The voice that answers the help number we call at 2 A.M. for technical assistance with our computer is speaking to us, more often than not, from a call center located somewhere on the other side of the world.

Clearly, we live in a time when the line that has separated countries, cultures, technologies, and finances in the past is a fuzzy one at best. The 20th-century word coined to describe such complex relationships is *globalization.*

In his book *The Consequences of Modernity* (Stanford University Press, 1990), sociologist Anthony Giddens, Ph.D., who is perhaps best known for his holistic view of global societies, defines *globalization* as the "intensification of worldwide social relations which link distant localities in such a way that local happenings are shaped by events occurring many miles away and vice versa."[7] Personally, I like the definition offered by sociologist Martin Albrow that identifies *globalization* as "all those processes by which the peoples of the world are incorporated into a single world society."[8]

Regardless of how we define it, the ways in which we generally share information, ideas, technologies, goods, services, money, and people have created a world where we are more connected with one another than at any time in history. It's this one world of globalization that's created what can often be a mixed bag when it comes to the big problems of the world and how we deal with them. There are now a number of drawbacks to a globalized world that are becoming clear.

In his book *Globalization* (Oxford University Press, 2009), Manfred B. Steger, director of the Globalism Research Centre at the Royal Melbourne Institute of Technology University, gives us a place to begin exploring such a huge concept. He breaks the effects of globalization into five separate yet related categories that offer us a way to honestly think about the pros and cons of each. These broad categories or dimensions of globalization are: *economic, political, cultural, ecological,* and *ideological.* While each of these affects our ability to live resiliently, there are two whose effects are obviously greater than others: a global economy and a global ecology. It's these that I'd like to focus on here.

A Global Economy

The effect of a globally linked economy is a great place to begin a discussion of globalization. For one reason, it's on everyone's minds right now in the first two decades of the 21st century. The world is in the throes of an economic crisis the likes of which we've never seen before. As mentioned in an earlier section, the amount of money that the world owes in debt is nearing the break-even point of what the world produces as income. Making matters worse is the fact that the interest on the debt is accumulating in such a way that we are on the fast track for our debt to *exceed* our income. In other words, as a global economy, we're spending more than we earn.

Among the largest economies in the world (including members of the G9 and the G20 nations) the solution has been to create more money to cover the debt in the near term. As described in Chapter 1, one of the effects of such a practice is that the world's money supply is flooded, and the value of the currencies is tremendously reduced.

While there are as many opinions as to where the economic crisis is headed as there are "experts" offering them, one thing is certain: the underlying reason why the whole world is in the same boat is because our economies are so deeply linked through globalization.

In a globalized economy, the effects of one troubled economy send ripples throughout the world that affect other economies to varying degrees. This is precisely what the world witnessed with horror in autumn 2008, when it was publicized that some of the world's largest financial institutions owed more money than they had in assets. When financial services firm Lehman Brothers declared insolvency on September 14 that year, an interconnected chain of events was set into motion that continues to this day. As some of the world's largest and most respected institutions, such as Lehman Brothers, Fannie Mae, Freddie Mac, and the insurance giant AIG, began to do what had previously been thought impossible—to collapse into bankruptcy—the vulnerability of our global economy was quickly realized.

In a 2010 interview, Henry M. Paulson, Jr., the former U.S. Secretary of the Treasury, stated, "If the system had collapsed, many Main Street companies of all sizes would not have been able to get short-term financing to maintain basic business operations, to pay their suppliers and employees who then wouldn't have been able to pay their own bills. This would have rippled through the economy, resulting in millions more jobs lost, millions more homes lost, trillions of dollars more in lost savings."[9] Such widespread and devastating effects of the banking crisis could only be possible in a globalized economy.

One of the consequences of globalization is that we share everything, including the hardships of an unsustainable economy.

A Global Ecology

Nature and natural resources are not bound by governments, nations, and borders. And it's precisely because of this fact that the most pressing environmental issues we face today are directly linked to globalization. When a local industry relies upon local resources for its needs, such as a specific kind of fish, for example, it's possible to meet that demand in a sustainable way that assures that the resource is not destroyed in the process. But when the same industry tries to meet a demand that has grown hundreds of times larger due to a global market for the fish, it can spell disaster. While larger markets and more customers can definitely be a boon for merchants, the downside is that they can also lead to the damage or loss of entire species if the market is not regulated. The present-day near extinction of the bluefin tuna is a perfect example of what can happen when a local industry goes global.

The Atlantic population of the bluefin tuna is found in two primary locations: the western population, which breeds in the Gulf of Mexico, and the eastern population, which breeds in the Mediterranean Sea. Before 1950, there was little interest in the western bluefin as a commercial source of food. For thousands of years, the bluefin in general had been caught using traditional methods and in low quantities that maintained a balance in their populations and supported their migration and breeding. When the Japanese fish market began to skyrocket in the 1960s, however, the thinking regarding the bluefin changed. Suddenly there was a tremendous demand on Japanese fisheries to provide the deep red, sushi-grade meat of the bluefin, not only to their own markets, but also to markets throughout the world.

In addition to creating a larger demand for the delicacy, globalization also allowed for the sharing of new large-scale commercial fishing technology, and the international relationships that meet the demand. In 1964, approximately 18,000 metric tons of bluefin tuna were caught off the New England coast, more than had ever been caught in a single year in the past. A 2011 report from the Pew Charitable Trusts reported that the numbers reached as high as 20,943 U.S. tons per year (approximately 19,000 metric tons) in the western Atlantic at one point, a level that "could not be sustained, and the population crashed."[10] As of 2011, the catch has dropped to approximately 1,984 U.S. tons. The continued pressure of such catches has now depleted the tuna population in the area *by 80 percent.*

Even though quotas to protect the tuna were enacted in 1998, lack of enforcement continues to plague the industry. In his research into the role of globalization and the tuna industry, anthropologist Theodore Bestor sums up the plight of the tuna in a single sentence, stating, "Sushi has become an icon of Japanese culture, but it has also become an icon of globalization."[11]

While the bluefin tuna gives us a specific example of what may happen in the unregulated environment of trying to meet the need of a globalized market through a local resource, this phenomenon is not limited to the tuna. The United Nations Food and Agriculture Organization published a study in 2005 showing that 70 percent of the species of fish now commercially exploited are already beyond their capacity to repopulate. The global demand for disposable paper products has led to approximately 11 million acres per year of forest that are cut for commercial industries. Ecological globalization refers to additional environmental issues as well. The expansion of what were once local supplies of goods for a few communities into global markets for thousands of communities impacts everything from population growth, access to food, and worldwide loss in biodiversity, to the gap between rich and poor and the human contribution to climate change.

The bottom line to these sobering statistics is that the attempt to supply new and emerging global markets from traditional localized resources is not only unsustainable, but causes tremendous hardship when the unsustainable market collapses. Recognition of this fact is the key to the thinking that allows for resilience in our families and communities.

Entire ecosystems can be destroyed when the needs of a globally connected market are filled from a limited local source.

The Bridge to Resilience

While we may not know exactly where globalization is leading the world, there is certainly no shortage of opinions about what it's meant so far. In an essay for *Newsweek* magazine, journalist Thomas Friedman describes how the riots that disrupted the 2009 G20 Conference held in Pittsburgh, Pennsylvania, reflected people's biggest fear for our global economy: that globalization is good for businesses only, and not so good for people. After describing the concerns expressed by the rioters, Friedman shared his belief that "globalization didn't ruin the world—it just flattened it."[12] In other words, he was arguing that the opening of global markets and making them accessible to everyone, including our neighbors and small businesses, leveled the playing field in a world that had been skewed in the past.

Friedman left no doubt in the minds of his readers as to how he believed that globalization "raises the global standard of living" and stated that "on balance [globalization] can benefit everyone, especially the poor."[13]

While the viewpoints that oppose Friedman's vary in their specifics, in general they argue that it's not the change in the standard of living for the world that the protesters fear. It's more about the evidence showing that huge corporations are gaining more control over our lives and the way we live. Perhaps even more relevant is the fear of the average person being powerless to stop these corporations from doing the things that are good for the bottom line of business, but bad for the human race and the sustainability of life on the planet.

Examples of where we see this kind of power emerging today are with the flooding of the markets with genetically modified seeds and foods, and also where corporations are harnessing technology that destroys farmland resources in exchange for the recovery of oil and gas. In both instances, fear is being generated in the hearts and minds of some members of the public that these things are mandated for business, while those most affected have little say in the defense of their homes and lives.

Clearly, globalization is a mixed bag. There are certainly some people and industries that have benefited. And some who have not. As globalization stands today, it's not a democratic process, and it's been largely driven by those who benefit from it the most. Just as clearly, it is a fact of life. We've definitely gone global, and there's no turning back. So while there's no doubt that economy, agriculture, and industry now work as global entities, what effect does a globalized world have upon our ability to live resiliently?

Drawing upon the best of today's leading-edge science and scholarly expertise, Judith Rodin, president of the philanthropic Rockefeller Foundation; and Robert Garris, managing director of the Rockefeller's Bellagio Programs, aimed at identifying solutions to critical global problems, have reported on the role of resilience in the 21st century. They describe how the "growing need for resilience as a counterbalancing force to the vulnerability driven by globalization means that development actors must act with greater urgency and sophistication to build the capacities of communities to adapt to change."[14] In other words, they're saying that the need is clear and now is the time for precisely the ideas that are identified in the pages of this book.

When we see the principles of such a shift in thought coming from influential institutions, like the Rockefeller Foundation, as well as from grassroots organizations, such as the Post Carbon Institute, we can be certain that the ideas are more than just a passing fad.

Learning to create resilient communities and cities is a trend that's here to stay.

The aspects of globalization that connected the world in the past may be destroying the world today.

Building Blocks of Resilience

Globalization in our world has changed everything. It's changed the way we live, the way we work, the way we think, and the way we solve our problems. It's even changed the kind of problems that we're presented with. Judith Rodin encapsulates precisely why we need to think differently when it comes to our communities and cities today: "What distinguishes today's threats from those of the past are the escalating rate at which they are occurring, and the growing interconnectedness of our planet. Building resilience is not a luxury. It's a 21st century imperative."[15]

I agree with what Rodin is saying, and the obvious question, then, is: *How?*

How do we go from creating personal resilience, as described in the last chapter, to building resilient families and forming resilient communities? Perhaps an even bigger question is: *How do we do so in the face of already-established systems that people have come to accept as "the way" things are done?*

The study of resilient lifestyles and communities is a relatively recent area of research. Some of the first studies to use the word *resilience* itself were published only in the early 1970s, referencing human illnesses: who gets sick, who doesn't, and how quickly do those who do get sick recover? I've had the opportunity to study many findings from the research of others. I've also witnessed resilience personally in the rural communities of northern New Mexico when conditions of nature and broken economies have created tremendous hardship where I live.

I can honestly say that I've yet to find a single theory or method of resilience that holds all the answers that seem to be necessary. Just as there are different kinds of communities that meet the needs of different populations, there are different kinds of resilience and a variety of ways to get there. At the end of this chapter, I'll share some of the resources describing case histories and real-world experiments in creating community resilience.

I'd like to begin here with the broad factors that apply to any kind of resilience, from a single family or neighborhood, to a digital community that extends worldwide. One of the best summaries of these factors draws from the expertise of hundreds of scientists and researchers contributing to resilience studies funded by the Rockefeller Foundation. These studies identify five key elements of resilience that are general enough to cover nearly any community situation, yet specific enough to give us a place to begin.[16] These core principles are identified as:

- Spare capacity
- Flexibility—the ability to change, evolve, and adapt in the face of disaster
- Limited or "safe" failure, which prevents failures from rippling across systems
- Rapid rebound—the capacity to reestablish function and avoid long-term disruptions
- Constant learning, with robust feedback loops

When we consider the turning points identified in Chapter 3 and the principles of personal resilience described in Chapter 4, we find that the general theme of the five principles of resilience listed above provides an umbrella under which we can adapt and customize according to our personal and community resilience needs.

Let's take a closer look at each of these five keys and see how it fits into the turning points within our communities.

Spare Capacity

There's a big difference between having our needs in the moment met easily, and thoughtfully planning ahead so the same can be true for the future. There is also a powerful difference between planning responsibly for the realities of life, and hoarding frantically at the last minute to compensate for a lack of planning. When it comes to our time of extremes, we're witnessing both of these scenarios.

I've met people who believe we're heading toward a world that reflects the worst-case scenarios portrayed by cable-television documentaries. These are frightening images that remind me of the classic 1979 movie *Mad Max,* showing a postapocalyptic world after climate change, war, and the end of oil.

I've also known people at the opposite end of the spectrum, who have found the seemingly endless supply of fresh fruits, vegetables, and household products at their neighborhood market so reliable that they believe things will always be this way and count on an ever-constant availability of produce and other food for each and every meal. They've become so accustomed to finding what they need on demand that they feel there's no reason to plan any further ahead than the day of the meal.

Clearly, I like the idea of eating the freshest fruits and vegetables possible, and enjoy daily trips to the market when I can. The concern here is the issue of what happens if the supply isn't available. How long can these people, or any of us, care for and nourish ourselves and our families with what we have today in our kitchen cabinets?

As creatures of habit, we tend to reflect the way we lived life at a particular time in our past. Once a habit is in place, we often give the idea of changing it very little thought. *This is where the resilient principle of spare capacity comes in.* In our time of extremes, we're finding that things simply don't work as reliably as they may have in the past. What was once the rare interruption of basic services, such as electricity and full grocery shelves, is becoming commonplace. The reasons range from "freak" storms, high winds, and deep snow to the economic realities of downsized workforces, shorter workweeks, and fewer stocks of available goods. Following are some examples of such interruptions:

- Electricity in the United States is becoming less reliable, following a trend that began 15 years ago. A study published by Massoud Amin, D.Sc., director of the Technological Leadership Institute at the University of Minnesota, states: "Since 1995, electrical grid power outages have steadily increased as R&D in new technologies steadily decreased."[17]

- Among the increasingly apparent effects of extreme weather are temporary disruptions of vital supplies to local markets. Brooklyn, New York, in winter 2010 is a perfect example. For nearly a week, supply trucks simply could not get to the grocery stores that needed replenishing. A quote reported at the time by a local media source summed up the city's dilemma. "Three days. No deliveries. You see all the shelves are empty," said a store clerk.[18]
- After Hurricane Sandy slammed into the Eastern Seaboard of the United States, 8.1 million homes in 17 states lost electricity. The rationing of gasoline at service stations in New York City lasted for 15 days.[19]
- In February 2011, as temperatures dropped to a record 36 degrees below zero, a state of emergency was declared in northern New Mexico. The natural gas used to heat homes and farms was shut off without warning due to rolling blackouts that were an attempt to address the increased demand for power.

Extreme weather conditions are catching multiple communities and entire regions unprepared. The effects are devastating, and the disruption of services can last from a few days to many months.

Because we're living a time of such extremes, the resilient principle of spare capacity makes more sense than ever. *It makes sense to expect periodic and temporary disruptions in the services that we've taken for granted for so much of our lives.* Far from the dismissive labels of "commando" and "preppers" that have been used to describe people who take such precautions, to create spare capacity is now a reasonable choice that reflects the facts of a changing world. To do so is simply responsible.

We're surrounded by wonderful models of spare capacity in nature. When the weather is good and food is plentiful, we see squirrels, for example, finding what they need for their daily nutrition. (This is like us going to the neighborhood market every day because we can.) We also see the same squirrels taking extra food and putting it away for the proverbial rainy day, the cold months when they instinctively know that food will become less available. We see something similar with bears and other forms of life that instinctively add to their body weight in the good times to sustain themselves when the times are not so good. (This is the equivalent of us creating spare capacity by stocking up on a few of the essentials that we rely upon every day, just in case there's a day when we can't get them.) In nature, we don't see these animals in a chaotic and last-minute frenzy, fighting tooth and nail out of fear of scarcity. They don't need to, because they've created the spare capacity in their lives that mirrors the reality of their world.

Flexibility

Whether we're talking about our lives or our communities, when it comes to creating resilience, the principles of flexibility and change go hand in hand. In the 6th century B.C.E., the Greek philosopher Heracleitus observed the role of change in our lives, stating, "There is nothing permanent except change. Nothing is permanent except change. The only constant is change. Change is the only constant. Change alone is unchanging."[20] Saying the same thing in five different ways, he leaves little doubt in our minds as to how he sees the role of change in our lives. His famous words are often shared today in an abbreviated form.

Science-fiction writer Isaac Asimov carried Heracleitus's wisdom one step further in the 20th century, when he said, "It is change, continuing change, inevitable change, that is the dominant factor in society today. No sensible decision can be made any longer without taking into account not only the world as it is, but the world as it will be."[21] When the reality of constant change is factored into our plans for resilience, it's easy to see the advantage of being flexible as well. It's our willingness to accept that the plans we've made, based upon what we knew to be true when we made them, are subject to change at a moment's notice.

Our flexibility to adapt to unexpected conditions, and then improvise and go to "Plan B," is one of the strongest links we can create in our chain of resilience. The potential-tragedy-turned-success of the Apollo 11 mission—not only once but twice—is a perfect example. Two times during the first manned mission to the moon, the plans that had been carefully thought out by the experts, that had been in place for years, and that had been described in the training manuals down to the smallest detail had to change at the last minute. The reason? The situation changed. The key to averting tragedy in the face of the change was flexibility.

On the first mission to the moon, one of the most important factors was the total weight that the spacecraft could carry. The men, their spacesuits, their food, their equipment, and their fuel were all carefully weighed and kept to an optimal capacity to ensure the safety of the crew and the mission's success. Only a slim margin of error was built into the plans that could mean the difference between success and failure, life and death.

As the astronauts in the lunar module approached the spot for their first landing, they could see that a field of boulders made it more dangerous than it had appeared on the radar screens and survey photos. In a last-minute decision, pilot Buzz Aldrin aborted the planned landing site in search of a safer place. As Mission Control nervously witnessed this unanticipated chain of events, Eagle, the lunar lander, found a smoother area and landed successfully *with only 15 seconds of fuel remaining.*

When the astronauts were ready to return to the orbiting module and come back to Earth, they noticed that a backpack had accidentally broken off the only ignition switch that could restart the engines. Once again, flexibility was the key. Thinking as a problem-solving engineer, Buzz Aldrin inserted the tip of a ballpoint pen into the base of the broken switch, allowing him to manually start the engines that would lift him and the crew from the surface of the moon.

While the flexibility to change our routines will probably never carry the magnitude of consequences that the first astronauts experienced on the moon, nonetheless we'll all be faced with situations where our willingness to embrace unexpected changes and make the best of a situation can save our lives—or those of others. In creating resilience for natural disasters, for example, there is often the need for multiple contingency plans—backup plans for the backup plans—to be used in the event that the conditions of nature prevent the first plan from working.

"Always realize you may encounter situations and circumstances that challenge the best plans," says Robert Cherry, M.D.[22] He should know. Speaking of his personal experience at a level-one trauma center in New York City after September 11, 2001, he saw firsthand what can happen when the situation doesn't fit the plan: "We felt the trauma center was prepared for disasters, until we found things that we simply hadn't planned for."[23] As well prepared as the hospital was, the teams discovered problems with the contingency plans, including limited resources of staff, equipment, communications, and fuel.

They discovered, for example, that the fuel supply for the backup generators was designed to last for only 36 hours. These were the generators that powered the lifesaving and life-sustaining equipment for the trauma victims. What if there was no additional fuel after that time? Dr. Cherry's experiences from that period led him to develop new programs at Penn State College of Medicine that now train people to be resilient in precisely such situations. Dr. Cherry sums up the role of flexibility in extreme situations: "You have to adopt an emergency plan that allows for change because it is impossible to adapt an inflexible plan during an emergency situation."[24]

Limited or "Safe" Failure

During one of my first assignments as a software engineer in the defense industry, I asked my customer a question that led both of us to rethink our entire approach to a problem. "If this program was to fail," I asked, "and it started to lose information, *how much* could you afford for it to fail? How much data are you willing to lose?" The question opened the door to our discussion of a way of thinking called *limited failure*. For an engineer, the idea of limited failure is common when it comes to a system or piece of equipment that's so vital to the success of a mission that it's actually called *mission critical.* If the component fails, for any reason, the idea is to find a way to prevent its failure from ending the entire mission.

For my client, before our conversation, his idea of failure and success had been black/white, either/or. Something either worked or it didn't. Discovering that it was possible for his software to break down, yet for the overall program to continue with a limited failure, was a new way of thinking—one he welcomed.

The thinking with respect to limited failure has been very much a part of scientific endeavors in America's space program. When NASA sent the first unmanned spacecraft to the surface of Mars, for example, its power system was considered to be mission critical. No matter how successful everything else on the mission was, if the spacecraft had no electricity, the mission was over. To ensure the mission's success, the engineers built backup power systems. But they didn't stop there, they built backups to the backups as safeguards called *redundant backup systems.* By creating alternative systems that could kick in during a power failure, the engineering team had stacked the deck of success in their favor by minimizing the effect that a failure would have for the rest of the mission.

It's this idea of limited failure that comes into play when we think of resilience as well.

When it comes to resilience in our communities, the idea of limited failure is a powerful tool that goes a long way toward creating peace of mind. I've spoken to families in rural areas of America, for example, who proudly announce that they have a backup well to supply water in the event the municipal water system breaks down. They feel that their backup well helps them be prepared for hurricanes, tornadoes, and unforeseen extremes. They commonly forget, however, that to get their backup water, they need electricity to run the pump that brings it to the surface. My question to them becomes, "If the power goes out, how long can you be without your well?" Their answer to the question tells them when they should be thinking about limited failure—in this case, a backup source of electricity for their backup source of water.

Although I've described physical systems to illustrate what I mean by limited failure, the idea also applies to the way we live our lives. We can create plans to limit failure in the event of job loss, family financial shortages, and even loss of communication with the people closest to us.

Rapid Rebound

The thinking underlying *rapid rebound* is precisely what the name suggests—our ability to resume function if something has been disrupted, and to do so in a way that serves us. This applies to human emotions and psychology, as well as physical systems such as power, water, and food.

As mentioned previously, we humans are definitely creatures of habit and routines. When our routines are interrupted for any reason, one of the most important factors for our emotional well-being is how quickly we can reestablish them in some form. We find this to be true in circumstances that range from people who have been in captivity for long periods of time and those who find themselves lost in the wilderness, to people stranded on deserted islands or confined to tiny lifeboats lost at sea. From real-life accounts after the fact, where people have survived under such unnatural conditions, we learn that one of the first things they attribute their survival to is their ability to create routines that give meaning to each day.

In an interview, one of the Iranian hostages mentioned in the previous chapter said that even in the small cell where he was kept isolated from the other hostages, he developed a daily routine of physical exercise, prayer, sleep, meals, and mental games that helped him rebound from the shock of being taken captive. I've personally witnessed the need for such routines following devastating snowstorms that leave entire mountain regions isolated, and in the aftermath of Hurricane Sandy, which left miles of the Atlantic coastline looking like a war zone.

One week after Sandy left homes, businesses, and neighborhoods in rubble, I was scheduled to speak at a conference in New Jersey that I felt certain would be canceled. To the contrary, the promoters opted to go forward with the weekend seminar to build a sense of normalcy, the *rapid rebound* for people who had lost so much in the storm. We discovered that the hotel where the event was held was one of the few that had a full complement of electricity, hot showers, phones, and meals, all of which would still be absent in some communities as long as five months later.

Rapid rebound is the key either to getting back to the old normal or to establishing a new normal to meet the new conditions of a changed world.

Constant Learning

Each of the previous elements of resilience is only useful to the degree to which it works in people's lives. Whether we're talking about a single family of four people living under one roof or many families in a digital community dispersed across an entire city, the key to success is the principle of *feedback* in learning. It's only possible to find out what works and what doesn't through feedback from people in the situation that's requiring them to be resilient. Formally or informally, it's good to identify mechanisms for your community's feedback. These can be as simple as a casual phone call or e-mail to let an organizer know of your experiences, or as formal as an organized meeting designated for a specific time and day. The key is that the way in which the feedback happens must be something that's easy and works for everyone. When we learn these lessons, then we discover for ourselves and our communities what to do more of, what to do less of, and how little things may be tweaked one way or another to become a real help.

A proven model for community resilience includes the principles of *spare capacity, flexibility, limited failure, rapid rebound,* and *constant learning [feedback].*

Principles of Resilient Communities

The idea of purposefully building communities of resilience is not a new one. Visionary individuals and groups of like-minded people have been working informally since the 19th century to find ways of living that are functional, are sustainable, and reflect the common values that bring the group together. As you can imagine, there are probably an infinite number of reasons for communities to form, and this fact is reflected in the number of communities that have come and gone over the years.

The community of Fairhope, Alabama, for example was originally founded in 1894 and based upon a system of taxes that worked for everyone in the community. Rather than owning their farmland outright, the members leased the land for 99-year terms, as do some Native American communities today. In this way, the land is used effectively by individuals and families during their lifetimes, yet stays in the community when the owners can no longer use it. The only tax in the Fairhope community was a land tax that paid for schools, roads, and community government. The vision that brought Fairhope together over 100 years ago continues to this day to sustain a small, successful, and thriving community.

Other communities are based upon core principles that vary from spiritual values to simple living and the desire to raise children in a communal environment. Examples of successful communities founded in the 20th century that remain alive today include the Findhorn Foundation, established in 1962 in Scotland; Ananda Village, founded in 1968 in California; and various other ecovillages. As different as the specific reasons why these communities formed may be, common threads have led to their continued success.

In 1992, the Berkana Institute was founded as a think tank for innovation when it comes to resilient living. In her own words, cofounder Margaret J. Wheatley describes the institute's function:

> Since 1991, we have been learning from life (living systems) about how to create systems that are interdependent, adaptive and resilient. Everything we have done has been a conscious experiment to better understand two of life's robust capacities:

> self-organization—life's process for creating order (effectiveness) without control; and emergence—life's means for creating system-wide change, taking things to scale.[25]

While there are many pioneering organizations now exploring what it means to live in community resilience, I'm sharing the example of Berkana here for two reasons:

First, in addition to my training as a scientist, I'm also a realist. My scientific training tells me that nature is simple: the laws of nature are simple, and they exist because they work. Nature surrounds us, and if we have the wisdom to recognize what works for all other forms of life on the planet, it will probably work for us as well. And this is the core of the Berkana philosophy. It begins with the belief that the community has within itself the intelligent systems that hold the key to solving its own problems as they arise. Briefly, these principles state that:

- Every community is filled with leaders.
- Whatever the problem, community itself has the answers.
- We don't have to wait for anyone. We have many resources with which to make things better now.
- We need a clear sense of direction, *and* we need to know the elegant, minimum next step.
- We proceed one step at a time, making the path by walking it.
- Local work evolves to create transformative social change when connected to similar work around the world.[26]

Second, while spiritual, economic, social, and political values have formed the core of many alternative, intentional, and resilient communities in the past, another factor is triggering the development of new and larger communities today: the surge of new community growth has come from the sense that someday we'll need what they've discovered to replace today's unsustainable ways of living that are sure to fail. When we take into consideration the effects of climate change, globalization, and the impact of other extremes described in previous chapters, it appears as if that time may have arrived.

A Template for Community Resilience

It's been commonly said that every journey begins with a first step. The corollary to this statement, which is heard less, is that it's what happens to get us to the first step that's often the hardest part of the journey. Our willingness to recognize the need, our choice to make a positive shift, our promise to commit to the work it takes to see it through, and the discipline that such a journey requires give credence to this statement. Formally or informally, every resilient community must begin somewhere.

I recommend using the philosophy described by the Berkana Institute as a template to start the process. If you and the members of your prospective community can honestly agree that these principles work for you, then you're already beginning your journey on the same page and you already have the foundation of a solid philosophy to base your next steps upon.

When it comes to creating a successful and resilient community, the key is to build the necessary principles into the model itself. One of the ways to do this is to holistically create each step with these ideas in mind rather than trying to retrofit them as an afterthought. In other words, these ideas must be considered in a way that *works* for the community. This can range from a formal set of written declarations describing the levels of community purpose and development, to a casual conversation and agreement between two families that accomplishes the same thing and ends with a handshake.

The real key is that the steps must work for everyone.

The following steps offer a template of guidelines that every resilient community must develop for itself, either formally or informally.

1. **Identify the needs of your community.** Why have you chosen to come together? Identify the common need that you hope to fulfill through your shared efforts.
2. **Identify the vision of your community.** Identify the goal or goals of your community, what success will look like, and how you will know when you get there. Some things to consider include: Are your goals specific and designed for a one-time need, or are they designed to become a way of life? Are your goals sustainable, and can they be accepted by the greater community or society at large? Be specific about what you hope to accomplish and the milestones that tell you when you're successful.
3. **Identify your plan.** Identify the steps that lead to accomplishing your goals. Determine realistic timelines, and assume roles and responsibilities to accomplish each step of the plan.
4. **Communicate.** Identify a way to share thoughts, ideas, feelings, and concerns that will inevitably arise with any community process. This can be as informal as an agreement to share such concerns when they come up or as formal as a specific time to meet for just such a purpose. In this way, the community is constantly informing itself of what works, what doesn't, and where there's need for a rethinking of the methods and processes.

This is an example of the kind of template that you may want in order to get your community up and running. It's intentionally general in nature so that it may be used for nearly any kind of community.

Now that we have the template, the best way to see how these principles work in the real world is through case histories. Having lived in a number of rural areas, as well as some of the largest urban areas in the United States, I've had the opportunity to witness various communities in action firsthand. I've also had the opportunity to see what works and what doesn't when it comes to a group of people taking on the tasks on a larger scale that have been accomplished by one or two people on a smaller one.

The minimum framework for successfully building a resilient community has been found to include: [1] identifying why your community is forming, [2] identifying the common vision for your community, [3] identifying your community plan, and [4] identifying how your community will communicate feedback.

Self-Reliance vs. Self-Sufficiency

When it comes to resilience in a community, two terms that often come up in conversation are *self-sufficiency* and *self-reliance.* Although the principles that I'm sharing in this book emphasize the more community-friendly ideas of self-reliance, I'd like to clarify the differences underlying each term.

Self-sufficiency is both a way of thinking and a way of living that strives for some aspect of complete autonomy. In its purest form, people living self-sufficiently would create everything they needed for all aspects of their day-to-day life, and consume only what they are able to create and provide for themselves. Clearly this is not practical in our modern world, and probably not even desirable. It's precisely because of the benefits that we find in a diversified community that we discover the power of group self-reliance.

Alternatively, self-reliance is a way of thinking and living where we learn to do as much as we can for ourselves while integrating our strengths and skills in complementary ways with others in our community. We can learn the skills of gardening and food preparation for ourselves and our family, for example—a form of self-reliance that's healthy for our bodies and frees us from commercial and store-bought foods. At the same time, we can share what we've learned, and grown, over the dinner table with friends in our community. In doing so, our self-reliance gives us the ability to share with others from a place of strength rather than need. While this may seem like a simple example, you get the idea of what I'm saying here: we can learn to be self-reliant within the context of our larger community.

As a point of clarity, there are certainly levels of self-sufficiency that fall between complete autonomy and community self-reliance. A self-sufficient source of energy for a family home is an example. I've met families who have been able to accomplish energy self-sufficiency through a combination of renewable sources ranging from passive and active solar farms to wind generators, and so on. So while they've made a choice to become energy independent for themselves, rather than being isolated survivalists living in fear, they've done so from the choice to be self-reliant. It's this choice, as well, that allows them the capacity to be there for others if the need arises.

The point here is that the benefit of community *is* the point. When it comes to creating resilience in the face of our rapidly shifting world of extremes, nature shows us that working to blend our skills, knowledge, and talent stacks the deck of success in our favor. The key is that we must have a plan when we work together. This is where our template of resilience comes in.

Perhaps the hardest part of building a resilient community is knowing where and how to begin. Some communities form after the fact following a devastating event such as the wildfires that have raged in recent years in America's Desert Southwest, Australia, and the forests of Italy. In these instances, the need to *recover from* their frightening and devastating experience brings neighbors together in community.

There are other resilient communities that form *before* the need actually arises. While the members hope they never face the fury of hurricanes, tornadoes, wildfires, or floods, these realities are built into their community plan. They're already resilient to our time of extremes.

For either kind of community, the steps are similar. Using the four steps identified in the template for community resilience offered in the previous section, let's consider a community based upon a real-life situation. In this way we can illustrate precisely how such a community is formed.

Building a Community

I've had the opportunity to see communities form and disband for a number of reasons. The irony of living in places that are an hour from the closest grocery store and acres away from your nearest neighbor is that the people typically drawn to live in such a way do so precisely because they *don't* want to be involved with other people. They don't particularly want to be part of an organized group, a community association, a road association, or any kind of association.

So while rural communities are sometimes the most difficult places to get people to work together, it's in doing so that they can find the strength to preserve the very qualities of the land and the way of life that have attracted them to such a lifestyle. I'm sharing this observation because it was through organizing and participating in precisely such a community in the early 1990s that I had the opportunity to witness the results of developing a community resilient to a number of changes that were threatening its way of life.

Every community begins with a reason to come together. In the case of my community experience, it was the threat of losing the rugged beauty and rural lifestyle that had drawn the people to the area to begin with. In the early 1990s, real-estate developers from out of state had come into the remote wilderness of north-central New Mexico in search of land for development. As they drove for miles seeing only sparse homesteads, ranches, and thousands of acres of undeveloped wilderness, to their eyes the land that was our home looked like wasted potential. The developers proposed building hundreds of homes, a shopping mall, two full-size golf courses, and a medical facility on our community's land. And to make the area more accessible to their development, they also proposed the expansion of a small community airport, the widening of existing roads, and the building of new ones.

Clearly, my informal community of ranchers, farmers, gardeners, beekeepers, carpenters, and artists was in danger of losing the pristine beauty that made our way of life possible. We needed to organize. On the night of our first meeting, we sat in a circle of chairs that had been provided by the local volunteer firehouse, looked at one another across the room, and asked the only question we could: "Now what?"

That question set into motion one of the most powerful, motivational, and successful communities that I've experienced in my life. And from the original community that rose up in response to the threat of the developers, new communities were also formed to create resilience in the face of a number of threats and changes that are unique to such a rural lifestyle. So while the needs may vary, the principles that worked for us can work for any situation where people want to build security for themselves and their children in a community environment.

In our example, this is how it was done:

Step 1: Identify the needs of your community. In the example of my rural mountain community, we began by stating our common needs: to preserve the open spaces, beauty, and unspoiled nature of the wilderness that we'd chosen for our homes.

Step 2: Identify the vision of your community. Once we were clear on what we wanted to happen, the next step in our planning was to create a vision of how we wanted the needs we'd identified to be met, and what the success of our vision would look like. This is always an interesting process that ignites the imagination with many possibilities, some more likely to become reality than others. Yet I've found that in addition to helping a community move into the process of working together, it's this step, perhaps more than any other, that opens the floodgates of communication and a deep sharing of people's thoughts, attitudes, experiences, loves, and desires for themselves and their families, particularly their children.

In our case, we followed the guidelines of community building and became very specific very quickly. We stated that the community was being formed to fill a one-time need (or so we thought) to preserve the land and the way of life that we cherished. We felt that we could accomplish as an organized group with a voice what we could not as individuals, by periodically working together on one aspect of the problem or another.

Step 3: Identify the plan. During this step in the process, we got down to brass tacks, by naming specific action items. As is to be expected in any group dynamic, some people were vocal and bubbling with ideas, while others sat quietly, listening and chiming in only when they felt they could contribute in a meaningful and useful way. I believe it's fair to say, for everyone in our community, that we were pushed to the edge of our comfort zones, and maybe a little beyond, as we made commitments and accepted responsibilities for the steps that would need to happen to ensure the success of our plan. While we all wanted the same thing—to preserve our way of life and the beauty of our valley—we quickly discovered that we were basing our goals on the emotions of our attachment to the land. As a geologist, I offered to take our efforts one step further and base our case on the availability of groundwater.

The magnitude and scale of the development being proposed would require huge amounts of water, which is an increasingly rare resource in the arid deserts of the Southwest. My role was to develop a factual assessment of the groundwater in the area, including the size of the reservoir, the thickness of the aquifer, and how many years it takes for the winter snow to percolate through the rock and recharge our water table. Using maps from the United States Geological Survey of the geology and water wells in the area, our community worked together to build a solid case. We presented evidence that the groundwater levels could not sustain the proposed development, as well as the data showing how the proposed development would compete for irrigation water all the way to the Texas border.

Step 4: Communicate. Staying in touch with members of a community while you're working toward a specific goal is the key to coordinating everyone's efforts. Because our community was so geographically spread out, we had to be especially creative in the ways that we communicated. We agreed to meet on a weekly basis for nearly eight weeks to put our arguments together. During that time, we shared phone numbers, fax numbers, and physical addresses, information that can be a hard to come by in rural areas. Members met over coffee, tea, family dinners, and late-night cookie feasts. And when all was said and done, our informal community of people who had reluctantly joined together to save their way of life became a close-knit community involving friendships that continue to this day.

One morning, just a few short months after we came together for the first time, I drove with four community members three hours to New Mexico's capital, Santa Fe, and met with one of the state senators who would help us present our case. I shared the groundwater assessments, the maps we'd created, and the impact that the proposed development would have upon communities throughout the state. The rest, as they say, is history. The State of New Mexico did not grant the permits the developers needed to proceed with their plans, and our valley has remained intact ever since.

What Does It Take?

I've shared the story of how a mountain community had to organize in order to illustrate how a real-life community can follow the template for resilience. In the case of the mountain community that I was part of, the members discovered a new strength within themselves as they got to know one another. And while the community was created at first for a specific purpose, it continued in various forms long after the original goals were met. It's because of the strength and diversity the members found among themselves that the relationships persisted even as the community faced new challenges beyond the ambitious land developers. These included evacuations during wildfires, aid in reaching stranded livestock during record-setting snowfalls that made the dirt roads impassable, and floods that washed away entire roads and kept some people away from their homes for weeks as the snow melted.

As we've seen in the previous sections, resilience is as much a state of mind as it is a way of life. It's about being willing to honestly embrace the immediate realities that we face in our everyday lives and to act responsibly to meet the conditions of those realities. Our mountain community coming together to preserve a way of life is one example of how a community can form and what it can accomplish. In our case, we found the knowledge, methods, and relationships that helped us in a specific instance. And in doing so, we created a process and reservoir of skills that we can now draw upon in future times of need. Our community became resilient to the things that threatened our way of life.

As we'll see in the next and final chapter, there are actions we can take immediately that will lead to the transformation of our own neighborhoods. The world is changing. It makes tremendous sense to adapt to the changes rather than fight them, and to do so alongside our friends and neighbors as we build healthy, resilient, and thriving communities.

What Is Your Threshold?

When we talk about resilience in general, one of the first questions that comes to mind is: *Resilience to what?* What is the actual force or condition that we are shifting our thinking and lifestyle to accommodate? It's a simple question and one that makes a lot of sense. The answer is simple as well.

We're learning to become resilient to the world we've created.

It's in precisely understanding what this answer means, and what it is that we've created, that we can begin to build the resilience that makes sense according to our specific needs.

When you consider creating a resilient community, the first question to ask yourself and other potential members is: "What would we like our resilience to address?" To get to the bottom of what this can mean, I invite you to consider the following:

1. What are the elements of your physical surroundings that you consider an absolute necessity in the short term (from a few hours to three days)?
2. What are the elements of your physical surroundings that you consider an absolute necessity in the long term (from three days to two weeks, or more)?

Different people have different thresholds of what they feel they can and cannot live without. This is especially true in times of crisis when we're often frightened, caught off guard, and unprepared.

For instance, people will generally say that they can do without electricity for a brief time, ranging from a few hours to a few days. For young people, such an experience can even seem like an adventure. During the time when the luxuries of life such as electricity are no longer available, the use of backup sources of light, such as lanterns, flashlights, and candles, will generally get people through the nights, and propane and natural gas will often sustain them for cooking and heat. Beyond this time, however, most people seem to need more. This is the time for long-term strategies to kick in.

The key here is to ask yourself what these questions mean to you. *What is your threshold?* Your answer will point you in the direction of what resilience means for you in a time of extremes. The way you answer these questions is your tip-off as to when you need to seriously consider measures that can assure you and your family of a sense of normalcy when faced with the vulnerability of extremes. In other words, your answer will be the key to know when to store extra food in your pantry, and what kind and how much. Only you can know for yourself when it's time to consider a backup source of power and whether yours needs to be a full-size generator to run your house or a large battery to power the lights in your living room.

While we sometimes feel reluctance, or even resistance, to putting our energy into thinking about such things, in view of the facts shared in this book and other sources of news and information, it actually makes perfect sense.

Community Resilience: It Just Makes Sense!

The first portion of this book identifies the rare conditions of climate, debt, population, and energy that are converging as a period of extremes and vulnerability in our lives. In light of the specifics, there can be little doubt regarding just how volatile things have become, and in all likelihood will remain for the foreseeable future. It's precisely the certainty of so much *un*certainty that gives even greater meaning to a culture of resilience. For example:

- It's *because* we're living amidst what the World Economic Forum's *Global Risks 2013* report, detailed in Chapter 1, called the "perfect storm" of conditions that it makes sense to expect volatility in places where life has been smooth sailing in the past.
- It's *because* climate change and a warming of the world's oceans is a fact that it makes sense to expect record-setting extremes in rainfall and snowfall, sizzling summers, and frigid winters.
- It's *because* the world's economies are weakened and fragile that it makes sense to expect cutbacks in manufacturing and the loss of jobs in supporting industries.
- It's *because* the already-reduced workforce and extremes in climate have placed a strain on the supply chain of services, food, and necessities that it makes sense to expect temporary disruptions in their availability.

It's because these extreme conditions, and others, are converging in our lifetime that the choice to create a resilient community is also the turning point from simply surviving change to thriving *through* the change. Just as we've seen with the turning points described previously, we now have two possible ways to deal with the reality of a shifting world that has unexpectedly arrived on our doorstep. We can choose either to:

1. Discount the facts that tell us the world has changed, and that we need to think and live differently, leaving ourselves and our families vulnerable to the new conditions.

or

2. Be honest with ourselves about the volatility that comes from the convergence of extremes, and learn to adapt our thinking and ways of life to minimize the negative impacts of the change.

With both choices, resilience plays a powerful role. In the first choice, we find a way to become resilient after the fact—after the crises of the superstorms, back-to-back tornadoes, record-setting floods and droughts, and the seemingly endless wildfires catch us surprised and unprepared. In the second choice, we can live resiliently, in a way that makes room for such changes in our lives.

Our answer to a single question makes all the difference in our experience. It changes the way we've lived and the way we've been taught to think about ourselves and our security. It's also the foundation for developing a new way of living. That question is: *In our time of extremes, what can we do to make our lives better?*

By the year 2050, only 36 years from the initial publication of this book, it's estimated that 75 percent of the world's population will be living in urban environments and large cities. Fifty percent does already. As the factors that contribute to our time of extremes continue to unfold, a shift in the way we build our cities and live our lives will, by necessity, be a part of that shift. When we take these factors into consideration, the conclusion is clear: adapting our lives to meet the uncertainties of a world of extremes is like packing what we need as we begin a journey to a place we've never been.

Just as it makes sense to begin any journey with the things necessary to maintain our daily routines, community resilience in our time of extremes makes good sense. A growing number of community leaders are recognizing this fact and beginning to act accordingly.

One of the innovative projects that has emerged from leaders recognizing our time of extremes is the 100 Resilient Cities Centennial Challenge, an opportunity to build proven strategies of resilience into 100 cities, using projects that will be selected through a nomination process ending in 2015. The stated goal of the challenge is "making people, communities and systems better prepared to withstand catastrophic events—both natural and man-made—and able to bounce back more quickly and emerge stronger from these shocks and stresses."[27]

Additional projects to create resilience on the larger scale of cities and beyond include Philadelphia's Reinventing Older Communities conferences[28], the San Francisco Planning and Urban Research Association (SPUR) project The Resilient City[29], and the Municipal Art Society of New York's Resilience Agenda.[30]

The transformation of societies, cultures, and living that has been envisioned by so many people for such a long time will come about only in response to a need that is shared across the board. From urban families and mom-and-pop businesses, to the home offices of global corporations, research institutions, and universities, we all need a society that works for us. The building of resilient communities on the scale of cities is an opportunity for just such a transformation. This is where the ideas of resilient community and the principles described in books like David Gershon's *Social Change 2.0,* Duane Elgin's *Voluntary Simplicity,* Lester Brown's *Plan B* series, Edmund Bourne's *Global Shift,* and others (see Resources) can become invaluable road maps on our journey of transformation.

CHAPTER SIX

Getting Serious about a World Transformed:

Real Solutions in the Real World

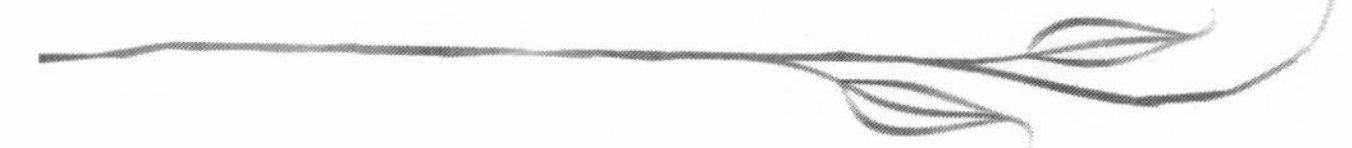

"Transformation in the world happens when people are healed and start investing in other people."

— Michael W. Smith (1957–), American musician

On October 5, 2007, one of the great visionaries of our time, Stanislav Grof, M.D., gave his acceptance speech for the prestigious VIZE (VISION) 97 Award. Each year, the foundation established by Dagmar and Václav Havel, the former first lady and president of the Czech Republic, presents this award in recognition of "ground-breaking prototypes with the potential to bring meaningful change to the future."[1] The magnitude of Grof's pioneering work in social transformation was summed up in the closing sentences of his speech:

> One of the most remarkable consequences of various forms of transpersonal experience is the spontaneous emergence and development of genuine humanitarian and ecological interests, and the need to take part in activities aimed at peaceful coexistence and well-being of humanity.[2]

Grof described why such a fundamental shift in the way we think of ourselves is so vital by saying, "It seems obvious that transformation of this kind could significantly increase our chances of survival if it could occur on a sufficiently large scale."[3]

The kind of shift that Grof is talking about is precisely where the journey described at the beginning of this book is leading us. It's the convergence point where the crisis in thinking, the extremes of the world, and the principles of resilience all come together as one big turning point on a global scale. This is the sign of a world transformed. The possibilities of such a world could take us in any number of directions. For the purposes of this book, I've chosen to approach this topic in a way that takes into account both the shift that's possible on the global level, as well as the things we can do personally to create positive transformation in our everyday lives.

For ease of reading, I've divided this chapter into two sections:

Section One: Transformation in the Real World identifies three scenarios of transformation that are possible, which one I believe is the most probable for us today, and the most likely ways in which we'll see the transformation show up in our lives in the short term, as well as the long term.

Section Two: Visions of Our Future explores two very different perspectives on leading transformed lives in a transformed world. One perspective comes from a grassroots level. This includes comments from individuals who describe the changes that are important to them. The second perspective comes from the insights of academic scholars and think tanks contributing to the visionary blueprints of our future. Whether we're talking about the future of next week or that of the next generation, the key is that whatever becomes of our world and our lives, the transformation begins with us.

SECTION ONE: TRANSFORMATION IN THE REAL WORLD

As we've seen in the previous chapters, there appear to be as many variations of what the world of our future can look like as there are people working to make it happen. Barring any unforeseen, or "black swan," events that could change everything we think we know about our future, a groundswell of innovative trends today is paving the way for a world transformed. So while we're definitely on the road of change, the big question is: *How will it come about?*

Three Scenarios of Transformation

When it comes to transformation, both personal and global, there are three basic scenarios that appear to be within the realm of possibilities. For our purposes, let's give them names that best identify these circumstances. The first possibility we'll call a *catastrophic transformation,* the second a *planned reset,* and the third an *evolutionary transformation.* While there are various combinations of these scenarios, the idea is that one is unplanned and happens abruptly, one is planned and still happens abruptly, and the last is also planned but happens gradually over a period of time. In the following subsections, I'll expand briefly on each scenario.

Scenario 1: A Catastrophic Transformation

I'm surprised by how many people envision, and even advocate, the sudden collapse of the world as we know it today as the best way to bring a radical shift in thinking and living to our lives. In this scenario, for any of a number of reasons, the transformation happens when the world as we know it abruptly comes to a screeching halt. Because our familiar ways of life would suddenly end, it's the kind of change that could not be ignored. Everyone would be involved, and for many people, such a sudden and radical shift would be nothing less than terrifying.

When I hear respected teachers and scholars talking about this kind of change, it always reminds me of the 1951 classic science-fiction film *The Day the Earth Stood Still,* which portrays an event so big that it commands everyone's attention (in the movie, it's a spaceship that brings a warning of destruction if the violence on Earth is allowed to expand to other worlds). In a scenario of catastrophic transformation, the world recovers from whatever the catastrophe is and begins to rebuild. The old systems that are corrupt and broken are replaced with new, life-affirming, and sustainable ones that work.

The situation that creates the sudden halt might be an apocalyptic event such as a global war, a pandemic disease, or the collapse of the world economy. In this scenario, it's the big event that makes way for the transformation and a new way of thinking.

I'm mentioning this scenario because it's one that's often talked about. When it is, people often ask, "Why not bring about the change in this way?" The implication is that a catastrophe might be a good opportunity to create change. My personal belief is that we don't need such a catastrophe to trigger big change. It would cause unnecessary hurt and undue hardship on the people of the world who are the most vulnerable and least prepared to manage such an abrupt shift. These people rely each day upon timely delivery systems for food, fuel, and the necessities of life.

We've already seen what can happen when supply chains are disrupted even briefly during times of natural disasters. With the wisdom and technology available to us in the 21st century, I believe we can transform our world without a catastrophe and the suffering that would come with it!

Scenario 2: A Planned Reset

Another possibility for an abrupt shift on both a personal and a global basis is "pushing the RESET button." In this scenario, the leaders of the world recognize at the highest levels that the very foundation of our global civilization is no longer sustainable. They recognize the approaching "zero hour," wherein the world's vital systems collapse under their own weight. This could include things such as the unsustainable burden of the global debt and the devastating effect it's having on the world's currencies, the destruction of global industry due to the unsustainable rise in the cost of energy, or the catastrophic levels of unemployment that have led to levels of welfare unsustainable for the world's economy.

A planned reset would mean that by agreement, on a predetermined day, the world's industries and commerce would temporarily stop and then rebuilding would begin. This is where things would get interesting, as governments and nations would have to work together to put a new, sustainable infrastructure into place. One of the ways this could happen is for each nation to employ every man and woman who wants a job as members of a global workforce that contributes to, for example, the retooling for the new industries and the building of new power grids and transportation systems based upon clean energy and the sustainable use of land and resources. When the new systems were in place, the switch for them would be turned to the "on" position and we would begin anew.

While my description here may be lacking in specifics, you get the idea. In a planned reset, allowances are made for debt, income, energy, and the essentials of everyday life while the rebuilding is happening. The thinking here is that the one-time cost of the reset, and the robust economy that would follow it, would more than offset the present-day skyrocketing costs of living and accumulating debt. While this option certainly sounds appealing in some respects, realistically the deep divisions between political parties, religions, cultures, and nations today make the cooperation needed for such a reset unlikely, at least for now.

Scenario 3: An Evolutionary Transformation

In light of the extreme nature of the previous scenarios, I believe that this third possibility is probably the one that we'll be most likely to see in our lifetimes, as well as being the healthiest of the options. In this scenario, as the unsustainable systems of the past strain, buckle, and break, they're replaced gradually with new systems that ultimately lead to the kind of future we all know is possible.

What sets this scenario apart from the previous ones is that the change is incremental. So while the complete transformation may take longer to appear in our lives, each of the steps to get to the transformation can happen quickly. Just as the temperature had to rise gradually before the last degree increase could trigger the boiling of our pot of water in Chapter 3, the gradual impact of peak oil upon our world, the role of increasing debt in our lives, and the growing awareness of just how fragile the world's supply chains of goods and services can be are all stepping-stones to the turning point of transformation. The big difference in an evolutionary scenario is that the gradual changes give us, our families, our communities, and our leaders the time to recognize the need for change, rather than reacting to an abrupt shift where the thinking is more about how to fix what's broken.

A Template for Change

The pioneering biologist E. O. Wilson once said, "It's obvious that the key problem facing humanity in the coming century is how to bring a better quality of life for eight billion or more people without wrecking the environment entirely in the attempt."[4] I believe there's a lot of truth to this statement, especially when it comes to the visions we hold of our future. When we think about what we'd like to see as our future, it's important to acknowledge what we've already tried in the past, and to look at what worked and what didn't so we can build the lessons of our experience into our future.

With these ideas in mind, let's compare how we get our needs met today with how we imagine getting our needs met in the future. What kind of thinking is involved?

In the following summary, the column to the left, labeled "The Need," identifies the vital needs that define the way our communities, cities, and nations function today. The center column, labeled "In the World Today," identifies the way those needs are met in the world as it is. The column on the right, labeled "The World Transformed," identifies how those needs will be met in our vision of a world transformed.

Comparison of Community Needs

The Need	In the World Today	In the World Transformed
Core values	Material wealth	Quality of life
Organization	Centralized/top down	Decentralized/ bottom up

This summary contrasts the two key elements that determine how information, ideas, and policies flow in communities of any size. These elements are *core values* and *organization*. So let's examine these needs more closely, beginning with the need for core values.

Core Values

Previously, we noted the need to identify a *common vision,* the shared idea that holds any community together. In the example of my mountain community, it was the rugged beauty of the wilderness that originally drew a group of diverse laborers, farmers, artists, and visionaries to the valley that became our home, and it was the threat of losing that beauty through development that brought us together to protect it. The values that define any community, from a mountain neighborhood to an entire nation, are the glue that holds them together through thick and thin—in the good times and in the times that are more difficult.

For much of the modern world, core values have been based, to one degree or another, around the idea of wealth and expressed in terms of the acquisition, storage, and protection of money. Without a doubt, money is important, and our financial systems are a reality that we must all accept in order to participate in the present-day world. What I'm suggesting here is that the meaning we give to money will change in a transformed world. It will no longer be the reason why we work, and accumulating it will no longer be the goal of our dreams in life.

For a core value to be sustainable for a local community, or for our global community, it must be based upon a principle that works for everyone and that's reflected in everyone's lives. For this reason, the core value of a transformed world will become the quality of life for our global family. While the indicators that tell us about the quality of life could fill a book, they must include honoring our relationship with the newly discovered biosphere boundaries that make life on Earth possible.

In 2009, the prestigious science journal *Nature* published a feature that provided a first step and the reasons for shifting the way we think of the natural systems that keep us alive here on Earth. The report drew from a study authored by Johan Rockström, professor of environmental science at Stockholm University and the executive director of the Stockholm Resilience Centre in Sweden, and his colleagues.[5] Providing a strong case for a much more integrated, almost holistic view of Earth's life-giving systems, it clearly shows, from a scientific point of view, what so many people have felt intuitively about nature and how natural systems work together to maintain the delicate balance of conditions for life.

While there are hundreds of science-based reports published each year documenting the damage that industry and our demand for natural resources has done to the planet, I'm mentioning the *Nature* report here for a specific reason. It carries us beyond simply knowing about the frightening statistics of destruction. What makes this report so meaningful is that it offers a powerful, new perspective identifying the harmony that must be protected among the systems that make up the bigger picture. So rather than focusing on a single facet such as greenhouse gases and global warming, for example—both of which are already acknowledged as vital parts of the equation—the report states that we must think *all* of the planetary systems.

In summary, these systems are identified as climate change, land use, biodiversity, freshwater use, the phosphorus cycle, the nitrogen cycle, ozone depletion, and ocean acidification. It's the combined effect of these eight vital systems—the climate; the land, freshwater, and oceans; biodiversity; the phosphorus and nitrogen cycles; and the ozone—*working together* that provides what the researchers call the *safe operating space* that supports us and life in our world.

Rockström and his team state that this bigger picture is vital if we: (1) are to understand the complete story; and (2) hope to have meaningful information to adapt to the changes that are present and those that are inevitable, and to prevent those that are still on the horizon.

The shift from a core value of materialism to a core value of quality of life will need to reflect this discovery of Earth's safe zone and these eight planetary boundaries.

Organization

The neighborhoods and communities that make up much of the modern world are governed by rules based upon the same kind of organization that we see in most corporations and governments. They employ a top-down approach to getting things done, and while top-down may work for a business or a corporation, it has its disadvantages when it comes to communities. The problem is that when there's diversity in a community that's spread across different time zones, climates, geography, lifestyles, and culture, such as we see in the United States, for example, it's rare that one solution created half a continent away can effectively meet the needs of those living in communities where the conditions are much different.

This reality is at the core of many of the divisions that have developed in nations undergoing large-scale change. In a transformed world, the ability of local communities to make the choices that are best for them will be the key to successful solutions and national unity.

Top-down vs. Decentralized

The Need	In the World Today	In the World Transformed
Food	Globally supplied/ corporate owned	Locally supplied/privately owned/seasonal
Energy source	Centralized/distributed	Local/based on renewables
Social participation	People feel powerless/apathy	People feel excited to participate
Innovation	Ideas concentrated, come from the top	Ideas diversified, come from the bottom

Food and Energy

Even with the diversity shown in today's neighborhood communities, there are needs shared by all. Among these are food; energy; and an economy that provides a way to share, purchase, and exchange goods and services. But while every community shares these needs, how they're met is where the difference between top-down and bottom-up organizations is felt.

Food

We've looked at very clear examples of how the globalization of markets, such as tuna and disposable paper products, can devastate local resources through overexploitation and the absence of sound management. Clearly when we rely upon global markets for our food, we support the depletion of the limited local resources that make these goods possible. There's another factor that comes into play with global markets as well. It's the huge carbon footprint that accompanies globalization. For example, when we find blueberries, a warm-weather crop, in our local North American supermarkets in the middle of December, it's because the berries have been grown and shipped from another place where the seasonal climate is the reverse of ours, such as South America.

The crop is possible because irrigation systems, powered by electricity from fossil fuels, have been used to raise greater numbers of blueberries to meet the global demand. The quick harvest of these huge crops is accomplished by farm equipment, which also runs on fossil fuels, in place of local laborers harvesting smaller fields by hand. The produce is washed using large amounts of water that's pumped using electricity produced by fossil fuels. The berries are packaged and shipped to North American cities using large commercial planes that burn fossil fuels, and then transported to local markets using commercial trucks that also burn fossil fuels. So while the growing of the berries has benefited South American communities by creating jobs, we have to ask if the joy of having blueberries in the winter is worth the environmental cost that makes it possible.

Consuming locally grown produce changes all of this. In our transformed world, communities will rely upon locally grown produce and adjust to the seasonal norms of their locations. The advantages are clear, and we know they're real because they're already apparent. When we eat locally grown vegetables, for example, we know the food we have on our table is fresh because it's been grown only minutes from where we're eating it. We also know that the money we pay for the food is supporting local jobs and is staying in the local community. And we know that the food is healthy, because most likely it's been grown from healthy seeds, in an organic and non-GMO environment, and in soil that's rich with natural minerals.

Examples of the benefits of this kind of thinking—"Eat only locally grown, organic food"—in my own community included avoiding regional health scares such as the *E. coli* outbreak from tainted spinach in 2007, the salmonella outbreak from tainted tomatoes in 2008, and the listeria outbreak from tainted melons in 2011, among others. I enjoyed eating worry-free salads and produce in the neighborhood cafés of Santa Fe, New Mexico, during each of these health scares because the businesses were already supporting what has been called farm-to-table produce. This is produce that's planted, grown, and harvested within close proximity of the places where it's prepared and served. The notation of "farm to table" on restaurant menus is becoming more common in many lifestyle-conscious cities throughout the world.

Energy

Just the way that a bottom-up approach allows local communities to determine the sources of food that best fit their needs, the same is true for energy. While centralized, powerful, and reliable energy sources may be good to run the hospitals, schools, high-rise office buildings, and apartments in some big cities, there are places where local sources can supply, and in some cases replace, the large centralized systems. America's Desert Southwest is a perfect example of what I mean.

The Four Corners area of Arizona, Colorado, New Mexico, and Utah is well known for the duration and quality of sunlight that it receives nearly every day of the year. Albuquerque, the largest city in New Mexico, for example, experiences an average of 278 days per year of sunshine, and some of the smaller communities in valleys in the northern part of the state receive an average of 300 sunny days each year. In places like these, it makes perfect sense to use solar energy to supply homes, offices, and small businesses with the electricity they need during the daylight hours that they typically operate.

In the same region, there are other supplemental forms of power generation that can be tapped as well. In addition to the sunlight of Four Corners, its weather patterns provide conditions that make wind energy a viable alternative to fossil fuels.

The good news regarding wind energy is that it's not limited to a particular time of day. It works day and night and in all kinds of weather, just as long as there's wind. And it doesn't take a lot of wind for the system to work. Commercial turbines are about 266 feet high, placing them above the trees and buildings in the zone where wind is more constant. The blades are designed to move easily, even when the wind is only blowing lightly. The Nine Canyon Wind Project in Washington State, for example, is made of 49 turbines, and while the optimal wind speed is about 30 miles per hour, these will begin producing electricity with winds speeds as low as 8 mph. There are times when faster isn't always better, and in this case, the turbines will actually shut themselves down when the wind reaches speeds of 56 mph or greater.

From the way we produce our food to where our energy comes from, in a transformed world the key to meeting our needs is that decisions are made locally. One of the basic tenets of the Berkana model for community resilience, described in Chapter 5, is acknowledging that the wisdom to address the community's needs already exists within the community itself. When it comes to decisions about food, energy, and jobs, the advantages of local thinking are clear. With respect to implementing local changes within the larger context of global transformation, the shift is already well under way, as the Nine Canyon Wind Project and many others illustrate.

Social Glue: Innovation and Participation

For any community, the factors of *social glue, innovation,* and *participation* seem to go hand in hand. Whether the community consists of a blood-related family under the same roof or a global community connected through Facebook or weekly blogs on the Internet, the principle that holds the members together is the same: we need to feel needed.

In a successful community, each member feels that he or she: (1) plays an important part in the processes at hand, and (2) has something to contribute that the community needs and wants. When these factors are present, everyone feels excited to participate and more willing to contribute time, support, and ideas. I witnessed these principles in action firsthand in my mountain community that I described in Chapter 5. I can say without reservation that they really work.

The ground rules of our 45-member community allowed each person to have a voice and chime in with opinions, options, and possibilities when it came to our open discussions. Because we live in land surrounded by Native American history, we elected to use an indigenous tradition to ensure that each of us had an equal opportunity to speak: a *talking stick.* The idea is simple. As it's passed around the room, whoever holds the talking stick has the floor and the right to speak, for an agreed-upon period of time, while all others listen.

Our talking stick was one that came into our community circle quickly and unexpectedly as a member stood up, walked out the door of the firehouse where our meeting was being held, and returned with the first piece of a tree branch that he found on the ground. That branch remained at our meeting place, and we used it during every meeting for the better part of the summer. And during that summer each member of our community became a necessary and integral voice in finding the decisions that worked for everyone.

Section Two: Visions of Our Future

When I think back to the television programs that were available to my family in the 1960s, I'm amazed by how few there were. There were no cable and satellite stations at the time. Networks like CNN, Fox, and BBC America didn't exist. My only view into the world beyond my neighborhood was through the eyes of the three major networks: ABC, NBC, and CBS. Apart from the six o'clock evening news that fascinated me each day, my favorite programs were those based upon science-fiction themes and the future of our world. I scheduled my swimming lessons, music classes, and homework around the next installment of *Star Trek, Lost in Space,* and even futuristic cartoons such as *The Jetsons.*

Through these programs, and others like them, we were given a visionary glimpse into what the world *could* look like only a few decades into our future. And the visions were powerful. In addition to time travel, space exploration, and magnetic cars with no wheels that move at lightning speeds, there was a common theme that was shown throughout these programs. In the futures that were portrayed, for the most part the world was at peace and everyone seemed happy. People had all the food they needed from what appeared to be an endless supply of automated gardens. There were robots to do mundane tasks so humans were free to do the creative, inventive, and visionary kinds of things that brought joy to their lives.

Fifty years later, the world that George Jetson, his wife, Jane; their children, Judy and Elroy; and their dog, Astro, enjoyed has yet to arrive. For the time being, we appear to be stuck in alternating cycles of war and peace, progress and regress, and abundance and poverty, in a world polarized between those who "have" and those who don't. Both the real-world statistics and our gut instincts tell us that something's wrong. We know that the polarized world of today simply can't last. Something's gotta give. Something *is* giving. And it's hard to miss it.

The symptoms of our unsustainably divided world are more than just a temporary deviation from the norm. They're the proverbial "canary in the coal mine" showing us where our attention is required and what needs to happen as the thinking of the past no longer fits into the world of the present. The turmoil of riots in Egypt's Tahrir Square during the Arab Spring of 2012 and again in 2013, the G20 protests in the American city of Pittsburgh in 2009, the groundswell of people risking their lives to cross treacherous oceans in fragile rafts and hike across hostile desert borders in the deadly summer heat in search of a better life . . . are all stops along the journey that began this book. The world itself is telling us that we're on our way to another world. What's important now is to make certain that the world we're going to is better than the one we leave behind.

The most obvious question we could ask ourselves at this point in our journey is also the most difficult one to answer: *What does a better world look like?* Interestingly, it's common to find that people are at a loss when it comes to answering this simple question.

What Does a Better World Look Like?

During a weekend seminar I led in autumn 2012, I opened the topic of "Visions of Our Future" as a point of discussion on the last day. Throughout the program, the participants had already told me that they believed the current chaos of our world is the prelude to a better world of the future. They felt that the realities of peak oil, broken economies, and the disparity of the world's wealth were the tipping points for big change. With their ideas in mind, I asked the next logical question: "Assuming that you're all correct," I said, "what does a better world look like?"

To my amazement, as well as that of most people in the program, there were nearly as many visions for what our future could look like as there were people in the room. My staff had set up two microphones on stands near the stage for participants who wanted to step up and share their visions. The lines were long, and we listened to each and every vision.

Throughout the sharing, the audience and I learned something about the world that people hope for. Each vision of the future was being offered through the eyes of the hurt experienced by the person sharing. For example, the teachers in the room envisioned a world with a better system of education where the teachers are respected for their contribution to our society and all people have similar opportunities to learn. The scientists in the room saw a future where they're allowed to apply the technology that already exists in the laboratory to ease the suffering in the world when it comes to issues of food and energy. The nurses, doctors, and health-care practitioners envisioned a world where everyone receives the full benefit of today's technology to give them the best chance for a long and healthy life.

While there was a general agreement on the need for a sustainable, clean, green, and equitable world, there was a definite *lack* of consensus regarding what such a world actually looks like and how to get there. As I listened to the heartfelt and passionate visions for their future that the participants shared, I remember thinking that I was witnessing a microcosm, in our conference ballroom, of what we're experiencing as a world while we move through our time of extremes. I also remember thinking that if a room with 1,000 people who've consciously dedicated a weekend of their lives to such a discussion can't agree on a common vision, then how can we expect a planet of 7 billion people with diverse backgrounds, religions, and needs to do so?

While we're quick to say we *want* a better world and we *want* changes to happen, where do we begin? How do we initiate the kind of changes each day that will shift the way we think and live?

Following are two reports from high-level, highly respected organizations that give us a perspective on how we may answer these questions. I have intentionally shared the work from large global organizations to show just how far the thinking along these lines has come. One is through the eyes of the academic world, scholars, think tanks, and futurists. The other is through the people who see the need for change. When we marry big-picture work with the types of grassroots changes that are being implemented by organizations such as the Post Carbon Institute, the Bioneers, Transition US, and others, we get an idea of how widespread the vision for a big change in our lives has become. I'm sharing these perspectives as the common ground for a place to begin.

The Global Trends Report

In addition to the futuristic thinking of individuals described in earlier chapters, entire organizations have been formed to draw upon the vast resources of many experts to offer a peek into the possibilities of our future. In this section I'll shared details about two of those organizations to flesh out the vision of what a transformed world may look like. From the broad spectrum of all of these, we can then identify the realistic trends and futuristic possibilities for our world transformed.

Among the visionary organizations attempting to gain insights into our future is the U.S. National Intelligence Council (NIC), formed in 1979. The purpose of NIC is multifold. One of the key functions of the organization is to provide each incoming American President a report of global scenarios and trends to help with the decisions that will be made during his or her term. The study is called the *Global Trends Report.*

Compiling the research, data, and opinions of hundreds of experts from nongovernmental sources, as well as from governmental organizations, universities, and think tanks, the report gives the President a powerful insight into the probable course of world events for 15 years, starting from the time of the election. It's delivered to the President-elect's desk sometime between the day of the election and the inauguration.

The *Global Trends 2015* report, released in the year 2000, was foundational to the Global Trends series because it identified key factors the experts believed would continue to be triggers of change for years to come.[6] These factors offer a global perspective for our discussion of what a world transformed may look like. The seven factors identified in this report are:

1. Demographics
2. Natural resources and environment
3. Science and technology
4. The global economy
5. National and international governance

6. Future conflict
7. The role of the United States in the future of the world

The *Global Trends Report* is just that, big-picture ideas of future scenarios based upon big events happening at the time the reports are compiled. These include studies of things like globalization and where it's headed, the role of China and India in the global economy, how terrorism may impact the way nations work together, how climate change affects our lives, and much more. The point is: these are the ideas of experts from a number of fields, across a number of disciplines, dealing with the world as they see it and the future that they see from their perspective. It's important to understand these ideas because, realistically, our transformed world will probably be a mix of their concerns being addressed through new and innovative solutions that few people are even considering today.

The United Nations My World Report

In December 2012, the United Nations and its partners launched a new program that may become a first step toward answering the question of what a transformed world looks like to everyday people. While the UN has many irons in many fires, and some have become the source of tremendous controversy, the organization still stands as the single most recognized opportunity for large-scale cooperation and change on a global basis. For this reason, I'm sharing the elements of a new program they've put into place as an opening to our discussion. In other words, it's a place to begin, rather than a final answer to the question.

The UN program is the first of its kind. Named *My World,* it's a well-designed and well-organized survey to allow "people across the world to tell the United Nations, global leaders—and in particular the Secretary General's High-Level Panel—the most important issues they would like the post-2015 agenda to address."[7] The UN survey was officially launched in January 2013 and is currently available online at www.myworld2015.org, as well as in a hard-copy format. So everyone in the world can participate, the website is translated into the six official United Nations languages: Arabic, Chinese, English, French, Russian, and Spanish.

The stated purpose of the survey is to gather the ideas from as many people as possible between the time of the launch in 2013 and its close in 2015, when the UN convenes to follow up on the Year 2000 Millennium Development Goals. The survey consists of 16 options. From these possibilities, participants are asked to check only the six options of change that would make the biggest difference in their own lives personally and those of their families.

My World

United Nations Survey Answers for a Better World

- Better job opportunities
- Support for people who can't work
- A good education
- Better health care
- Affordable and nutritious food
- Phone and Internet access
- Better transport and roads
- Access to clean water and sanitation
- Reliable energy at home
- Action taken on climate change
- Protecting forests, rivers, and oceans
- Equality between men and women
- Protection against crime and violence
- Political freedom
- An honest and responsive government
- Freedom from discrimination and persecution

Along with capturing information that includes gender, age, country, and educational level, the goal of *My World* is to gain input from the greatest cross section of the global population possible. The results are constantly compiled and updated on an ongoing basis. I'm mentioning the survey here as a first step in understanding just what we, as a global family, really mean when we say that we "want a better world."

My World Results

While the *My World* survey is new and will continue until 2015, the results so far show a number of interesting, and possibly telling, trends that are worth mentioning here. The survey data is available in real time at the website, where it is broken down into categories that include male; female; and three age ranges identified as "less than 34," "35 to 54," and "over 55." As of this writing in summer 2013, there appears to be a high level of agreement for both men and women under 34 regarding their priorities.

On a global basis, without question, the top-listed priority is:

1. A good education

For the same age-group, both men and women selected the following categories in descending order of significance in their lives. They want:

2. Better health care
3. An honest and responsive government
4. Better job opportunities
5. Access to clean water
6. Affordable and nutritious food
7. Protection against crime and violence

While there is near-unanimous agreement on the priorities that include these seven parameters, beyond this point the ideas become mixed with no clear trends evident. For example, men tend to see the category of *Better transport and roads* as the eighth level of priority. This is not surprising when we consider that it's the men who are generally using the roads more often to provide goods for themselves and their families. For women, the next level of priority becomes *Equality between men and women.* This is also not surprising, as there is a near-universal struggle in every nation of the world regarding women's rights. Not only do these issues pertain to economic equality, but also to protection from victimization and abuse during the vulnerable years of raising children.

Also not surprising is what the survey shows in terms of priorities for the next age range, the 35–54 group. It's at this age boundary that the *Better health care* category does a flip-flop with *A good education* as the number one priority. It's no surprise, for the obvious reason that this age reflects a greater need and dependency on the health-care system, as age-related health conditions begin to show up in their lives.

To be clear at this point, I'm not suggesting that the future portrayed by the UN's *My World 2015;* the NIC's *Global Trends;* Lester Brown's *Plan B* series; or any of the other books, projects, or ideas I've mentioned is *the answer* to a transformed world. Each of them is a microcosm of the world, precisely like the microcosm I see in my seminars, and what we all see every day of our lives.

There are many different ideas of what a better world looks like—probably as many as there are people in the world itself! I'm sharing them at this point to ground our view of the reality of so many different ideas and to lay the foundation of facts for where we go next. It's from this point that we'll have the information to bring in new possibilities—new turning points—with the potential to lead to new outcomes and, perhaps, very different worlds than those described in the reports.

Cuba, 1990: An Example of a Real-World Turning Point

While think tanks and visionary scholars speculate on how a future of broken economies, the loss of corporate agriculture, and the peak-oil scenarios *might* play out, history gives us a real-world example that takes the guesswork out of the equation. Following the collapse of the former Soviet Union in the 1990s after the Cold War, Cuba became a prime candidate for the benefits of community resilience. What happened for Cuba in the early '90s is difficult to imagine. But because *it did happen* in our lifetimes, it provides a living laboratory that shows us the power of a turning point of resilience.

For a number of reasons, including the continuing U.S. trade embargo upon the island nation, during the Cold War years Cuba's livelihood depended heavily upon the imports, exports, oil, and support of the former Soviet Union. When the U.S.S.R. disbanded, Cuba's imports fell dramatically. The post–Cold War economy was not only devastating for the people of Russia, it was even worse for Cuba because of its geographic and political isolation.

Suddenly Cuba lost 80 percent of its export and import markets. Seemingly overnight, the gross domestic product dropped by 34 percent. Its oil-fed system of transportation and agriculture screeched to a halt. For a period of time, it could take three hours to catch a bus, and food consumption was reduced to as little as one-fifth of what it was before everything changed. The nation's oil-fed power system could no longer produce electricity, and there were rolling blackouts that lasted for much of the day. Without electricity, the cities were dark, businesses closed, restaurants stopped serving food, and the Cuban economy went into a tailspin. During this time, the ripple effect of the sudden loss of oil—effectively an artificial post-peak-oil scenario—became painfully clear.

Cuba doesn't produce its own oil. It relies on imports. And when they stopped, there was no substitute fuel, because the nation hadn't developed one. The conditions became dangerous. The agriculture that Cubans had depended upon was possible only because of the oil that had made it possible to grow, irrigate, and harvest a lot of food quickly. Without the oil, agriculture declined and people needed food. The combination of the collapse of agriculture, the loss of imported oil, and no foreign markets created the perfect storm that is often referred to in Cuba today as the *Special Period in Time of Peace,* or simply the Special Period. It was during this time that the Cuban people made the decision to *adapt to the extremes* they faced. What happened next will sound like it's taken from the highlights of this book. I'm sharing it here as an example of, and a testament to, the power of communities to create local solutions that work for them in a healthy and sustainable way.

In cities throughout Cuba, including the capital of Havana (population approximately 2.1 million), the residents formed neighborhood communities. I'm not suggesting that they went through all of the steps identified in this book or that they followed a formal protocol of assigning responsibilities or a structure of authority. What I am saying is that they recognized the need to come together as a community to address a problem that they all shared. At the time, it was survival that motivated them: the communities needed to eat, and this became the driving value of their community vision.

One of the first things they did was to identify public lands that were not being used. As communities, they cleaned up the land and began to plant inner-city gardens. During this time Australian experts came to Cuba and demonstrated the value of permaculture farming under such conditions. Permaculture is a form of ecological design that models self-sustained gardens from natural ecosystems. Carmen López, the director of one of the permaculture centers, described the effect of the Australians' teaching: "With this demonstration, neighbors began to see the possibilities of what they can do on their rooftops and their patios."[8]

The gardens were successful. The communities began to produce enough food not only to feed themselves, but also people in other communities. Today, the gardens continue. They're now organic and have made the neighborhoods and communities they serve so economically sustainable that their presence has had an effect upon the policies of the government itself.

Seeing the value in the resilient response of the people to the conditions they faced, the Cuban government has changed its motto from "Socialism or Death" to "A Better World Is Possible."[9] They've also taken the steps toward more *bottom-up* government by shifting decision making down to the community level, rather than enforcing policies that are made at a higher level from a location that is less in touch with the local issues. In this way, government officials are encouraging greater community participation and the people feel that they have a voice in their lives, their communities, and their future.

The success of Cuba's response is not limited to agriculture alone. The same principles of community resilience and local solutions that kept people alive during the Special Time have now been applied to other areas of Cuban life, including energy, education, and health care.

Finding the Turning Point

One key to an evolutionary transformation for today's world is to find a pivot point—the turning point of change—where a shift in a community's thinking triggers life-affirming change *before* the tipping point of collapse and suffering. Such a turning point for Cuba would have minimized the suffering from the loss of oil imports, because the resilience principle of spare capacity would have already led the nation to find alternative fuel sources. The fact that the Cuban people adapted after the fact is a testament to the power of resilient thinking and the fact that it's never too late to implement the changes that get us there.

When we consider the potential of discovering such a turning point for the world today—before we reach the global tipping points of peak oil and imploding economies—the implications are immense. In the following section I'll identify just such a point.

During the years I worked for Fortune 500 corporations, I was trained in crisis management and as a problem solver. So it's very natural for me now to think of our time of extremes from this point of view. When I look at the convergence of big shifts in our world today, it definitely appears that we're in a time of crisis. Just as corporate projects are often over budget and looking for eleventh-hour solutions, the problems we face have become more expensive to address, and, especially in the case of greenhouse emissions, we're now *beyond* the eleventh hour. But as I mentioned before, the fact that the crisis—or in our case, the multiple crises—still exists is the best news we could hope for.

Because the crises are still with us, it means that we still have the time to meet them with the turning points that lead to transformation. And because the key issues we're facing are on a global scale, it means that the scale of transformation that's possible is global as well. The key here is to find a place to begin. We need to identify a turning point issue that addresses multiple crises while meeting as many of the human needs identified in the studies and reports as possible.

Once such an issue is identified and demonstrates the benefit of resilient thinking, it will lay the foundation of trust and goodwill for the next big change, or milestone, on our journey of transformation.

So what is our turning point issue? When I look at the crises, the consequences, and the needs stated from so many different perspectives, two choices stand out beyond all others.

The first turning point is that the thinking to make resilience a priority must be in place.

Assuming that this is, in fact, the case:

The second turning point issue is energy.

The reason energy is a perfect candidate for the turning point we need now is that energy is the common denominator that touches nearly every aspect of our individual and global lives. It's a factor in each of the crises dominating the landscape of our future, including climate change, food production, and the world's economy. The source of energy that we choose to meet the needs and demands of the world directly impacts the concerns stated in the World Economic Forum's *Global Risks 2013,* the UN's *My World,* and the NIC's *Global Trends Reports,* and indirectly addresses others as well. It also lays the fertile ground for solutions of social change, a new economy, and environmental action shared almost across the board.

Clearly, energy can be the game changer that eliminates the competition and the use of war for securing limited resources, such as today's fossil fuels. *If we can get the factor of energy right this time around in the equation of transformation, the trust and goodwill created will make transforming the remaining factors, such as food and economies, much easier to accept.*

The energy that powers the world is the key to elevating each member of our global family to a higher standard of living. Just to be clear, however, this higher standard would not be measured by today's guidelines, where the accumulation of goods at the expense of limited resources is the means to a better life. Rather, it's by the sustainable and holistic standards of a transformed economy that we see the elevated standards. I invite you to reexamine the items from the *My World* survey and do so with the thought of how having a source of affordable, clean, sustainable, and abundant energy would make a difference.

How can we transform the energy equation of the world in an evolutionary way? With the understanding that Scenario 3, evolutionary transformation, is the most likely and most realistic path to our future, the following describes how the transformation of energy may unfold.

The Turning Point of Energy

When people ask me where the energy of our future will come from, I begin my answer with a question: "Are you willing to accept an honest answer based upon the reality of our world today, or are you hoping to confirm an opinion that you have already formed for yourself?"

It's a good question to ask, because there's so much misinformation about energy and our future circulating that many people are genuinely confused regarding the realities of where we're headed, what's possible, and what's likely.

Depending upon the way the first question above goes, if there's a follow-up question, it generally relates to what is often called *free energy*. Even the word *free* means different things to different people. In general, however, when this topic comes up, it's mentioned with regard to technologies that tap the immense energy potential that exists in the quantum realm.

As an engineer, I've certainly studied the theories of free energy, zero-point energy, torsion-field physics, and quantum potential throughout my adult life. I've seen what appear to be references to it on ancient temple walls, and I've heard it described in the oral traditions of indigenous elders. As a member of the Nikola Tesla Society, based in Colorado Springs in the 1980s (the home of Tesla's laboratory from 1899 to 1900), I had firsthand access to Tesla's lab notes, his working models, and his insights that might have led to the free energy, also known as *broadcast* energy, described earlier in this book.

In all honesty, while I've seen prototypes of energy devices that work in unconventional ways, I've yet to see one that genuinely runs on free energy—energy from a universal source delivered without wires or cables—and I've yet to see a technology that is something you and I would like to hinge the energy needs of our daily lives upon.

To be absolutely blunt: Is free energy possible?

Yes, I believe it is.

Is the technology available for commercial use today?

No. Not in a way that I'm personally aware of.

Will it be in the future?

Yes. The promising study of zero-point energy and torsion-field technology holds the potential to revolutionize the way we think of energy and, ultimately, the way we power our world.

Will we see it soon?

While anything is certainly possible, it's probably not going to happen before the tipping points from our time of extremes appear on the horizon. And this is precisely why we need to be honest with ourselves and embrace the turning points of energy that are available today, immediately.

Earth, Wind, and Water: Energy from the Elements

The next question I hear is generally with regard to today's alternative and renewable sources of energy. Will these be the answer to peak oil and the world's appetite for energy? The alternative and renewable energy sources that we are most familiar with today will probably not be the primary energy sources that power the world in the future. I wish that I could say they will be. Without a doubt, the energy that's available from solar, wind, wave, geothermal, and hydroelectric power are all viable sources to *supplement* the types of energy that we currently use in our homes, schools, offices, and hospitals. And there's nothing that I would like more than to say to you that these alternatives to conventional energy sources of today will be where we get our energy from tomorrow.

The reality is that: (1) the technology is far from being perfected to the point where we could even begin to think of these sources on a global scale, and (2) even if the technology were perfected today, these alternatives are designed to make use of regional conditions that support them rather than be imposed as a national or global energy policy. In other words, one solution does not fit all needs.

When it comes to the energy that we depend upon each and every day for reliable, high-quality, and continuous power in our hospital operating rooms and air-traffic control towers; the transfer of critical financial and life-support data; and the monitoring of the world's nuclear reactors, water-pumping stations, weather stations, and satellite communication systems, what alternatives remain? What will the energy resource of our transformed future look like?

My sense is that the answer is really two answers, because it depends upon when in the future we're talking about: the near-term future or the long-term future. I'm going to share the most likely candidates that will unfold as the gradual transformation described in Scenario 3 from Section One of this chapter.

In Chapter 1, we saw the peak-oil curve and the science that accurately predicted the shrinking reserves of easy-to-access high-quality crude oil. The reality of Dr. Hubbert's predictions appears to tell us that we reached the peak of the peak-oil curve in the mid-1980s. An unexpected development, however, has redefined what peak oil means in our lives. The late-20th-century discoveries of mammoth-sized fields of natural gas, and the innovations that allow the gas to be recovered, have changed the role of crude oil in our lives. While the general public is still thinking about oil as the primary source of the world's energy, the energy industry has already moved on with a very different vision.

We know that the new technology is working because, beginning in 2011 and 2012, the world's energy markets were flooded with more natural gas than the demand could deal with. As prices dropped and new storage facilities were developed, one thing became abundantly clear. Oil is becoming less of a factor in the energy equation of the world, and various forms of natural gas, including liquefied natural gas, are here to stay in our lifetimes and for the next few generations to come. The reason: the same technologies that predicted Hubbert's curve for oil tell us that the world has reserves of natural gas that can last as long as 250 years if it's used at the current rates.[10]

Is this a good thing or a bad thing? When we look at the properties of natural gas and how it can be used, within the context of today's world, it's better than the coal and oil that we use today and is a step in the right direction.

The illustration that follows is a comparison of the emissions of coal, oil, and natural gas. Because the reduction of CO_2 is a critical requirement for any new source of energy, natural gas is a good candidate.

Natural Gas vs. Coal and Oil

(pounds per billion btu of energy produced)

	GAS	OIL	COAL
Carbon Dioxide	117,000	164,000	208,000
Carbon Monoxide	40	33	208
Sulfur Dioxide	1	1,122	2,591
Particulates	7	84	2,744

Figure 6.1. A comparison of coal, oil, and natural gas, showing the advantages and disadvantages of each, including the CO_2 emissions. Source: International Energy Agency.

Natural gas burns approximately 50 percent cleaner than its counterparts of oil and coal, and is less expensive, making it more accessible to everyone. If natural gas can be extracted wisely, and if we factor in the local use of renewable sources, including solar, wind, and geothermal and hydroelectric power, where it makes sense to do so, it's possible that natural gas will be a stepping-stone to meet the world's energy needs while we develop an ultimate source of abundant and clean energy.

Big Energy with No CO_2?

If I said to you that there is a source of energy that is abundant in the earth, cannot be made into a weapon, cannot melt down in a reactor, and emits no greenhouse gases, it would sound as though we had a nearly perfect energy source. Well, what I'll describe here is not perfect, but it may be another step in our journey to the ultimate source of energy.

During the super-secret Manhattan Project of the mid-20th century, the race was on in the United States to find the mineral that could run the nation's nuclear reactors and produce by-products that could be made into weapons in the Cold War era. The wartime thinking opted for uranium with its by-product of plutonium as the mineral of choice. Since that time, uranium has continued to be the fuel source for most of the world's 430 or so reactors. While most people are generally aware that this is the case, they're also surprised to learn that another mineral was discovered that had many of the qualities of uranium as a fuel source, but without the harmful by-products. This element, *thorium,* is number 90 on the periodic table.

If we're really serious about creating large amounts of electricity, and doing so from an energy source that creates zero greenhouse gases, until we have free-energy technologies, thorium should be at the top of our list. Here's why. It works on principles that are a little different from the uranium that we're all familiar with, and those differences make it an attractive alternative.

In essence, the purpose of conventional power generators is to create the heat that drives the turbines to produce electricity. There are many ways that the heat can be created. The familiar technologies of the past include the burning of coal, oil, and natural gas. Nuclear reactors generate heat as well, and do so through a controlled chain reaction. The process generates so much heat, in fact, that separate cooling systems have to be built and maintained to help the reactors' temperatures stay within safe limits. When a reactor "melts down," or gets so hot that the shielding is destroyed, it's often because the cooling systems have failed, such as we saw with the 2011 Fukushima power-station disaster in Japan.

I'm describing these principles here, because while thorium is used in a form of reactor, it works on a principle that makes it impossible to melt down. The liquid that the fuel is made of—a thorium and fluoride salt solution—is the same liquid that cools the system. One of the interesting properties of a thorium generator is that there's a direct relationship between its ability to generate heat and its temperature, and that difference is probably not what you'd expect.

In the case of thorium salts, the warmer they become, the less ability they have to generate the heat. This means that if they were to reach a dangerous temperature, by the time they did so the reactivity would already be in a very low state. Safety plugs made of the same hardened salts that make the fuel itself would melt away, allowing the slurry to drain away into another container. In other words, the stuff that's producing the reaction *while* cooling the system would empty into a separate vessel, thereby preventing any further reaction from continuing.

From local economics to global policies, there are a number of reasons why the mainstream energy industry and the mainstream press may have been reluctant to embrace thorium as an energy source in the past. In light of its implications for climate change, low cost, and energy security, those reasons may now be less of a factor. Thorium energy is beyond theory at the present time, and a number of thorium generators have already been built and are being used successfully for research and commercial applications in different countries, including India, Germany, China, and the United States. In the U.S., there have been two thorium generators: the Indian Point facility, which was operational between 1962 and 1980, and the Elk River facility, which was operational between 1963 and 1968.

So while we need more research to hone thorium technology to meet the large-scale needs of the world, it holds the promise of a clean, abundant, and relatively safe alternative to tide us over while we engage in our search for the ultimate source of energy.[11]

Thorium Facts

- 1 ton of Thorium produces the energy of 250 tons of Uranium*
- Thorium power costs approx. $1.98/watt vs. $2.30/watt for Coal*
- 99% of Thorium fuel is consumed vs. 1% for Uranium*
- Thorium cannot 'melt down' in an emergency situation*
- Thorium produces no weapons-grade by-products*
- Thorium is over twice as abundant as Uranium
- Thorium by-products can be reused as fuel*

*When used in a Molten Salt Reactor (MSR)

Figure 6.2. Thorium is safer than conventional uranium reactor fuels. It's impossible to create a meltdown in a thorium reactor, such as we saw in the Chernobyl and Fukushima disasters. Its by-products cannot be weaponized, and it creates zero CO_2 emissions, while being inexpensive and abundant in the earth.
Source: International Energy Agency.

I believe that our civilization will ultimately perfect the technology to tap the potential of "empty" space and torsion fields to fill our energy needs. The evidence suggests that after oil, we'll probably pass through two more phases of energy production on our way to the best futuristic source. The first of these phases is the era of natural gas that weans the world from oil and coal and reduces the greenhouse emissions from each. The second phase is the combination of renewable sources and thorium reactors that provide abundant energy with no harmful greenhouse emissions.

There are many possibilities that could become global turning points in our time of extremes, including revamping national currencies and meeting new greenhouse emission standards to minimize the effects of climate change. While these and other turning points are certainly viable, the development of new energy sources not only addresses the needs of the world economy and climate standards, it's also a direct step toward raising the standard of living for all people. The added benefit of goodwill that could come from such an effort, combined with the elimination of the conflict that has come with exploiting finite energy sources in the past, makes a turning point of new energy very attractive.

Advanced Technology or Sophisticated Wisdom?

During an emotion-charged exchange that I had with a regional archaeologist working in New Mexico in the 1990s, the conversation turned toward the role of the past and what it can mean for our future. We happened to meet at one of the most intriguing archaeological sites I've ever explored, the mysterious remnants of Chaco Canyon.

Located in the Four Corners area of northwestern New Mexico, Chaco Canyon is an enigma of such significance that it's now recognized as a UNESCO World Heritage Site to ensure that the sophisticated observatory, the perfectly formed underground *kivas* (circular ceremonial chambers typical of some North American native traditions), and the 2,400 known archaeological sites are preserved for future generations. Part of the mystery of Chaco is that while some aspects of the site show an advanced knowledge that's about 1,000 years ahead of that of people in the surrounding communities, other aspects appear to be crude and primitive.

During the conversation, I suggested to the archaeologist that we may be standing on the remnants of one of the most technologically advanced civilizations to have existed in North America before the 20th century. This obviously was an idea that wasn't part of her training, and she was in no mood to entertain new theories. "If they were so advanced," she asked, "then where are the gadgets? Where are their toasters, microwave ovens, and VCRs?" It was clear to me that we had very different ideas about the meaning of an advanced civilization and what the evidence it left behind would look like.

It was also clear that we would not agree on an interpretation of the mysterious complex sprawling in front of us. I never saw the archaeologist again, and I often wonder if the newer discoveries in places like Göbekli Tepe, Turkey, which now push the date of advanced civilization into the end of the last ice age nearly 13,000 years ago, have changed the way she thinks of Chaco Canyon.

As I've mentioned in previous books, I find it so interesting that our interpretation of ancient civilizations hinges largely upon the *things* that they built. *What about the thinking that underlies what they built?* While, to the best of my knowledge, it's true that we've never found a television or VCR in the archaeological record of the American Southwest—or anywhere else, for that matter—maybe the reason why we haven't is what we're missing here. And maybe that's precisely the clue to what the future of a transformed world would look like as well.

The native peoples of America tell a story about our past that sounds more like a science-fiction story of another world. They say that a long time ago, the people of the earth lived very differently from those of today. There were fewer people to use the resources of the land. There were no wars in which people hurt one another or destroyed the land. And the people lived close to the land. They honored themselves and their relationships to one another and to the elements that gave them life. During this time, people were happy, healthy, and lived to advanced ages of hundreds of years that we can only imagine today.

Then something happened. Although the elders don't always agree on precisely what that something was, the outcome for each of the stories is the same. The people of the earth began to forget who they were. They began to forget the power they held within themselves to heal and work together. And they forgot their relationship to Mother Earth herself. They became lost, frightened, and lonely. In their loneliness, they longed for a deeper connection with the world. They began to build machines outside of themselves that could duplicate the powers they dreamed of. They built machines to enhance their senses of sight and sound that had become dull and other machines that could send healing into their bodies just the way their bodies used to create healing from within.

The elders say that the story isn't finished and that we're part of the last chapter. They say that we continue to be lost, frightened, and lonely. And until we remember who we are, we will continue to clutter our lives with the machines that mimic our greatest powers.

When I hear such stories, I feel sure the elders are describing us and our world today. With the few exceptions of isolated cultures and remote pockets of tradition that remain, our civilization certainly places its focus more on the world *around* us and less on the world *within* us.

Is it possible that when we see the remains of advanced civilizations, like those in Egypt, Peru, or Chaco Canyon, we're actually seeing the remains of a technology that's *so advanced* that they no longer needed toasters and VCRs? Maybe they outgrew the need for a cluttered and complex outer world. Maybe they knew something about themselves that gave them the *inner technology* to live in a different way, something that we've forgotten, as the elders suggest. We spend billions of dollars each year defending ourselves from disease and trying to control nature. In doing so, we have perhaps strayed further from our balance with the natural world than ever before.

The elders say that our cluttered world serves a purpose. Once we remember who we are, we will no longer need the machines and our lives will become simple again. But here's the key: our lives will become simple *because we've achieved the sophistication* that frees us from the technology. So rather than reverting to a primitive way of living, we actually become so advanced in the way that we live that our lives look simple to the casual observer.

This is what I believe the archaeologist and I were witnessing that day in Chaco Canyon. Whoever lived in that place knew of our relationship with the sun and the moon with a precision that was not even recognized again until the mid-20th century. The people living there built perfect roads that radiate for hundreds of miles in all directions and could only be recognized when modern satellite images revealed them. Clearly the people of Chaco Canyon had advanced knowledge and used it to make their lives simpler.

If this is true, then we need look no further than nature to understand who we are and what the future of a world transformed can look like.

Whatever world we bring into existence, to be successful it will have to work for everyone. And I believe this is the key to our future as a species as well. While it's possible to transform our world in such a way that the standard of living is raised for everyone (rather than elevating it for a few at the expense of many), to do so requires a choice. This choice brings us back to the unspoken crisis that was described as the "elephant in the room": the crisis in our thinking. To transform our world to reflect the possibilities that I've described requires a fundamental shift at the very core of the values that we claim as a global community. But once we replace the core value of money, for example, with the core value of quality of life and well-being, we're on our way.

Just to be clear, this is not a statement that money is the root of our problems or that it is bad in any way. Money is a means of exchange and, in all honesty, a means that will probably be with us for a long time. My comment is not about the money itself. It's about us. It's about the way we think of money, the significance we give to money, and the role that we've allowed money to play in our lives.

When we make this choice in our lives and it becomes the standard by which we measure every policy and each action, including the development of technology and the application of science, the current of change will be unstoppable. By reading of these possibilities in this book, and others, we ignite the realization of such a world.

Creating Your Turning Point

Throughout this book, I've shared elements of a lifestyle and a shift in thinking that can help us create turning points of resilience in our lives. Everyone learns differently, and it's for this reason that I've done my best to offer different perspectives that allow us to see how these ideas play out in the real world. With the information in the previous chapters still fresh in your mind, you now have everything you need to answer the question: *How do I create my own turning point of resilience?*

The following is a possible sequence of steps, a template, for doing just that.

A Template for Creating Your Personal Turning Point of Resilience

The bullet points below represent a high-level summary of steps to create resilience in your life. While this book describes these turning points with respect to the bigger changes occurring in our world, the principles of resilience are also designed to foster any kind of change in your life. Regardless of whether these changes are triggered by our world of extremes or your personal processes, these steps will guide you through the thinking to discover which actions are right for you.

Each bullet point is an invitation. It's the opportunity for you to: (1) consider your life and the way you've thought about your life in the past, and (2) decide whether or not your way of thinking still suits conditions in the world. If you find that it's time for a change, the bullets will guide you to the places in this book, as well as additional resources, that will help you in your change.

Remember, these bullet points represent proven steps, those that have created turning points for other people and communities. Because they've worked for others, you can be confident that each one can bring you closer to the thinking and living of a world transformed.

Your Lifestyle

- **Be honest with yourself.** Ask yourself if the world feels different today, now.

- **Acknowledge our time of extremes.** Identify what makes this time in your life different from your life in the past. Embrace the fact that your life and our world are changing faster than we've been prepared to accept. Pinpoint what this means for you.

- **Identify your core values.** Ask yourself what your core value system is based upon. Is your answer based upon material wealth, personal well-being, family and/or group well-being, spirituality, religion, or a combination of these values—or any other values? Your answer will give you clarity when it comes to difficult decisions regarding lifestyle and your daily life.

- **Develop personal and heart-based resilience.** By developing the strength of your inner resilience first, you will be better prepared to meet the challenges of our changing world and the needs of your loved ones who depend upon you.

- **Reread Chapter 4.**

Your Finances

- **Support the things that you believe in.** Invest your money and energy in ways that you can feel good about. This sets an example for your children and other family members, while giving you the satisfaction of participating in positive change on a global scale with your investments, as well as on a local scale with the impact they have upon your community.

- **Embrace money as a powerful tool, yet keep its role in your life in perspective.** The relationship between value and worth is changing in our lives. Explore what this means for you and use your hard-earned money and resources wisely to reflect the new economic realities.

- **Acknowledge that the meaning of money is changing.** A new economy is emerging, and the way we've thought of money in the past is changing. We've entered a time where the long-term investments of the past now carry a greater risk because of the fragile nature of the world's markets. This means that assets based in "paper," such as stock certificates, can lose their value in a matter of hours, whereas tangible assets—commodities such as energy, water, and food—will never be worth zero. This fact is your invitation to adjust your financial plans.

- **Reread Chapter 1.**

Your Politics

- **Support people and ideas that align with your values and beliefs.** In the present top-down system of government and decision making, the people we choose from our local communities to represent us are our opportunity to have a voice in the bigger picture. There are candidates out there who can be trusted to carry the message that you and your community want to be heard on a larger scale. These candidates can only work for you if you get behind their message.

- **Be informed.** Look deeply into the major issues of our time. Learn to research for yourself rather than depending upon a flyer that comes to your door or the endorsement by a newspaper or an organization for your information. Seek out sources of news and information beyond the bias of mainstream television and radio networks, web portals, and publications. Make the time required for such research a priority in your life.

- **Follow your choices.** After the elections on any level (citywide, statewide, national), make it a point to follow the results and see if your candidates continue to represent your values once they're in office. This is one place where community can be invaluable, as the time and effort for such research can be distributed throughout the community on an as-needed basis and the results disseminated at community gatherings.

Your Community

- **Gather your community.** Now is the time to gather your community—whether it's your family under one roof, neighbors in separate homes, or people of like mind being connected through clubs and associations in the same city or virtually in cyberspace—and embrace the fact that our lives and our world are changing faster than we've been prepared to accept in the past.

- **Acknowledge our time of extremes.** Identify what this means for you and your community. What has changed, and how can your community make the changes easier in members' lives?

- **State the goals of your community: Why have you come together?** Define what you hope to accomplish as a community. This is one of the keys to the success of your community and what you do at this point will become a point of reference in the future when questions arise as to the scope of your community goals.

- **Identify your community's core values.** Ask yourself if your community's core value system and organization is based upon things such as material wealth; personal, family, and group well-being; spirituality; religion; or a combination of these or any other principles. This is a key that will help assure your community members that everyone has clarity when it comes to difficult decisions.
- **Develop a plan of community resilience.** This step is directly related to the way your community feels about our time of extremes. It's also the step where you and your community members can voice your concerns, reservations, and fears, as well as identify your strengths and the conditions that you honestly feel may need the greatest levels of resilience. If you are in a seaside community that is becoming more prone to superstorms that impact the necessities of daily living, or in an area that is especially susceptible to wildfires or any natural disaster, a plan of action creates resilience before a community needs it, along with the peace of mind that comes from having done so.
- **Reread Chapter 5.**

Welcome Home

When we consider separately the facts of our time of extremes, the records of Earth's ancient history, and the experiences of our indigenous ancestors from thousands of years ago, we're presented with interesting information. When we marry these facts, they tell us a story. It's *our* story, and we're completing a chapter that we began over 5,000 years ago.

We're living the repeat today of the cycles of change that our ancestors experienced in their time. The big difference is that we're sharing the experience with a family of 7 billion people. Although we can't know precisely how our story will end, we can know with certainty that our time of extremes is the birth of a new normal and a new way of life. Our lives are changing to reflect this transition.

Our ability to thrive through the transition while turning our time of extremes into a time of transformation hinges upon: (1) our willingness to acknowledge the emergence, and (2) how we learn to adapt to it. It's because we're living a time of extremes that it makes sense to expect volatility where life has been smooth sailing in the past. It makes sense to expect record-setting weather and plan accordingly; it makes sense that the weakened economies of the world point to the need for new strategies in our ideas of savings and retirement; it makes sense to plan for temporary disruptions in supplies and services as the strain of climate change and the world's reduced workforce is reflected in our lives.

These are among the realities that we face as our world and our lives make way for the new normal. They're inconvenient, but they're temporary. We're not being honest with ourselves or one another if we pretend that they don't exist. To turn such extremes into transformation, we must be willing to acknowledge what the world shows us and accept our role in adapting to what we're being shown.

Because our time of extremes *is* so very different from times past, it makes perfect sense to expect that our lives must change and our thinking must change as well. It makes perfect sense to live resiliently and *adapt* to our emerging world rather than to thrust the solutions of the past onto the problems of today. We've already tried those. When it comes to the world's economy and climate change, it's clear that the old solutions aren't working. It's also clear that to adapt to the transition we're living through, we must cross the traditional boundaries that have kept us from knowing ourselves in the past. When we do, something wonderful begins to happen. And it all begins with the turning points that we can build into our everyday lives.

Each of the items in the preceding template represents an important element in your life. Each bullet is like a rubber band of possibilities that can only stretch so far. In our time of extremes, each aspect of our lives is being stretched to its limit. The question is: *Will you choose the turning points that ease the tension in your rubber bands of possibilities?* Will you embrace the greatest transformation of power, wealth, and resources in the history of the world? The shift is all about you. It's your journey.

The new world has arrived. Welcome home.

RESOURCES

Organizations

Berkana Institute

Berkana.org

"The Berkana Institute and our partners share the clarity that whatever the problem, community is the answer. Berkana has worked in partnership with a rich diversity of people around the world who strengthen their communities by working with the wisdom and wealth already present in their people, traditions and environments. For twenty years our work has been preparing for unknown futures by creating strong and sustainable relationships, by wisely stewarding the earth's resources and by building resilient communities."

Bioneers

www.Bioneers.org

"The overarching mission of Bioneers is the advancement of holistic education pertaining to global social, cultural and environmental issues. Bioneers identifies progressive yet nature-honoring solutions to rising challenges of instability, inequality, and unsustainable growth and disseminates this knowledge via independent media, events, and community action networks."

Institute of HeartMath

www.HeartMath.org

"The Institute of HeartMath is an internationally recognized nonprofit research and education organization dedicated to helping people reduce stress, self-regulate emotions and build energy and resilience for healthy, happy lives. HeartMath tools, technology and training teach people to rely on the intelligence of their hearts in concert with their minds at home, school, work and play."

Post Carbon Institute

www.PostCarbon.org

"Post Carbon Institute provides individuals, communities, businesses, and governments with the resources needed to understand and respond to the interrelated economic, energy, environmental, and equity crises that define the 21st century. We envision a world of resilient communities and re-localized economies that thrive within ecological bounds."

Resilient Communities

ResilientCommunities.org

"How do we live our lives in ways that make enough of a difference to make a difference? I think we do it by turning to one another. I think we do it by rediscovering our own wisdom and our capacity to whatever is needed for the health and safety of our families and neighbors. I think we do it by remembering how deeply interrelated we all are."

Transition United States

www.TransitionUS.org

"Our vision is that every community in the United States has engaged its collective creativity to unleash an extraordinary and historic transition to a future beyond fossil fuels; a future that is more vibrant, abundant, and resilient; one that is ultimately preferable to the present."

Recommended Reading

Edmund J. Bourne, Ph.D., *Global Shift: How a New Worldview Is Transforming Humanity* (Oakland, CA: New Harbinger Publications, 2008).

Lester R. Brown, *Plan B 3.0: Mobilizing to Save Civilization* (New York: W.W. Norton & Company, 2008).

Doc Lew Childre, Howard Martin, and Donna Beech, *The HeartMath Solution: The Institute of HeartMath's Revolutionary Program for Engaging the Power of the Heart's Intelligence* (New York: HarperOne, 2000).

Duane Elgin, *Voluntary Simplicity: Toward a Way of Life That Is Outwardly Simple, Inwardly Rich* (New York: HarperCollins, 1981).

David Gershon, *Social Change 2.0: A Blueprint for Reinventing Our World* (White River Junction, VT: High Point/Chelsea Green, 2009).

Bruce Lipton, *The Honeymoon Effect: The Science of Creating Heaven on Earth* (Carlsbad, CA: Hay House, 2013).

ENDNOTES

Author's Note

1. Lao-tzu, Chinese philosopher, 6th century B.C.E., as quoted on the website: http://www.byzant.com/mystical/biography/Quotations.aspx?id=30.

Chapter 1: Now Is Different

1. Johan Rockström, Will Steffen, and Kevin Noone, et al., "A Safe Operating Space for Humanity," *Nature,* vol. 461 (September 24, 2009): pp. 472–475. Website: www.nature.com/nature/journal/v461/n7263/full/461472a.html.

2. Omar Baddour, as quoted in an article by Sarah Lyall, "Heat, Flood or Icy Cold, Extreme Weather Rages Worldwide," *The New York Times* (January 10, 2013): p. A4. Website: http://www.nytimes.com/2013/01/11/science/earth/extreme-weather-grows-in-frequency-and-intensity-around-world.html.

3. Dim Coumou, as quoted in an article, "Global Warming Has Increased Monthly Heat Records Worldwide by a Factor of Five, Study Finds," *Science Daily* (January 14, 2013). Website: http://www.sciencedaily.com/releases/2013/01/130114101732.htm.

4. Ibid.

5. Craig Loehle and J. Huston McCulloch, "Correction to: A 2000-Year Global Temperature Reconstruction Based on Non-Tree Ring Proxies," *Energy & Environment,* vol. 19, no. 1 (2008): pp. 93–100. Retrieved from: http://www.econ.ohio-state.edu/jhm/AGW/Loehle/Loehle_McC_E&E_2008.pdf.

6. Joel E. Cohen, "Human Population Grows Up," *Scientific American,* special edition "Crossroads for Planet Earth" (September 2005): p. 48.

7. Central Intelligence Agency, "Population Growth Rate," *The World Factbook.* Retrieved June 21, 2013, from: https://www.cia.gov/library/publications/the-world-factbook/rankorder/2002rank.html?countryName=Fiji&countryCode=fj®ionCode=au&rank=136.

8. Reported in "How Much Coal Is Left?" *Greenbang.* Website: http://www.greenbang.com/how-much-coal-is-left_21367.html.

9. Alfred J. Cavallo, "Hubbert's Petroleum Production Model: An Evaluation and Implications for World Oil Production Forecasts," *Natural Resources Research,* vol. 13, no. 4 (December 2004): pp. 211–221.

10. A commonly accepted definition for *reserve currency.* Retrieved June 21, 2013, from: http://en.wikipedia.org/wiki/Reserve_currency.

11. "The Global Debt Clock," *The Economist.* An interactive debt clock with up-to-the-minute calculations for the combined debt of the world's largest economies. Website: http://economist.com/content/global_debt_clock

12. Table of gross domestic product to debt ratios for the world's advanced and emerging economies from 2010 through 2016, with estimates beyond 2013, found in "Comparing Debt Ratios," *The Wall Street Journal* (April 20, 2011). Website: http://online.wsj.com/article/SB10001424052748703789104576272891515344726.html.

13. Tim McMahon, "What Is the Inflation Adjusted Price of Corn?" InflationData.com (November 16, 2011). Website: http://inflationdata.com/Inflation/Inflation_Articles/Corn_Inflation.asp.

14. Tim McMahon, "Inflation Adjusted Gasoline Prices," InflationData.com (July 16, 2013). Website: http://inflationdata.com/Inflation/Inflation_Rate/Gasoline_Inflation.asp.

15. Peggy Noonan, "A Time of Lore: We Live Through an Agincourt a Day, Yet Life Goes On," *The Wall Street Journal* (July 26, 2002). Website: http://online.wsj.com/article/SB122418845573142011.html.

16. Lonnie Thompson, as quoted in an article by Earle Holland, "Major Climate Change Occurred 5,200 Years Ago: Evidence Suggests That History Could Repeat Itself," *Ohio State University Research News* (December 15, 2004). Website: http://researchnews.osu.edu/archive/5200event.htm.

17. Ibid.

18. George Musser, "The Climax of Humanity," *Scientific American,* special edition "Crossroads for Planet Earth" (September 2005): pp. 44–47.

19. Abstract and link to full report by World Economic Forum, *Global Risks 2013,* Lee Howell, editor in chief. Website: http://www.weforum.org/reports/global-risks-2013-eighth-edition.

20. "The Climax of Humanity": pp. 44–47.

21. Stephen Konarik, as quoted in an article by Childs Walker, "Magnitude of Friday's Storm Shocked Meteorologists, Utility Workers," *The Baltimore Sun* (June 30, 2012). Website: http://articles.baltimoresun.com/2012-06-30/news/bs-md-storm-unexpected-20120630_1_utility-workers-storm-bge.

22. Ibid.

Chapter 2: No Shortage of Solutions

1. Garson O'Toole, Quote Investigator, "The Chains of Habit Are Too Light to Be Felt Until They Are Too Heavy to Be Broken." Website: http://quoteinvestigator.com/2013/07/13/chains-of-habit.

2. Peter Drucker, *Management Challenges for the 21st Century* (Burlington, MA: Elsevier, 1999): p. 62.

3. Excerpt from the public declaration by President John F. Kennedy (1917–1963) that America would focus its resources to accomplish the first lunar mission before 1970. National Aeronautics and Space Administration Website: http://www.nasa.gov/vision/space/features/jfk_speech_text.html.

4. "One Small Step, Corrected Transcript and Commentary by Eric M. Jones," NASA (1995). Video of the historic lunar landing is also available. Website: http://www.hq.nasa.gov/alsj/a11/a11.step.html.

5. "2013 World Hunger and Poverty Facts and Statistics," *Hunger Notes*. World Hunger Education Service Website: http://www.worldhunger.org/articles/Learn/world%20hunger%20facts%202002.htm.

6. Ibid.

7. Ibid.

8. United States Environmental Protection Agency, "Natural Gas." Website: http://www.epa.gov/cleanenergy/energy-and-you/affect/natural-gas.html.

9. Advances in renewable energy sources will make them more viable as local alternatives that supplement regional energy systems. Green Progress, "Alternative Energy." Website: http://www.greenprogress.com/alternative_energy.php.

10. The UN Millennium Development Goals 2015 goal for poverty reduction was achieved ahead of schedule. United Nations Website: http://www.un.org/millenniumgoals/poverty.shtml.

11. Lester R. Brown, "Is Our Civilization at a Tipping Point?" *Hunger Notes*. World Hunger Education Service Website: http://www.worldhunger.org/articles/09/editorials/brown_tipping.htm.

12. David Gershon, "Social Change 2.0: A Blueprint for Reinventing Our World," *Sustainable City Network* (November 12, 2010). Website: http://www.sustainablecitynetwork.com/blogs/david_gershon/article_5b8f63d2-eea0-11df-8077-0017a4a78c22.html.

13. From the Paolo Soleri community of Arcosanti website: http://www.arcosanti.org.

14. Edmund J. Bourne, *Global Shift: How a New Worldview Is Transforming Humanity* (Oakland, CA: New Harbinger Publications, 2008): p. 322.

15. Ibid.

16. Gregg Braden, *Deep Truth: Igniting the Memory of Our Origin, History, Destiny and Fate* (Carlsbad, CA: Hay House, 2011): pp. 219–222.

17. Ibid: pp. 139–183.

18. Gregg Braden, *The Divine Matrix: Bridging Time, Space, Miracles, and Belief* (Carlsbad, CA: Hay House, 2007): pp. 101–122.

19. Ibid.

20. *Deep Truth:* pp. 93–138.

21. Ibid.

22. Ibid: pp. 219–222.

23. Ibid: pp. 139–183.

24. *The Divine Matrix:* pp. 61–100.

25. Ibid: pp. 37–58.

26. Lawrence H. Keeley, as quoted by R. Brian Ferguson in "The Birth of War," *Natural History,* vol. 112, no. 6 (July/August 2003). Website: http://iweb.tntech.edu/kosburn/history-444/birth_of_war.htm.

27. Ravi Logan, Prout Institute, "Opening Address for the Symposium on the Humanistic Aspects of Regional Development," Birobidzhan, Russia (September 1993).

28. Opinion voiced by Sir Martin Rees, Royal Society Research Professor at Cambridge University, and quoted by Andrew Walker, "Sir Martin Rees: Prophet of Doom?" *BBC News* (April 25, 2003). Website: http://news.bbc.co.uk/1/hi/in_depth/uk/2000/newsmakers/2976279.stm.

29. George Musser, "The Climax of Humanity," *Scientific American,* special edition "Crossroads for Planet Earth" (September 2005): pp. 44–47.

30. Ibid: p. 47.

31. Ibid.

32. Tad Williams, *To Green Angel Tower, Part 1* (New York: DAW Books, 1993): p. 771.

33. Paul R. Ehrlich, *The Population Bomb* (New York: Ballantine Books, 1968): p. xi.

34. Paul R. Ehrlich and Anne H. Ehrlich, "The Population Bomb Revisited," *Electronic Journal of Sustainable Development,* vol. 1, no. 3 (2009): pp. 63–71.

35. Ibid.

36. World auto-production statistics, Worldometers. Website: http://www.worldometers.info/cars.

37. Paul Chefurka, "How Tight Is the Link between Oil, Food and Population?" (February 15, 2011). Website: http://www.paulchefurka.ca/GrainOilPop.html.

38. Ibid.

39. "UN Raises 'Low' Population Projection for 2050," *Worldwatch Institute* (July 2, 2013). Website: http://www.worldwatch.org/node/6038.

40. Food and Agriculture Organization of the United Nations, "Global Hunger Declining, but Still Unacceptably High" (September 2010). Website: http://www.fao.org/economic/es-policybriefs/briefs-detail/en/?no_cache=1&uid=45361.

41. Ibid.

Chapter 3: The Turning Point

1. Tom Stoppard, as quoted by Jacques Steinberg, "Stoppard Overwhelmed by World's Problems," *The New York Times* (July 11, 2008). Website: http://www.nytimes.com/2008/07/11/arts/11arts-STOPPARDOVER_BRF.html?_r=0.

2. Ibid.

3. "Q and A with Malcolm," Malcolm Gladwell, the author's official website: http://gladwell.com/the-tipping-point-q-and-a.

4. Zach Van Hart, "How Weight Loss Saved My Life: The Story of Bill Smith," *SparkPeople*. Website: http://www.sparkpeople.com/resource/motivation_articles.asp?id=79.

5. Spoken by Neil Armstrong, "One Small Step," Corrected Transcript and Commentary, *Apollo 11 Lunar Surface Journal* (Last Revised January 18, 2013). Website: http://www.hq.nasa.gov/alsj/a11/a11.step.html.

6. "How Weight Loss Saved My Life: The Story of Bill Smith."

7. The Harvard School of Public Health, "Fats and Cholesterol," *Nutrition Source*. Website: http://www.hsph.harvard.edu/nutritionsource/fats-and-cholesterol.

8. The term *cognitive dissonance* is defined in Leon Festinger's book *A Theory of Cognitive Dissonance* (Stanford, CA: Stanford University Press, 1957).

9. Ken Kuhne's website for all-weather hoop greenhouses built in Santa Fe, New Mexico: http://www.raisedbed.biz.

10. James A. Blumenthal, a professor of medical psychology at Duke University Medical Center in Durham, NC, links emotions to heart disease in an article by Rebecca Clay, "Research to the Heart of the Matter: Psychologists are producing clear evidence that psychosocial factors contribute to cardiovascular disease and

are coming up with interventions that may help patients live healthier lives," *American Psychological Association,* vol. 32, no. 1 (January 2001). Website: http://www.apa.org/monitor/jan01/coverheart.aspx.

Chapter 4: Getting There

1. This statement comes from the opening quote for the *Time* special edition "Beyond 9/11." Website: http://www.time.com/time/beyond911/#.

2. Ibid.

3. A definition of *resilience* from the American Psychological Association. Website: http://psychcentral.com/lib/2007/what-is-resilience.

4. An expanded definition of *resilience* that may be applied to nature as well as society, from the Stockholm Resilience Centre. Website: http://www.stockholmresilience.org/21/research/what-is-resilience.html.

5. Janice Harris Lord and Kevin O'Brien, "Core Elements and Strategies for Victim Service Providers to Develop Resilience," an excerpt from "Chapter 10: Developing Resilience," in *National Victim Assistance Academy Track 1: Foundation-Level Training* (March 2011): pp. 9–18. Website: https://www.ovcttac.gov/downloads/views/TrainingMaterials/NVAA/Documents_NVAA2011/ParticipantText/10_NVAA_MAR_2011_Developing_Resilience_PText_final.doc.

6. Peter Corbett, "Ex-Iran Hostage Survived on Faith, Power of Prayer," *The Arizona Republic* (November 9, 2012). Retrieved from: http://www.azcentral.com/community/articles/20121106ex-iran-hostage-survived-faith-power-prayer.html.

7. Terry Anderson, as quoted by Pierre Tristam, "Terry Anderson Remembers His Ordeal as a Hostage in Lebanon," *Middle East Issues.* About.com Website: http://middleeast.about.com/od/lebanon/a/me081206f.htm.

8. Scott Barry Kaufman, "The Will and Ways of Hope," *Psychology Today* (December 26, 2011). Website: http://www.psychologytoday.com/blog/beautiful-minds/201112/the-will-and-ways-hope.

9. Ibid.

10. Jennifer Holmes, M.A., "Healthy Relationships: Their Influence on Physical Health," *BC Council for Families* (2011). Website: http://www.bccf.ca/all/resources/healthy-relationships-their-influence-physical-health.

11. Eleanor Roosevelt, *You Learn by Living: Eleven Keys for a More Fulfilling Life* (Louisville, KY: Westminster John Knox Press, 1960).

12. Bruce Lipton, *The Biology of Belief: Unleashing the Power of Consciousness, Matter & Miracles* (Santa Rosa, CA: Mountain of Love/Elite Books, 2005): pp. 146–150.

13. Rollin McCraty, Bob Barrios-Choplin, Deborah Rozman, Mike Atkinson, and Alan D. Watkins, "The Impact of a New Emotional Self-Management Program

on Stress, Emotions, Heart Rate Variability, DHEA and Cortisol," *Integrative Physiological and Behavioral Science,* vol. 33, no. 2 (1998): pp. 151–170. Website: http://www.heartmath.org/research/research-publications/impact-of-a-new-emotional-self-management-program-on-stress-emotions-heart-rate-variability.html.

14. Ibid.

15. Kahlil Gibran, *The Prophet* (New York: Alfred A. Knopf, 1923): p. 30.

16. Rollin McCraty, Raymond Trevor Bradley, and Dana Tomasino, "The Resonant Heart," *Shift* (December 2004–February 2005): pp. 15–19.

17. This quote is one of my favorites regarding the interrelated nature of community, life, and us. M. Scott Peck, *The Different Drum: Making Community and Peace* (New York: Touchstone, 1987).

Chapter 5: The Next Level

1. Zerihun Kassa, as quoted by Bethany Marinelli in "Herds to Harvest: A Community Transformed," *Global Hope Network International* (February 20, 2013). Website: http://globalhopenetwork.org/herds-to-harvest-a-community-transformed.

2. Ibid.

3. Michael Krasny, "What Is Community?" *Mother Jones* (May/June 1994). Website: http://www.motherjones.com/politics/1994/05/what-community.

4. Ibid.

5. Ibid.

6. *Back to the Future* (1985), directed by Robert Zemeckis, with Michael J. Fox, Christopher Lloyd, Lea Thompson, and Crispin Glover.

7. Anthony Giddens, *The Consequences of Modernity* (Stanford, CA: Stanford University Press, 1990): p. 64.

8. "Glossary: Globalisation," United Nations Educational, Scientific, and Cultural Organization. Website: http://www.unesco.org/new/en/social-and-human-sciences/themes/international-migration/glossary/globalisation.

9. Henry M. Paulson, Jr., "It Could Have Been A Lot Worse: A Conversation with Henry Paulson," *The American Interest* (May/June 2010). Website: http://www.the-american-interest.com/article.cfm?piece=815.

10. Lee Crockett, "Overfishing 101: Protecting Tuna with Technology," *National Geographic* (posted September 27, 2011). Website: http://newswatch.nationalgeographic.com/2011/09/27/overfishing-101-protecting-tuna-with-technology.

11. Theodore Bestor, as quoted in an article by Ken Gewertz, "Fish Story: Anthropologist Bestor Looks at Globalization and Culture Through Study of Sushi Market," *Harvard University Gazette* (December 6, 2001).

12. Thomas L. Friedman, "Overblown Fears, #10: Globalization," *Newsweek* (2010). Website: http://2010.newsweek.com/top-10/most-overblown-fears/globalization.html.

13. Ibid.

14. Judith Rodin and Robert Garris, "Reconsidering Resilience for the 21st Century," an essay based on prior research and writing done by several colleagues at the Rockefeller Foundation, including Heather Grady, Claudia Juech, Anna Brown, Ashvin Dayal, Bethany Martin-Breen, Stefan Nachuk, Cristina Rumbaitis del Rio, and Fern Uennatornwaranggoon. *The Rockefeller Foundation.* Website: http://www.rockefellerfoundation.org/blog/reconsidering-resilience-21st-century.

15. Judith Rodin, as quoted by Arianna Huffington, "Worldwide Resilience Key to Our Future," *Chicago Tribune* (January 23, 2013). Website: http://www.chicagotribune.com/sns-201301232030--tms--ahuffcoltq--m-a20130123-20130123,0,1817267.column.

16. Ibid.

17. Massoud Amin, "U.S. Electrical Grid Gets Less Reliable as Outages Increase and R&D Decreases," University of Minnesota College of Science and Engineering (February 22, 2011). Website: http://tli.umn.edu/blog/security-technology/u-s-electrical-grid-gets-less-reliable-as-outages-increase-and-rd-decreases.

18. "Some Grocery Store Shelves Empty in NYC," *ABC New York News* (December 30, 2010). Website: http://abclocal.go.com/wabc/story?section=news/local/new_york&id=7870930.

19. Kayla Webley, with reporting by Christopher Matthews, "Hurricane Sandy by the Numbers: A Superstorm's Statistics, One Month Later," *Time* (November 26, 2012). Website: http://nation.time.com/2012/11/26/hurricane-sandy-one-month-later.

20. Attributed by Diogenes Laërtius to Heracleitus, 6th-century B.C.E. Greek philosopher. Website: http://en.wikiquote.org/wiki/Heraclitus.

21. Isaac Asimov (1920–1992), Russian-American science-fiction writer."My Own View," published in *The Encyclopedia of Science Fiction*, ed. Robert Holdstock (1978).

22. Robert Cherry, Medical Director of Penn State Shock Trauma Center, "Business Testimonials: Penn State University," Federal Emergency Management Agency. Website: http://www.ready.gov/business/business-testimonials.

23. Ibid.

24. Ibid.

25. Margaret J. Wheatley's description of the scope of her work at the Berkana Institute. Website: http://berkana.org/about.

26. Summary for the Berkana Institute philosophy of community. Website: http://resilientcommunities.org.

27. To enable 100 cities to better address major 21st-century challenges, the Rockefeller Foundation is inviting cities from around the world to apply for the 100 Cities Challenge. Website: http://100resilientcities.rockefellerfoundation.org/resilience.

28. A series of conferences designed to create greater resilience for the city of Philadelphia. Website: http://www.phil.frb.org/community-development/events/2012/reinventing-older-communities.

29. A description of San Francisco's efforts to "retrofit the buildings and infrastructure that sustain city life. Our goal is to ensure San Francisco's resiliency and our capacity to not only survive but thrive when a disaster strikes." Website: http://www.spur.org/initiative/resilient-city.

30. An innovative initiative in New York that emphasizes the need for a holistic resilience agenda and answers the question: "How resilient is New York City? Can we absorb sudden shocks to our economy, to our natural environment, to our way of life?" Websites: http:/mas.org/mass-resilience-agenda and http://mas.org/video/building-resilient-cities-future-model-sustainability-community.

Chapter 6: Getting Serious about a World Transformed

1. "Stanislav Grof, M.D., Receives Prestigious VISION 97 Award," *Merlian News* (October 25, 2007). Website: http://merliannews.com/People_36/Stanislav_Grof_M_D__Receives_Prestigious_VISION_97_Award_printer.shtml.

2. Excerpt from Stanislav Grof's acceptance speech for the VIZE (VISION) 97 Award in 2007. Website: http://www.realitysandwich.com/acceptance_speech.

3. Ibid.

4. Attributed to American biologist E. O. Wilson. Website: http://www.goodquotes.com/quote/e-o-wilson/it-s-obvious-that-the-key-problem-faci.

5. Johan Rockström, Will Steffen, Kevin Noone, et al., "A Safe Operating Space for Humanity," *Nature,* vol. 461 (September 24, 2009): pp. 472–475. Website: http://www.nature.com/nature/journal/v461/n7263/full/461472a.html.

6. Prepared under the direction of the National Intelligence Council, *Global Trends 2015: A Dialogue about the Future with Nongovernment Experts,* National Foreign Intelligence Board (December 2000). Website: http://www.dni.gov/files/documents/Global%20Trends_2015%20Report.pdf.

7. *My World: The United Nations Global Survey for a Better World.* Website: http://www.myworld2015.org/index.html.

8. Megan Quinn, "The Power of Community: How Cuba Survived Peak Oil," *Energy Bulletin* (February 25, 2006). Website: http://www2.energybulletin.net/node/13171.

9. Ibid.

10. "IEA Lauds Unconventional Gas Reserves," UPI.com (January 19, 2011). Website: http://www.upi.com/Science_News/Resource-Wars/2011/01/19/IEA-lauds-unconventional-gas-reserves/UPI-83531295444312.

11. While there are a number of technical research papers on thorium as an energy source, I'm sharing this particular one because it is nontechnical and clearly identifies the advantages and disadvantages of this technology. Victor Stenger, Ph.D., "LFTR: A Long Term Energy Solution?" *Huffington Post* (January 9, 2012). Website: http://www.huffingtonpost.com/victor-stenger/lftr-a-longterm-energy-so_b_1192584.html.

ACKNOWLEDGMENTS

The writing of this book is only the first step in the process that carries it from my desk to your purse, briefcase, bookshelf, or nightstand. Along the way, copyeditors, proofreaders, graphic designers, marketing representatives, publicists, event producers, and bookstore buyers have arranged their lives and schedules around my commitment that *The Turning Point* would be ready at the time that I promised. Although I will never meet most of these people personally, I know they're there. I'm deeply honored to share our journey and eternally thankful for all that they do each and every day to help this world become a better place. These pages are my opportunity to express my gratitude specifically to those whose efforts have directly contributed to making this book possible.

I'm especially grateful to:

Each and every one of the greatest group of people I could ever imagine working with, the members of our Hay House, Inc., family. To Louise Hay and Reid Tracy, thank you both so very much for your continuing vision and personal dedication to the truly extraordinary way of doing business that has become the hallmark of Hay House's success. *The Turning Point* marks my seventh book with Hay House and the ten-year anniversary of the journey that we began together in 2004. To Reid Tracy, President and CEO: my deepest gratitude for your support, rock-solid advice, and your trust in me and my work. I look forward to seeing where the next ten years lead us!

Erin Dupree, my worldwide publicist extraordinaire; Alex Freemon, my most amazing and talented copyeditor; Richelle Zizian, my big-picture-of-the-world publicity manager; Margarete Nielsen, COO, and the powerful link between my desk and the big publishing world; Christy Salinas and her staff of patient and gifted designers and artists; Nancy Levin, the most awesome event director anywhere on the planet; Rocky George, the perfect audio engineer, with the ear for just the right sound; and all of the always-smiling, hardworking people from the California warehouses to the perfectly stocked book tables at our I Can Do It! events—you're all absolutely the very best! I couldn't ask for a nicer group of people to work with, or a more dedicated team to support my work. Your excitement and professionalism are unsurpassed, and I'm proud to be a part of all the good things that the Hay House family brings to our world.

Ned Leavitt, my literary agent—thank you so very much for your wisdom, integrity, and the human touch that you bring to every milestone we cross together. Through your guidance in shepherding our books through the ever-changing world of publishing, we have reached more people on Earth in more countries than ever with our empowering message of hope and possibility. While I deeply appreciate your impeccable guidance, I am especially grateful for our friendship and your trust in me.

To Stephanie Gunning, my editorial guru extraordinaire for over a decade, and now my friend, you have my deepest respect for your knowledge of the world, your dedication to our projects, and your editorial skills that you shower onto each of our projects. I'm forever grateful for all you do to help me share the complexities of science and the truths of life in a joyous and meaningful way. Thank you for always asking just the right questions, in just the right way, to lead me to the clearest choices.

I am proud to be part of the virtual team, and the family, that has grown around the support of my work over the years, including my dearest Lauri Willmot, my favorite (and only) office manager since 1996. I admire you tremendously, respect you deeply, and appreciate the countless ways that you're there for me always, and especially when it counts. Thank you for representing me in a way that honors the blessings we've been given.

To my dearest friends who have crossed the veil into the next world: Robin Miner (founder of Source Books) and Debbie Ford (my sister on the path). You both left this world while I was creating this book, and your strength, your courage, your choices, and your passing are a part of my writing. I miss you both and thank you for all of the ways you shared your love with me and the world.

To Rita Curtis, my business manager extraordinaire, and now my friend: I deeply appreciate your vision, your clarity, and your skills that get us from here to there each month. Most of all, I appreciate your trust, your openness to new ideas, and especially your friendship.

To my mother, Sylvia, and my brother, Eric: Thank you for your unfailing love and for believing in me even when you don't understand me. Though our family is small, together we have found that our extended family of love is greater than we've ever imagined. Thank you for all that you bring to my life each day.

To the one person who's seen it all from my best to my worst, my beautiful wife in life, Martha: Knowing that your acceptance of me, your lasting friendship, your exquisite and gentle wisdom and all-embracing love is with me each day of my life is the constant that I count on to get me through. Along with Woody "Bear" and Nemo, the furry beings we share our lives with, you are the family that makes each journey worth coming home from. Thank you for all that you give, all that you share, and all that you bring to my life.

A very special thanks to everyone who has supported my work, books, recordings, and live presentations over the years. I am honored by your trust, in awe of your vision for a better world, and deeply appreciative of your passion to bring that world into existence. Through your presence, I have learned to become a better listener, and heard the words that allow me to share our empowering message of hope and possibility. To all, I remain grateful in all ways, always.

ABOUT THE AUTHOR

New York Times best-selling author **Gregg Braden** is internationally renowned as a pioneer in bridging science, ancient wisdom, and the real world. Following a successful career as a computer geologist for Phillips Petroleum during the 1970s energy crisis, he worked as a senior computer systems designer with Martin Marietta Defense Systems during the final years of the Cold War. In 1991, he became the first technical operations manager for Cisco Systems.

Since 1986, Gregg has explored high mountain villages, remote monasteries, and forgotten texts to merge their timeless secrets with the best science of today. His discoveries are now shared in 33 countries and 38 languages through such paradigm-inspiring books as *The God Code, Fractal Time,* and *Deep Truth.* His 2007 bestseller, *The Divine Matrix,* was recently selected as the source for the made-for-television feature *Entanglement,* and is now used as a textbook for college-level courses exploring new discoveries of science and our relationship to the world.

Gregg has received numerous awards in recognition of his insights and innovation. His work has been shared on every continent of the world through his presentations and trainings with Fortune 500 companies, the U.S. military, and international businesses, and is featured in media specials on the History Channel, Discovery Channel, National Geographic Channel, NBC, and ABC.

For further information, please contact Gregg's office manager at:

Wisdom Traditions
P.O. Box 14668
North Palm Beach, FL 33408
(561) 799-9337
Website: www.greggbraden.com
E-mail: info@greggbraden.com

Hay House Titles of Related Interest

YOU CAN HEAL YOUR LIFE, the movie,
starring Louise L. Hay & Friends
(available as a 1-DVD program and an expanded 2-DVD set)
Watch the trailer at: **www.LouiseHayMovie.com**

THE SHIFT, the movie,
starring Dr. Wayne W. Dyer
(available as a 1-DVD program and an expanded 2-DVD set)
Watch the trailer at: **www.DyerMovie.com**

CELEBRATING THE UNIVERSE!: The Spirituality & Science of Stargazing,
by James Mullaney

THE HONEYMOON EFFECT: The Science of Creating Heaven on Earth,
by Bruce H. Lipton, Ph.D.

MIND OVER MEDICINE: Scientific Proof That You Can Heal Yourself,
by Lissa Rankin, M.D.

ONE MIND: How Our Individual Mind Is Part of a Greater Consciousness and Why It Matters, by Larry Dossey, M.D.

QUANTUM CREATIVITY: Think Quantum, Be Creative,
by Amit Goswami, Ph.D.

YOU ARE THE PLACEBO: Making Your Mind Matter,
by Dr. Joe Dispenza (available April 2014)

All of the above are available at your local bookstore,
or may be ordered by contacting Hay House (see next page).

We hope you enjoyed this Hay House book. If you'd like to receive our online catalog featuring additional information on Hay House books and products, or if you'd like to find out more about the Hay Foundation, please contact:

Hay House, Inc., P.O. Box 5100, Carlsbad, CA 92018-5100
(760) 431-7695 or (800) 654-5126
(760) 431-6948 (fax) or (800) 650-5115 (fax)
www.hayhouse.com® • www.hayfoundation.org

Published and distributed in Australia by: Hay House Australia Pty. Ltd., 18/36 Ralph St., Alexandria NSW 2015 • *Phone:* 612-9669-4299
Fax: 612-9669-4144 • www.hayhouse.com.au

Published and distributed in the United Kingdom by: Hay House UK, Ltd., Astley House, 33 Notting Hill Gate, London W11 3JQ • *Phone:* 44-20-3675-2450
Fax: 44-20-3675-2451 • www.hayhouse.co.uk

Published and distributed in the Republic of South Africa by:
Hay House SA (Pty), Ltd., P.O. Box 990, Witkoppen 2068
Phone/Fax: 27-11-467-8904 • www.hayhouse.co.za

Published in India by: Hay House Publishers India, Muskaan Complex, Plot No. 3, B-2, Vasant Kunj, New Delhi 110 070 • *Phone:* 91-11-4176-1620
Fax: 91-11-4176-1630 • www.hayhouse.co.in

Distributed in Canada by: Raincoast Books, 2440 Viking Way, Richmond, B.C. V6V 1N2 • *Phone:* 1-800-663-5714 • *Fax:* 1-800-565-3770 • www.raincoast.com